My Mother's Witness

The Peggy Morgan Story

Also by Carolyn Haines
Crossed Bones
Splintered Bones
Buried Bones
Them Bones

Summer of the Redeemers
Touched

MY Mother's Witness

The Peggy Morgan Story

By
Carolyn Haines

RIVER CITY PUBLISHING
Montgomery, Alabama

Printed in the United States.
Designed by Lissa Monroe.

Library of Congress Cataloging-in-Publication Data:
Haines, Carolyn.
My mother's witness : the Peggy Morgan story / by Carolyn Haines.
p. cm.
ISBN 1-57966-042-8
1. Morgan, Peggy, 1947- 2. Women--Mississippi--Biography. 3. Poor
women--Mississippi--Biography. 4. Abused women--Mississippi--Biography.
5. Evers, Medgar Wiley, 1925-1963--Assassination. 6. Trials
(Murder)--Mississippi. I. Title.
HQ1438.M7H35 2003
305.42'092--dc21

2003010250

For those who taught us to speak the truth

Foreword

Invariably as witnesses appear and stand before me, left hand on a Bible, right hand raised, and swear to tell the truth, I cannot help but wonder certain things about them. Just who is this person? Do they really understand the oath that they are taking, and more significantly the ramifications of telling the truth versus a lie? What brought them to my courtroom? In essence, what's the story behind their story?

It's been said that adversity introduces a person to oneself. There is a lot of truth in that adage; I know that I learned quite a bit about myself during my years as a prosecutor at the District Attorney's office of Hinds County, Mississippi, especially throughout the reinvestigation, reprosecution, and third trial of Byron De La Beckwith for the 1963 murder of civil rights leader Medgar Evers. That journey, chronicled in my memoir, *Never Too Late*, was not by any stretch of the imagination along a straight or direct path to justice. John Donne stated it best: "No man is an island"; and my story is necessarily intertwined with those of many others.

I have been given a lot of credit for helping obtain Beckwith's 1994 conviction, but, as Sir Isaac Newton said, "If I have seen further, it is by standing on the shoulders of giants." Indeed, but for the strong shoulders of several "giants," upon whose shoulders I stood, Medgar Evers's assassin would have forever eluded any earthly accountability for his dastardly act. Justice, to Byron De La Beckwith, may have come at a leaden pace, but when it struck, it did so with an iron fist. The Mississippi Supreme Court, in affirming Beckwith's conviction, wrote:

> Miscreants brought before the bar of justice in this State must, sooner or later, face the cold realization that justice, slow and plodding though she may be, is certain in the State of Mississippi. . . . Final

resolution of this conflict resulted from voices, both present and past, who showed the courage and will, from 1964 to 1994, to merely state the truth in open court. Their voices cannot be ignored.

Indeed they cannot, and this book, *My Mother's Witness*, is the story of one of those voices—of Peggy Morgan. The courage and will to speak the truth in the face of adversity are not intuitive. What is instinctive in that situation is self-preservation.

According to nineteenth-century Swiss writer Henri Frederic Amiel, "A lively, disinterested, persistent liking for truth is extraordinarily rare." Peggy's story is that of a voice arising from a once petite girl; a voice smothered daily throughout years of poverty and brutality in the Mississippi Delta; a voice that somehow managed to pierce the blanket of adversity that seemed to envelope its owner's life and finally be heard. Her story is the epitome, in Amiel's words, that "truth is not only violated by falsehood, it may be equally outraged by silence."

Through adversity that many of us can only imagine, Peggy Morgan was introduced to herself and now, through this superbly written biography, writer Carolyn Haines introduces her to the reader. I am quite certain that Amiel's famous journal did not enjoy a place in the Morgan household, but Peggy's memoir, shared in *My Mother's Witness,* is no less a masterpiece of self-analysis. It is certainly a victory for Peggy and her mother, but most importantly it is a victory for the human spirit and truth. It is consequently a true story of substance, a story that will endure. I am thus grateful, personally and as a jurist, that Carolyn Haines has shared it through her skilled pen, and I am honored to recommend it to the reader.

The Honorable Bobby B. DeLaughter

Circuit Judge, Hinds County, Mississippi,
and author of *Never Too Late: A Prosecutor's
Story of Justice in the Medgar Evers Murder Case*

Author's Preface

In 1955 Emmett Till, a fourteen-year-old black youth from Chicago, was murdered in Money, Mississippi. Eight years later, NAACP field secretary Medgar Evers was gunned down in the carport of his Jackson, Mississippi, home. Both murders were racially motivated. Both committed by Mississippi men.

Peggy Albritton Morgan's story is not about these murdered men or about the white men who committed the murders. Not directly. But no story of that time and place could be told outside the framework of men. Men who had wives and children, families who bore the brunt of their violence and hostility on a day-to-day basis. These women, wives and daughters, became unwilling accomplices to murder, repositories of secrets that allowed murderers to range free.

Inez Albritton and Peggy Morgan, a mother and a daughter, shared a world that was in torment and transition—a mirror image of the turmoil and violence within their family. Within their society.

In a twist of fate, both women were connected with two of the most notorious racial murders committed in Mississippi. They were drawn into brutality and viciousness by the men in their lives—husband, father, uncle—and by the very geography of the Mississippi Delta. The rich soil that sprouted cotton so abundantly was also the dividing line of a rigidly enforced social order.

Shortly after the murder of Emmett Till, Inez Albritton became privy to information regarding the details of his kidnapping and subsequent death. Till was visiting relatives in the Greenwood area, a city boy who may not have taken the "rules" of Delta society seriously. He allegedly whistled at a white woman, an advance that was not tolerated. Only fourteen, he was beaten, shot, and his body thrown into the Tallahatchie River with a seventy-pound cotton fan bound to his neck with barbed wire.

Inez's small knowledge of this event—not even first-hand knowledge—was instrumental in her destruction. Like many women of her social class, Inez was a faceless female, the bearer of children, the provider of meals, sexual pleasure and some small income, the object of drunken abuse—in other words, a wife. Property of the man who gave her his name.

In an irony that is bitter beyond words, Peggy, Inez's sixth child, found herself in possession of knowledge that would set her on the path to repeat her mother's fate. In the early 1970s Peggy was in a car with her husband, Lloyd Morgan, and Byron De La Beckwith, who had caught a ride with Lloyd to Parchman State Penitentiary. On that trip, Beckwith confessed to the 1963 murder of Medgar Evers. For twenty years that secret festered in Peggy. Fear, abuse, and a world where a woman had no right to expect decent treatment, much less justice, all combined to keep her silent. In 1990, when Peggy heard that Hinds County assistant district attorney Bobby DeLaughter had reopened the Evers murder case, Peggy made the call that changed her life.

I came to know Peggy through one of those twists of fate that seem to abound in her life. I was sitting at my desk in the public relations office at the University of South Alabama when the phone rang and a timid female voice asked me if I was really from Mississippi. When I confirmed that I'd been born in Lucedale, Peggy gave me her name and said she wanted help in writing her life story.

Nonfiction has never been a goal of mine, and though I had no thought I'd be interested in the project, something in her voice intrigued me. I went to see Peggy.

Once the thread began to unravel and Peggy's story spilled out, I knew there was no way I could walk away from it. It is a story that must be told.

Peggy's motivations for pursuing this book are multiple. Years of therapy have given her the courage to look back on her life and accept the consequences of her choices. Peggy has assumed responsibility for herself, and that has given her the power to move forward. She wants her story told for the women who find themselves in similar circumstances—so they will know they can escape and find a better life. She is living proof of that.

Second, she wants to vindicate her mother's death. Inez is still a presence in Peggy's life, a woman who loved her children with a child's heart. The abuse her mother endured will not prove futile if this book helps someone.

The suffering that Myrlie Evers and Mamie Till-Mobley endured is a constant on Peggy's mind. Nothing can undo the past or change the fact that Medgar Evers and Emmett Till were murdered. But Peggy has learned that while justice heals no wounds, truth does. She wants justice, for the Evers family and Mrs. Till-Mobley. More than that, though, she wants to tell the truth of a time and place and a way of life. Only truth holds the power of healing.

Prologue

Dec. 1, 2002

Peggy Morgan held the telephone in one hand and the newspaper in the other as she sat at her kitchen table. She'd read the article several times—Mamie Till-Mobley had written a book about her son, a fourteen-year-old boy murdered in Money, Mississippi, in 1955 for allegedly whistling at a white woman.

Peggy listened to the telephone ring and wondered if anyone would pick up on the other end. It was a bold step, calling Mamie Till-Mobley. But Peggy had her reasons.

When Mrs. Till-Mobley answered, Peggy almost couldn't talk she was so choked with emotion. Fate had dropped this chance into her lap, though, a chance to speak for her mother, Inez Albritton.

"Mrs. Mobley, my name is Peggy Morgan. I grew up around Money, and I was eight years old when your son was killed. I just wanted to tell you how sorry I was."

In the lengthy conversation that followed, Peggy told Emmett's mother about her mother's attempts to tell what she knew about Emmett's murder.

"I want you to know, my mama tried. She did try."

Mrs. Till-Mobley talked about her desire for justice, her hope that her son's murder would be reopened.

"I'm sending you a picture of me," Peggy said. "It isn't much, but whenever you look at it, you'll know that little girl cared about what happened to your son. A lot of folks still care."

Chapter One

It was hot for early March. The sun burned down in the cloud-less sky like a big, angry eye. Inez Albritton thought maybe it was God, looking down at her, checking to make sure that she was a fit vessel for a new child. No matter how hard she tried, she was always in trouble over something. Mostly from her husband, but some-times she felt as if she had displeased even God.

Lifting her hoe, she chopped at the weeds that threatened the tender young cotton plants that were the future of Coahoma County's economy. The fertile soil and, later, the thick bolls of fiber, were the past, present, and future of the entire Mississippi Delta. Cotton, sun, hard work, and her children were the best components of life for Inez. Like all of the other women in the field, she wore a calico dress and a straw hat. The men wore loose shirts, cotton pants, and straw hats. As she looked out over the rows of cotton that stretched to the end of the earth, she noticed there were more men working than the year before. The war was over, and more and more men were finding their way back into the cotton fields. The compe-tition didn't bother her. She worked hard. No matter what else the folks around Clarksdale said about her, no one could say she didn't give a good day's work.

The familiar dull pain stabbed low in her back, moving around the mound of her belly and centering somewhere deep inside. She leaned on her hoe and rubbed a hand over the tautness of the baby. Her stomach was hard, unyielding. Ripening. The other workers teased her about her belly, saying how she could rest on it as she leaned over to hoe. The truth was, her back ached with a constant grinding, and her legs, never strong, were being pulled from their sockets. She hadn't felt like working today, but there was no choice. If she didn't work, she couldn't be certain there would be money for food.

When the first sharp pain hit, she wasn't exactly surprised. She straightened up and gauged the distance to the field supervisor. With her first step, another pain hit, and she braced on the handle of her hoe to keep from falling in the hot, black dirt.

"Get Gene!" she called out. "Get someone to find him." She staggered and worn black hands grabbed her, holding her up.

The baby coming was her sixth. Though Inez was small, she was strong and wiry, and giving birth was part of her duty. Women were made to carry and deliver children, and there was nothing to make a big fuss over. Except for the bulge of her belly, there wasn't an ounce of extra flesh on her frame. She was fit and ready.

In her head, she timed the pains, walking forward a dozen steps before the next one struck. Little by little, she made her way to the edge of the cotton field.

The supervisor had sent someone running up to the big house to use the phone to find Gene Albritton. Inez knew that he might not be at work. Gene's work habits were sketchy, and more often than not he wasn't where he said he was going. But Clarksdale was a small town. Someone would get word to him that his wife had gone into labor in the middle of a cotton field.

She was almost to the road when her water broke.

The worker came running back, a worried black face under a straw hat not much different from the one Inez wore. "Mr. Gene's on his way."

Inez heard the words, but she knew it would be too late. Wherever Gene had been, there was no time to make it to the hospital. The child was coming. She looked back over her shoulder once. Except for the woman who steadied and supported her, the other choppers had gone back to their rows. Labor was labor. A furrow of cotton or another mouth to feed, it was all in a day's work.

The stutter of the Ford's engine came to her as another pain caught her with a wrench so violent she lost her breath. In the distance she saw the ancient car approaching. So they'd really found

Gene. She tried to hold back the pain, to clamp down on the relentless struggle of the baby as it shifted and positioned itself to enter the world. At the hospital there would be nurses, a clean place, someone to catch the child and make sure it was whole. She didn't want this new life to begin in a ditch beside a cotton field.

Chugging and puffing, the car pulled up beside the worn-looking cluster consisting of Inez, the woman helping her, and the supervisor.

"Get in," Gene said.

"It's the baby," she told him. "It's comin'."

Gene got out and helped his wife into the back seat, trying to arrange her so that she could lie down. She was almost small enough to fit across the seat.

"Can we make it to the hospital?" Inez asked.

"We'll try." He got back behind the wheel and drove away, leaving the supervisor and the woman standing a moment longer beside the ditch before they, too, turned back to the long rows budding green with new life. Valuable life that would be fed and nurtured with the greatest of care.

Less than two miles down the road, Inez cried her husband's name. "It's comin', Gene. I can't wait!"

He pulled the car over to the side of a field. Getting out, he eased into the cramped back seat. Like many men in the late 1940s, he'd helped bring at least one of his children into the world. It was women's work, but he could assist if there wasn't a midwife or a doctor to help. Inez knew what to do.

Inez surrendered her mind to the pain and let her body take over. When at last she felt the baby move out of the birth canal and into Gene's hands, she was exhausted.

"It's a girl," he said, handing the baby to her. The calico dress was already soaked in blood. He used his pocket knife to cut the umbilical cord and tie it off.

"A girl," Inez whispered. The infant was small, destined to be petite. "Peggy," she pronounced.

Gene got out of the car and lit a cigarette. "Ruth," he said. "From the Bible."

"Peggy Ruth," Inez agreed. Peggy was a happy name. She didn't object to Ruth, which was biblical, but there was something attached to that name, a shadow of suffering and woe. Peggy was joyful, the name for a beautiful little girl who would play in the sunshine and grow up to be strong and healthy. "Peggy Ruth Albritton." Saying the name almost exhausted her. "Born March 7, 1947." She would have to remember to get Gene to write it down in the Bible or it would get lost. Every child needed a proper birthday.

Gene finished his cigarette and got back behind the wheel of the car. There was no need for the hospital now. He headed home where he could wash the blood off his hands.

Chapter Two

It was 1948 when Gene Albritton decided to move his family from Coahoma County south to Leflore County. Though he was a talented carpenter, he left behind no sterling work record or community reputation. Those who knew Inez—her field supervisors, the merchants she had occasion to know, the teachers of her older children—felt a sense of relief. There was something not right in the Albritton family, a hint of brutality in the occasional bruises on Inez's arms or a too-quiet child. Folks knew that Gene Albritton drank, and many suspected that he made 'shine. For a man who held no regular job, he often had money. What Inez made in the fields was spent on necessities.

Gene loaded his pregnant-again wife, six children, and assorted possessions and drove due south, then east, crossing Sunflower County where Parchman State Penitentiary is located, settling just north of Greenwood in the small community of Money.

Clarksdale flourishes on the Sunflower River. The Tallahatchie, Yazoo, and Yalobusha nourish Leflore County. Greenwood is known as "the city of three rivers that run two ways." A network of these slow, yellow rivers enriches the Delta, offering water for irrigation, recreation, and distillation. The rivers and the small springs and creeks that feed them are ideal for the stills, capable of creating everything from fine sippin' whiskey to rot-gut poison that can result in blindness, meanness, and insanity. The purchase of 'shine from an unknown bootlegger was a game of Russian roulette. It wasn't an uncommon practice to use the radiator of an old car to filter the whiskey. Lead poisoning was the result. Some bootleggers used any cheap, available organic material to help the fermentation process along.

Even though national prohibition laws had been repealed, bootlegging was a problem because the manufacturers failed to pay state taxes. The 1940s were a time when independent mash-makers fought bitterly to avoid the federal revenue agents. In many instances, even local authorities protected the bootleggers against the "outsiders" who wore federal badges.

Gene was cunning when it came to keeping his still safe. Whenever a location was jeopardized, the still was broken down and moved to another deep-woods location.

The home site Gene chose for his family was a shack on the Tallahatchie, where he promptly opened a small fish market that served as a front for his bootlegging operation. The Albritton mash developed a reputation for being good, if not good for you, and the family finances gradually improved. Inez continued to work the cotton fields and take care of the children, cooking every day the flour gravy, biscuits, and fish that came out of the Tallahatchie. Gene was a good fisherman when he chose to work at it.

Beyond the cultivated fields of cotton and vegetables, Leflore County was still wild. The banks of the Tallahatchie were perfect for Gene's thriving gambling and moonshine operation. But Inez was unhappy in the isolated location. Clarksdale had been a small town, but it was the county seat of Coahoma County. Money was barely a crossroads. Though she constantly asked to move into Greenwood, Gene ignored her. His business was growing daily. He managed to maintain a working vehicle, but it was used for his exclusive needs. Inez and the children caught a ride or walked when they needed to get somewhere.

Peggy's first year passed, long summer days and sweet nights, when it seemed the Albritton fortunes were on a slow, steady rise. They were still poor, but the moonshine and dice were bringing in extra money. No one was sick. The years of depression and war were behind America. Prosperity was the promise and the dream, and Inez knew if Gene didn't get caught by the federal revenue agents or killed in a knife or gun fight, there were better times ahead for her family.

It was early afternoon, a day just right for stoking up the stove and baking a pan of cornbread. The new baby, Sheila Diane, was asleep in her crib by the kitchen table while Sammy, Melinda Faye, and Peggy stayed home, too young for school or work. Inez hummed as she made the cornmeal batter that would bake up light and crisp for the cornbread that Gene and the children loved with fresh butter.

Gene had gone off, either fishing or tending to the still. He seldom said where his business took him, and even when he did say, it wasn't a guarantee that was where he'd be. Once old enough to be considered a man, men didn't answer for their actions or whereabouts. Inez suspected Gene was cooking more mash. The best she could tell, Gene had sold almost all he'd made.

Inez didn't drink or sell the whiskey, but she knew that the men around Money favored Gene's brew. There was more cash in the household, and with the cotton harvested and the fields resting for the winter, Inez was glad of the income, and glad not to have to wield a hoe for twelve hours at a stretch.

It was another dry day, real winter just a faint promise in the stack of cut wood Gene and the older boys had piled up behind the fish market for cooking and heat. The day before, Gene and his brother-in-law Bob had caught a mess of buffalo catfish, German carp, and the ugly gar used to make sausage. The fresh fish had sold fast. Inez had been able to tuck away a few dollars for some new shoes for Boyd. He needed them for school so the other children wouldn't tease him. With seven children it was always something, but Inez loved her babies.

Peggy toddled over to her, clutching at her dress before she fell on her diapered bottom. Inez stepped to the window, searching the backyard where honeysuckle and scuppernong vines tangled the tree limbs together. There was no sign of the two older children.

"Sammy! Faye!" Of all her children, she worried about Sammy the most. Gene had taken an unreasonable dislike to the boy. She saw flashes of it in his questions about Sammy, his hints that Sammy wasn't his child. Ridiculous, but a storm warning of trouble to come. Gene's suspicions could turn into hard fact with one or two slugs of

21

whiskey. Once he was convinced it was true, there was no telling what he might do to her, or to Sammy. All over something he'd made up in his head.

Though Gene may have given her cause, Inez had never fooled around with another man. There had been times when she'd considered leaving her husband, but she'd never broken her vows of marriage. Never. Though Gene didn't always act as if he believed in them, the wedding vows were sacred to her. A woman had to be faithful to a man, even if he didn't abide by the same rules. There had been rumors about Gene and a woman from Greenwood. Talk. Ugly talk which she tried not to hear as she worked her way up and down the long rows of cotton. It was a relief to be out of the fields, away from the talk, home with her babies.

But it had occurred to her that another woman might be one reason Gene seemed determined to keep her and the children stuck out in the woods on the river. A family in town might interfere.

She poured the drippings from their breakfast of gar sausage into the large cast iron pot where hot water simmered. Using both hands to lift the turnips from the wash basin into the boiling pot, she crushed the tender young greens into the hot water, watching them turn dark and cook down. Fresh turnips would be good with the cornbread.

Peggy crept under her feet, and Inez deftly stepped around her as she leaned down to check on the sleeping baby and then shifted to the window to call once more. It worried her that the children weren't in sight. Not that they were bad or troublemakers. There was just no telling with the kind of men who stopped by to do business with Gene. Some of them would do anything for money. "Sammy and Faye, you two better get in here right now!"

Sammy and Faye were too little to be wandering out of the yard alone. Panic made her slightly breathless as she stuck her face to the window and searched for them. They were not by the big trees where they had a pretend house drawn in the dirt. They weren't by the rope swing. The panic blossomed, crowding her small rib cage.

She tried to think back. There had been no vehicles on the road in front of the house. No one, to her knowledge, had stopped by the fish market. But there were animals in the woods that could bring down a grown man. An armed man. Wild boars with long tusks. Panthers. Even a bobcat could get little Faye. She was hardly bigger than a minute.

Lifting the baby to her chest, she hefted Peggy up on one hip. At twenty-nine, Inez weighed seventy-two pounds and had given life to seven children. With her youngest babies in her arms, she ran out of the house and into the front yard.

"Sammy! Melinda Faye!" She called again and again, turning in a tight circle as she examined the yard and surrounding woods for some sign of movement, for a giggle or something that would give the children's hiding place away. When she got hold of them, she'd make them understand the consequences of driving her nearly mad with worry and fear.

"Samuel Herbert! Melinda Faye!"

Her voice flushed a covey of quail from the dead Johnson grass beside the road. There was no other movement. Still holding Peggy and Sheila, she started down the narrow path that led into the woods and to the river. Dear God, what if they'd fallen down the bank! She increased her speed, hugging her babies as she started to jog.

There was no sign of them in the woods, no little footprints in the dry soil, no way to tell if they'd come this way or not. After a thorough search, Inez turned back to the house.

Black smoke spiraled straight up into the air. There was no wind to blow it. Too afraid to even speak her worry, Inez started home as quickly as she could. Her legs were weak from exertion and fear. Her left leg was slightly crooked, but it only troubled her when she was near exhaustion. Though she limped slightly, she forced herself to hurry. She knew the difference between the yellow-gray smoke of a field burning and the black smoke of seasoned, dry timber and tar paper. The house was on fire, and still there was no sign of Sammy and Faye.

She burst through the tangle of vines and stepped into the yard. Sammy and Faye were standing together. Faye rubbed her eyes as if she'd just awakened from a nap. They stared at the house, now a roaring ball of orange flames and black smoke.

Inez joined them, too relieved to even punish them for frightening her. Slowly she eased Peggy to the ground but kept the baby in her arms. There was nothing to do but watch it burn.

The house fire resolved the issue of living in Greenwood. The house was a total loss. The family relocated at 2012 Basket Street in Greenwood, where Gene promptly tar-papered a shed on the right-hand side of the house and opened his fish market. There were advantages to living on the fringes of town. Cars were still hard to come by, and living closer into town meant more business. It also distanced Gene from his stills, in case there was a bust by the federal agents.

The Basket Street address was only a few blocks off Highway 82, and it quickly developed a reputation for toughness. Another family of Albrittons lived nearby, Gene's brother, Buddy, his wife, Josie, and their brood of six children. The rough-and-tumble cousins stuck together, defeating any outside children who might be inclined to look, linger, or laugh at the Albrittons, who were often called the Albritches because they frequently didn't have enough money in the household to buy shirts.

The lack of money was heightened by neglect. The children sometimes went days without having their hair combed. Peggy and her cousin Molly, who shared so many of her problems, developed a united front. They learned to lash out first before the other children could hurt them.

Basket Street and the surrounding area, though it was on the eastern side of town, became known as The Western Front because of the "wild west rule." It was as open and dangerous as Tombstone had ever been. It was not a place to linger, but the Albritton children had no other place to go. The drinking and fighting of the adult men was a pattern that defined their childhood days and nights.

Gene's still, which was moved around the Tallahatchie and Yazoo wilderness to avoid revenuers, was now constantly in operation, tended by Gene, his brother-in-law Bob, or some of Peggy's older brothers as they grew big enough to be saddled with the responsibility of cookin' the mash. The boys were not given a choice in this work.

The Albritton family now consisted of Boyd W., ten years old; Mary Jean, nine; William Earl, seven; Samuel Herbert, five; Melinda Faye, four; Peggy, two; and the infant Sheila. Ronald Eugene and Michael Gale were born later. Another child, a boy, died in infancy with a heart condition.

The older Albritton children did well with their studies at school. They were able to push the growing violence at home away enough so that they could study. For Peggy, though, worry about her mother was constant.

She was just four when she became aware that her father hurt her mother. It was late summer, a time of heat and harvest in the Delta. Since it was Saturday, Peggy's older brothers and sisters were home, always a source of pain and pleasure as they played and fought amongst themselves.

"Let's go for a ride," Gene called, rounding up the four youngsters who were outside playing in the yard. The babies were inside under the care of Becky, the Albritton's occasional maid. Since moving into town and with the fish market prospering, Inez was sometimes able to afford a little help with the children. When Gene allowed her the money. On this one day, he had agreed that Becky could watch the babies.

Inez, clean and dressed in one of her best outfits, slid into the seat beside her husband. In the back seat the wind lifted Peggy's hair, and she closed her eyes and enjoyed the cool breeze and the movement. Sometimes a ride in the car meant a treat. Maybe an ice cream cone.

The cooked custard ice cream sold in downtown Greenwood at the drugstore was the best thing Peggy had ever tasted. She was deep in her choice of whether she'd get chocolate, vanilla, or strawberry when an argument broke out in the front seat.

Gene halted the car at one of Greenwood's most established places, the Crystal Grill. "Get out," he ordered the children. "Get out, and you wait right here until I come back for you."

Peggy had known slaps and punches from both her parents and her siblings, but she had never been afraid. She clung to the car seat as her brother pulled her out of the car. Something terrible was going to happen, and she tried to resist without drawing her father's wrath down on her own head. As soon as the car door slammed, Gene roared away with only Inez in the car. Peggy was left at the curb of the restaurant wearing only the drawers Inez had made for her from a flour sack.

For several hours the children stood in a small clump, watching first the evening shift, then the customers slowly begin to arrive at the Crystal. Afraid to leave, getting more worried by the minute, they watched the sun set and the night start to creep over them. At last one of the older children made the decision to start walking home along the railroad track that would take them to Basket Street.

They were all under ten years of age, and they got confused about the direction home. They headed north toward Money rather than east. When the solid earth beneath the tracks dropped away leaving only the railroad ties and rails over a fast moving creek, Peggy balked. She had never been so afraid. Her mother had gone, and she could sense the growing panic of the older children. The woods crept closer to the railroad tracks, and the night sounds of crickets and frogs were mingled with the rushing sound of the water that only waited for Peggy to step on the railroad ties. She knew she would fall through and be swept away.

Working together, the older children forced her over the creek, and they kept walking. At last they passed the house of a man they knew. Lonnie Neal was a moonshine friend of Gene's.

"Where you goin'?" Lonnie called out. Perhaps it was sympathy that made him ask. If the children were running away, they would be in big trouble from Gene. When he learned they were headed home, he took pity and gave them a ride home.

Gene and Inez returned at long last. Her mouth was cut, with blood dried on her lips and chin, and the next morning there were bruises over her face and body.

It was the last time Gene bothered to take her away from the children before he beat her. For Peggy, it marked the beginning of a reality that forged her character.

Violence shimmered around the fringes of the household. The dice games Gene conducted in the fish market beside the house often turned deadly. Fistfights and cuttings were the more common event, but gunfights weren't unheard of.

It was a world where every frustration was justification for an act of violence. The men beat each other when they were in a mood for it, they beat their wives and children on a whim, the children beat and tormented each other and any other children who crossed their paths. And when there was time left over, there were always the blacks to intimidate and injure.

For men like Gene Albritton and his patrons at the fish market, there was a growing sense that they were losing control of their world. While the decade of the fifties held the promise of prosperity, there was increasing conflict in the Delta. Where once a Negro had known his or her place, some were now asking for equal wages, wanting the same things that whites took for granted. In the class stratification that was a comfort to Gene and his friends, the lower rung was beginning to rumble. The fear, unspoken and unacknowledged, was that any groundswell of movement at the bottom might buck the next rung off. The talk about Negroes, always laden with superiority and contempt, took on a nastier edge.

Chapter Three

The first years of the 1950s brought a regular rhythm to the Albritton family. Gene's success as a bootlegger kept a jingle in his pocket. Though there was money for expansion, there was never enough to feed the children that Inez birthed every twelve to twenty-four months. Before Sheila was up and toddling, Jimmy Eugene was born. Although all eight previous Albritton babies had been born in good health, Jimmy's heart was not strong. He died shortly after his birth. Inez returned to work in the cotton fields.

By mid-February, the field hands were out on the frost-crusted ground, preparing the rich Delta soil for planting. As soon as the ground thawed, the seedlings were transferred by hand, and then came the long months of chopping and weeding, of fighting against disease and drought, of checking for the dreaded boll weevil that could destroy a cotton crop in little more than a blink of the eye. Harvest came in the fall, and for Peggy, now five, the entire world seemed to be eye-level fluffs of white cotton perched on brown stalks.

Inez often worked the fields of Alton Hadden. The Hadden plantation was located not far from the area where Inez and Gene had first settled on the banks of the Tallahatchie. Through the planting and growing season, the rich fields shifted from the bright green of young plants to the darker, fuller green of maturity, and then finally brown. When the large bolls burst open, spilling the long, valuable fiber from their husks, it was time to bring in every able-bodied worker to pick—to harvest the bolls, one by one, before rain or frost could destroy the crop.

Some harvests were better than others, but the early fifties passed with plenty of work for a woman of Inez's abilities. The only changes she saw were the different stages of pregnancy and the number of children she took to the cotton fields.

When Ronald was old enough to endure the seemingly endless hot days, he went along with his mother, Peggy, and Sheila. Though the work of harvest was some of the hardest, at least there was the hope of cool weather and rest ahead. If the crop was good, but not so good that the prices fell, it was generally a time of promises fulfilled for the land owners. For the day workers, it would determine whether they would eat through the winter or starve. Those with the most to lose were the families living on the old plantation properties. Not only their food but their shelter depended on the cotton yield and their ability to bring it in.

September had rolled around once again. The older Albritton children had returned to W. C. Williams Elementary School, and Inez stood with Ronald in her arms while Peggy guarded Sheila and the large flour sack that contained their food for the day.

"Watch those jugs," Inez admonished as Peggy carelessly spun around, almost knocking over the three jugs of water that would do all of them for the long day in the field.

Down the road the rumble of a truck motor came. Peggy grinned. It would be fun to ride in the back of the truck, even if she did have to keep Sheila from falling—or jumping—out and breaking her neck. At three, Sheila was active and had not yet learned that life was filled with things that looked like fun but often hurt.

Scampering onto the road, Peggy forgot about the food, the water, and her baby sister. She cast a sidelong glance at Inez. Her mother was looking fat again. Another baby would be along. She felt no emotion about an additional baby sister or brother. More siblings were the rule, not the exception. There was nothing to get excited about, or distressed. Her daddy liked her mama to be pregnant. He didn't particularly like the children who appeared year after year, but he liked the pregnancy.

"Hey, Willie." Peggy waved at the driver of the pickup, who tooted the horn at the little blond girl and slowed to a stop.

Willie didn't bother to kill the engine or offer to help Inez and the children into the back. Any woman who could pick three hundred pounds of cotton on a good day could get herself into the back of a truck.

Peggy clambered up the tail pipe and bumper into the flat bed of the truck where two other women, both white, held their lunches. They nodded as the truck took off toward the Hadden fields.

Along the way they passed several Negroes, all walking to the cotton fields to work. The truck never slowed, but Peggy waved at the men and women who would arrive to work beside her mama. They waved back, smiling at the irrepressible little girl who often drove her mother to fits of anger. They knew Peggy and Inez, but they were more familiar with the reputation of Gene and the men who tended to spend more time than necessary at the grocery store he ran. Even if it meant adding an extra mile or two onto the walk, the Negroes knew to avoid the Basket Street area. It was a dangerous place for a white man. For a Negro, it was suicidal. Gene and his drinking buddies had been known to rough up a Negro who happened by at the wrong time. In the summer heat they saw the bruises on Inez's arms and legs, the black eyes, and cuts.

The truck rumbled north, then headed toward the river. In the clear September day, Inez could smell the river. She'd always been afraid one of the children would drown in it. The Tallahatchie looked peaceful, but it was as deceptive as many other things in her environment. As they bounced off the road and into the field where she would work for the next ten hours, she smiled. She didn't mind hard work. There was a china cabinet she'd seen in one of the furniture stores in downtown Greenwood. Gene had fixed up his grocery store a little, putting a huge fan in the hallway that connected the store to the house. Maybe he would let her buy the china cabinet. She could save a dime or two here and there from her own earnings. Besides, why should he care if she bought some nice furniture? He stayed in the store more than he did in the house.

During the day, Gene liked to sit behind the counter by the cash register and let the fan blow over him while he waited on customers. At night, the large, spinning blades sometimes helped to cool tempers in the dice games that went on until the men were too drunk to stand or someone was badly injured. Inez did her best to keep the children away from the store at night, but as they got older, they paid less and less attention to her orders. They never obeyed Gene, unless he was close enough to grab them or hit them with something.

Her mind on the older children, Inez climbed out of the truck and held out her hands for Peggy to give her the food and water, and finally, the baby. They were getting away from her. Boyd was thirteen, or thereabouts, and looking like a grown man. She'd been fifteen herself when she'd married and had Boyd, her firstborn. And now Gene had him off in the woods, tending the still, cooking the mash. Inez tried to argue against it, but Gene didn't like her having an opinion about men and their work.

"Mama?" Peggy's face held a question. "Mama?"

Inez found herself standing at the back of the truck, one arm holding Ronald and the other stretched out before her as if she were beseeching the empty truck bed. Peggy had already hopped to the ground and now stood, staring up at her mother.

Inez turned to find that the other women had already picked up the empty sacks and were headed into the rows that burned white under the pale sun. The rows of cotton blistered in the distance, seeping into the blue-white horizon.

"Get your sack," Peggy reminded her mother. Peggy held her own sack made from a ten-pound flour bag. At the age of five she could pick a ten-pound-sack full and help her mother toward the coveted three-hundred-pound goal. Even Sheila, who was barely above toddler stage, had a sack. Inez gave Peggy the baby to hold until she got enough cotton in the sack to make a nest for him. Then she would place Ronald on the sack and drag him along behind her as she picked the bolls that looked so white and inno-cent—and which could tear tender hands to shreds.

Inez plucked the bolls and started filling her sack. The Negroes they'd passed along the road were finally straggling in. Some of them would not make the day's minimal quota of two hundred pounds. Mr. Hadden would tell them they couldn't come back and pick for a few days, or a week. Or a month. That type of punishment meant financial ruin. Inez ducked her head lower and tried to get her fin-gers to move faster. Most of the pickers were Negroes. As hard as it was for her to find the money for the necessities and a few pleasures, the Negroes had it much worse, especially those who lived on the plantation property. It seemed no matter what they did, there was always something to set them back.

Like the P-scales where the cotton was weighed each evening to determine the picker's pay.

Inez looked around to see if Peggy had Ronald and to check that Sheila was following her down the row. Today she'd make cer-tain to watch the way the men weighed the cotton. Hers and the Negroes'.

"Miss Inez."

She heard the surprisingly deep voice of the small Negro man who hurried toward her. Straw looked upset.

"Becky said you were going to pick today, Straw." Inez didn't stop plucking the bolls as she talked. "She said Mr. Hadden was goin' to get over being mad and let you go back to work."

"He said, but that ain't what he done." Straw looked over the fields. "He said not today."

Inez nodded. She knew Becky and Straw were having it hard. Straw lived not too far away along the river, and he fished and worked the fields, and did more than his share of drinking. Often with Gene. The difference was that Gene could sit on his stool and work or not the next day. Straw needed to be out in the fields or on the river. Becky worked as the maid for both Albritton families, when they could afford some extra help. But her wages were a pittance compared to what Inez earned in the fields.

"What did you do to get Mr. Hadden so mad at you, Straw?" Inez asked. She'd often wondered.

Straw shrugged. "Didn't finish my two hundred."

"That's a week off at most. You ain't picked in a month."

He shrugged again. "Didn't make my two hundred for a few times."

Inez nodded. She caught sight of Peggy drifting through the cotton rows, Ronald in her arms. "Peggy Ruth, come on back here with that baby."

Peggy hesitated, then turned to peep through the brown stalks and see if her mother could really see her. She met Inez's steely gaze and knew she was trapped.

Since thinking about the way her children were falling away from her, Inez had determined to take a firmer hand with Peggy.

"Mr. Hadden keeps a whip. A big, ole black whip made from snake hide, and he's going to flail the skin off your legs if you take that baby off and upset me," Inez warned. Of all her children, Peggy seemed the most headstrong and determined. She challenged Inez on a daily basis. Almost moment to moment.

Peggy slipped through the brown stalks and deposited Ronald on the tail end of the long sack. The baby blinked his eyes against the bright sun and finally squinched them shut. Peggy stood back, watching.

"Is Mr. Gene up to the store?" Straw asked.

Inez hesitated. One thing Becky didn't need was for Straw to go down to the store and start with the whiskey before noon. "He said something about runnin' the trot lines." She shrugged. Gene did what he wanted, when he felt like it. Chances were that he might have gone fishing.

Straw nodded, looking over the field where men and women made slow progress down the rows, dragging the twenty-foot sacks behind them. He shifted from foot to foot. "Maybe Mr. Gene got somethin' for me to do."

"Maybe." Inez kept picking, ignoring the heat that would build with each passing hour. It was not yet eight o'clock, and already a sheen of perspiration had formed on her face. She looked back to see that her sack of provisions and the jugs of water were still at the end of the row. "Peggy! Peggy! Take that water and food over to the shade. No point making it hotter than it has to be."

Peggy grabbed two water bottles and took off for the big white oak that grew at the edge of a field. The carefully tended brown soil felt wonderful to her bare feet. Next year she'd have to get shoes. The teachers at school made the children wear shoes, whether it was cold weather or not.

When she turned back, she saw Straw tip his hat and amble away. Straw was in trouble. She didn't understand how, but she knew that he was. She went back for the last jug of water and placed it against a tree root in the shade then retrieved the food. She shook the sack, knowing already that it contained cheese and crackers and peanut butter crackers. That was what they had for lunch most days. Good, mellow rat cheese and saltines. Peanut butter spread thick on the same saltines. Water. And maybe an RC Cola. She glanced up at Inez and wondered if her mama would spare the nickel today for the soft drink Mr. Hadden sometimes brought out to the field. Maybe if she were good. But Peggy knew from experience that being good didn't always bring a reward. Often as not, it didn't prevent punishment. She picked up her flour sack where she'd dropped it and started to the row where her mama worked. She'd pick cotton for a while and see what lunch brought.

Chapter Four

Peggy opened her eyes and watched the squawking blue jay in the branches of the oak tree. He hopped from branch to branch, moving ever closer to where she lay on the ground, half awake and half asleep. Even though she hadn't done a single thing, the bird was putting some kind of cussin' on her. She squinted her eyes closed and thought that Sammy could put an end to the bird's awful fussing. If she had a gun, she'd end that fretful racket. Twisting onto her side, she found the empty RC bottle and remembered the satisfaction of the sweet cola. Sheila was asleep beside her. Peggy sat up slowly and scanned the distance until she spotted Inez's small frame, stooped and moving inch by inch down a row far across the field. Rolling in the warm grass, Peggy eased away from Sheila and turned toward the river. Her mama had told her to stay away from the Tallahatchie. During the hot weather there were water moccasins all around the banks. And alligators sunning themselves in the yellowish mud. Peggy had seen the reptiles and knew they were very dangerous, but that wasn't what was on her mind.

Adventure was to be had among the tangle of trees and vines and the thick layer of dead leaves. It was possible to catch a rabbit or squirrel, to discover something of value hidden in the secret heart of the woods. Quickly, Peggy slipped from the shade of the oak toward the thicket of trees, taking care not to attract anyone's attention.

Out in the field, Inez wiped the sweat from her forehead. Her dress clung to her, and her hair was soaked. Behind her, Ronald fretted in the depression she'd made for him in the cotton sack. It was over half full, and she pulled it with each step. If she kept up the pace, she'd make three hundred pounds today. That was no guarantee the scales would weigh her in at that. It would all depend on who worked them and how they'd set up the weights. Since she could neither read nor write, the suspicion that the men at the scales sometimes cheated her was difficult to prove. Today, though, she'd count the counterweights. Boyd and Billy both were good with figures. She'd ask them when she got home.

She shaded her eyes with one hand and looked toward the tree where she'd left Peggy and Sheila. She could make out what looked to be the two little girls still stretched out asleep. A few cheese crackers on top of several hours of steady work had finally taken the starch out of Peggy. Inez nodded to herself with grim satisfaction. They were good girls. Hard workers. Peggy had picked a good bit of cotton, and Sheila had tried to help, too. Inez could work faster, though, if both children slept on. She turned back to the rows that seemed to stretch for eternity. Her middle and forefingers and her thumbs were tough and calloused, but the prickly cotton husks had managed to snag a few cuticles that had begun to bleed slightly. She ignored them and picked on.

Moving steadily toward the woods, Peggy kept an eye on the cotton field and her mother. When Inez stopped and stared toward her, she froze, waiting until Inez went back to work before she scampered the rest of the way to the trees. Peggy stopped in the dense shade of the woods. It was at least ten degrees cooler, and the leaves, still green with summer, fluttered with secret promises. Peggy moved stealthily, as Boyd had taught her, so as not to warn any of the rabbits that might be out of their warrens and unaware. The boys brought home rabbits and squirrels for supper, and that brought praise from Inez. Sometimes even a grunt of approval from Gene. Peggy knew she could kill a rabbit, too, even if she didn't have a gun. Boyd and Billy had told her she could knock it in the head with a stick and kill it. Searching the thick carpet of leaves, she finally found a stout walnut branch that wasn't too rotted. Now all she had to do was find the rabbit. Her mama would be excited. They'd have something good for supper, and none of the children would have to sneak into the grocery store and steal food.

Carried away with her own fantasies, Peggy wandered farther from the field. The trees grew thick, laced with scuppernong vines that, only a month before, had yielded the wonderful wild grapes. Boyd and Billy had brought home sacks of them and Inez had cooked them down with some of the sugar she'd snitched from Gene's moonshine supply. The resulting jelly was wonderful, a deep purple color that was not too sweet but just perfect on biscuits. Now all traces of the grapes were gone, the vines empty. Peggy kicked at the ground and turned up a few dried hulls. Staring up into the dizzying blend of tree branches and sky, she could see that the scuppernong leaves had taken on the first tinge of yellow. They were always some of the first leaves to predict cool weather.

Peggy heard what sounded like wood striking metal, and then the man's voice. "Hey! What're you doin'?"

She froze, one foot ready for the next step. Her daddy had talked about people comin' round his still and how he'd shoot them. If she'd stumbled on men making moonshine, they might shoot her, too. She held herself motionless until she had to breathe.

"What you got there, boy?"

The man's voice was angry. Peggy thought she recognized it, but she wasn't certain.

"I ain't got nothin'."

That voice Peggy recognized. It was Straw, and he sounded so scared she knew he had done something wrong. Knowing that the men had not seen her and were not talking about her, she inched toward a big bay tree and crouched down at the base of the trunk. She couldn't see them, but she could hear them, and in the distance there was the glint of the Tallahatchie winking the afternoon sunshine back at her. She hadn't realized she'd strayed so close to the river. She was a long way from the cotton field. A long, long way.

"What you got in your hands?"

"Nothin'."

"You lyin' nigger, hold out your hands!"

There was a moment's silence.

"You thievin' bastard. You're worse than an egg-suckin' dog. Where'd you get those eggs? Hey! I'm asking you a question. Where'd you steal those eggs from?"

Peggy forgot her own troubles as she listened to the exchange. Straw sounded terrified. A breeze gusted off the water and shivered the leaves above her. Peggy thought it was Straw's fear, rattling the leaves like dry bones. She heard it in his voice, could almost taste it. She braced her bare hands against the smooth trunk of the tree. Her brothers and sisters had stolen eggs before. They'd never gotten caught, but raiding a henhouse was more on the lines of a prank. Why was the man so mad?

"I found 'em. Here in the woods."

"Like hell you did. You stole 'em from the shed."

"No, sir, they was here. Where the chickens had come over in the woods to nest."

"Don't you lie to me, nigger. There's folks who can get the truth out of you."

"I ain't lyin'."

Straw's voice broke, and Peggy thought he was going to cry. She held her breath. Crying didn't do any good. She wanted to tell him that. She'd seen her brother cry when her daddy was getting ready to hand out punishment. It seemed that crying only made it worse. She wanted to tell him, but she was too afraid to do anything. At home, sometimes when she tried to stop Sammy's beating, her daddy would turn on her and punish her instead.

"You're lyin'. Niggers can't help lyin'. But I tell you what, there's ways to stop a nigger from stealin'. There's men in this town that know how to break a nigger of egg suckin'."

"I foun' the eggs in the woods."

"You own those chickens that laid them eggs?"

"No, sir. Ain't my chickens."

"Then those ain't your eggs, are they?" The man didn't wait for Straw to answer. "Niggers around these parts are gettin' way too full of themselves. You one of those, Straw?"

"No, sir, me and Becky was just hungry. We ain't had eggs in a while, and I foun'—"

"You knew those eggs weren't yours. You already said you didn't own the chickens, and there can't be eggs without chickens. So whoever owns the chickens owns the eggs, right?"

"They was in the woods."

"Let me tell you, Straw, this here's a free warnin'. Folks don't like the attitude you people are gettin'. You can't take what you see just 'cause you want it. Hard work is the ticket. You don't work, you don't eat eggs. Now if we have to pay a visit to you and make you understand this, we'll come a-callin'."

"No need for that." There was a rustling in the leaves. "No need to come visit me."

"You tell your other black cousins and friends that we won't have no agitatin' in Leflore County. Folks here act respectable. Black and white. We know our places, right?"

"Yes, sir." The leaves rustled again.

"You get a hankerin' to vote, you remember this day. You remember . . ." the man's voice grew even more menacing and leaves crackled as someone walked, "how I could have . . ."

Straw's voice cried out in pain and fear.

"Left you out here for the buzzards to pick."

Peggy leaned her forehead against the tree. The man was going to hurt Straw. Straw shouldn't have gotten caught stealing the eggs. Even taking them from the woods was stealing. This land was Hadden land. Everything on it was Hadden. The wild grapes, the firewood, the rabbit, even the dead leaves. Where Straw found the eggs didn't matter. He was going to get punished, and Peggy only wanted to get back to her mama so she didn't have to see or hear it.

She started inching back, her head tucked down, her bare feet feeling behind her for the clear path. The blackberry brambles that edged the fields didn't grow much in the dense woods, but there were bamboo briars and a host of other prickly, hurtful things to avoid. She moved cautiously, turning slowly on her hands and knees.

Her hand found the slick, cool surface of the snake. She felt it, her brain registering fear before her eyes even found the curvy, brown-patterned body buried in the leaves. The forked tongue flicked at her, not a foot and a half from her face.

Peggy's scream filled the air. She rocked on her heels and spilled backwards, falling onto her bottom. The snake didn't move. It simply stared at her, tongue moving in and out.

Peggy's scream hit the canopy of tree leaves and echoed back. There was the sound of running, and the underbrush beside her crashed as a body ran through it. She screamed again.

Straw powered his way through the bushes, stumbling as he nearly tripped over her.

"Miss Peggy," he said, his breath hard and fast, his body shaking. "What's wrong? What you screamin' for?"

"Snake." Peggy pointed to the area where the snake had been.

Straw scooped her into his arms. "Snake's gone," he said, scanning the brown earth again. "Was you bit?"

Peggy shook he head. She'd begun to notice a distinct gooeyness on Straw's clothes. An unusual smell. She drew her hand away from his chest and found that it was coated with clear slime. She recognized it as egg white.

"I'm takin' you to yo' mama, and she's gone tan your hide." Straw looked back over his shoulder, stepping away even before he'd finished looking. "She's gone tear you up, girl. What you doin' off in these woods? You coulda got lost or hurt. What if that ole snake had bit you? Where you be then? Lying out in the leaves moanin' and dyin', that's where you'd be."

Peggy held onto Straw's neck and gave in to the safety of his arms. When he got to the edge of the cotton field, he would put her down and leave her. Peggy knew he wouldn't tell Inez where he'd found her. He never told. Straw didn't care to bring trouble down on anyone's head. With stolen eggs smashed all over his clothes, he had enough of his own.

When they stopped at the edge of the woods, Straw put her on her feet. "You better git on to your mama," he warned. "Now go before I change my mind and tell her how far I found you in those woods."

Peggy started to run through the last few yards of woods. Her feet hit the tilled earth of the cotton field and she picked up speed.

"Stay out of them woods, Miss Peggy," Straw called softly to her. "Stay out of them woods. Bad men hiding out on that river. They'd snap you up faster than a ole gator."

Peggy ran on. She could just make out Inez's small figure in the middle of the field. With a squeal of relief, Peggy tore down the row, dodging the pickers who either gave her a smile or a curse. She ran and jumped onto the nearly filled cotton sack that looked like an enormous, bloated earthworm. Sheila was already riding the sack, and Ronald was sitting on top of it, steadied by Sheila's arms.

"You been back in those woods." Inez never stopped picking, but her voice held danger.

"I went to hunt a rabbit for supper." Peggy had almost forgotten why she went into the woods. "Straw got caught stealin' eggs."

Inez stopped. "He got caught? Is he okay?"

Peggy nodded. "The man was going to hurt him, but . . . he didn't." Best not to mention the snake. It would only upset her mother.

"Straw better quit that foolishness and find himself some work or he's going to be in bigger trouble than he knows." She wiped the sweat from her brow with the back of her bare, brown arm. When she pulled the sack, a muscle bulged, a hard knot jumping out on

41

delicate bone. She paused a moment, looking over the field. The pickers were bent to the work. Not twenty yards away two black women picked side by side, talking as they worked. When they felt Inez's gaze on them they looked up and hushed.

"I'm gone have to talk to Becky when we get back to town." Inez seemed to be talking to herself. "Straw has to watch it. Folks don't like a shiftless nigger, and Straw's gettin' that reputation." She grabbed the sack where it fitted across her chest and held it away from her sweating skin. In the late afternoon hours she'd lost momentum with her picking. She still had a good twenty pounds to go before hitting three hundred. "Peggy, go get me some water." She turned back to the cotton without even waiting to see if her daughter responded. She had to make three. That would give her seventy-five cents for the day. She could save twenty for that china cabinet that she'd day-dreamed about for most of the afternoon.

Chapter Five

Willie stopped the truck in front of the Albritton store. Though he didn't kill the engine, he looked longingly in the open door where he could barely make out Gene's upper torso behind the counter.

"Care for a cold drink, Willie?" Inez asked. She offered him an RC Cola in payment for the ride.

"No thanks, Mrs. Albritton. I got to be getting home."

She nodded. "Will you be by tomorrow?" The arrangement of the ride was day to day. Willie owed Inez no commitment on his time or his truck. If he worked and felt like stopping, he did.

"Yes, ma'am, if the truck runs, I'll give you a ride to the field tomorrow."

"Thanks, Willie." Inez lifted the angry baby and the empty water jugs that clanked together in the food sack. Sheila stood at her leg, but Peggy was already gone. Inez searched the front yard with quick glances. That girl had disappeared in a flat second.

As the truck moved away, Ronald began to cry. His diaper was wet and soiled, and Inez knew he would have a rash as angry as he sounded when she finally got a chance to get him into a clean diaper.

"Mama!" Sammy ran off the porch. His eyes were troubled. "Daddy says he wants supper right away. He's got a game tonight."

Inez jostled the baby in her arms. "Get the water jugs for me, Sammy." She started toward the house.

"I got a project in school," Sammy said. "It's about storing energy. Do you think I can get a battery for my science project?"

Inez didn't bother to answer. There wasn't an answer to that question. There was never enough money around for food, much less foolishness for school projects.

"Inez!"

She was on the porch when she heard Gene's yell. The baby in her arms screamed in frustration and irritation. She started into the house to change Ronald, then thought better of it and turned back into the yard and went to the open doorway of the store.

"Get some food on the table. We got a game tonight, and we want to get started early."

Inez eyed the supplies in the store. She went and got a bag of flour, testing the water to see if Gene would yell or throw something at her. When he didn't, she ventured a step further. "Got any fish cleaned?"

Gene pointed to a paper wrapped parcel. "Traded for that 'possum. Cook it up with some sweet potatoes and some peas and okra."

Inez picked up the bundle, still warm. "Straw got caught stealin' some of Hadden's chicken eggs."

"I know." Gene grinned. "He came by here. Chicken mess on his shirt and near abouts somethin' else in his pants."

"He's gone get in big trouble, Gene. You'd best not be sellin' him anything else to drink."

"It ain't my fault he gets a bad head and can't work."

"It may not be your fault, but you aren't helpin' it any either."

"Straw ain't my worry." Gene's tone took on an edge. "Is he somethin' to you?"

Inez took a breath. "He's Becky's husband. She depends on him not to get himself beat to a fare-thee-well, or to bring trouble to their home. They live out there by themselves." Gene's lanky body straightened, a slight difference in his posture, in the way he looked at her. Inez knew it too well. "It's just that bad things could happen out there. No neighbors around to help." She slowed to a stop.

"Do you know somethin' about bad things, Inez?"

"Nothing." She spoke sharply. "I don't know anything about bad things. And I don't want to know. I just don't want Becky and Straw to know either."

Gene grinned. "You been listening in on my talks out here in the store?"

"Gene, I got children to put in bed, dishes to wash, clothes to fold and mend. I don't have time to listen to your talk."

He nodded, easing back in his chair. His point was made. "Put that 'possum on to cook. I don't want it too greasy."

Inez turned. Her legs were trembling worse than they had been from working all day in the cotton field. She hadn't seen the jug down by Gene's feet. She didn't need to see it to know that he'd been slowly sipping at it all day. It was getting to the point that he drank every day. No matter how much he sold, there always seemed to be plenty for him to drink. And as for his talks, she'd be glad when winter came and the bedroom windows would be shut tight. She did hear them late at night. What she heard was hate and meanness that seemed to boil out of their very souls. They came over to the store, lost their money at dice, got themselves worked up and angry on wild talk and liquor, and finally went home to wives and children who cringed at the sound of their arrival. Inez knew it all too well. But lately, the talk had become more focused, more dangerous.

The men who threw dice and drank were all agitated over the idea of Negroes voting. Inez didn't follow the comings and goings at the Leflore County Courthouse, but she had heard the talk. Some Negroes had tried to register to vote. They'd somehow gotten the idea that they could cast a ballot like anyone else. Outsiders had come into the area trying to stir up the voting mess, and now a few Negroes who either wanted trouble or didn't understand what stink they'd stepped in were determined not to back down.

They were determined to vote. As if it would make a difference. Why would they want to vote, and why would anyone care if they voted? Most Negroes she knew wouldn't bother voting if they had the right. Like her, they didn't have time to go to the courthouse. There was work to be done. Inez herself had never cast a ballot. Gene took a big interest in the sheriff's election every four years, but other than that, politics was only something the men fussed and complained about.

Why should it matter to them if a handful of Negroes straggled in to the courthouse and voted? What possible difference could it make? Those were questions she'd never dare ask. Never. Not if she wanted to keep her bones unbroken and her eyesight and senses. A constriction in her chest made her pause, hand on the screened door to the house. For a split second, she thought she was dying, baby Ronald and the 'possum clutched against her bosom with one hand. The pain passed, and she recognized it as a bolus of fear that had traveled through her, as if she'd swallowed it. Now it was lodged in her stomach, nesting beside the tenth baby she had carried in her twenty-nine years of life. Gene's beatings were getting more and more vicious. He was itching to find a reason to beat her now. She could smell it on him, the desire to hurt her. Maybe to hurt the baby. He'd made it clear he didn't want another mouth to feed. He was always pleased when she went to him and told him she was carrying a new life. As the term of the pregnancy wore on, though, he grew more and more resentful. Yet when she'd delivered, he was at her right away to start another child.

She caught her breath and her tattered courage and went into the house to start supper. The 'possum weighed better than four pounds. At least it was dressed so she wouldn't have to skin it and clean it. On the way to the kitchen she put Ronald down on a pallet that served as a makeshift playpen. His cries had turned to painful whimpers, but she didn't have time to tend to him now. Gene wanted his supper. Ronald would have to toughen up, like the rest of the children had done.

Hiding under the porch, Peggy listened to the exchange between her parents. As her daddy's tone had hardened, she'd backed deeper beneath the house. The hunger she'd ridden home in the truck with completely disappeared. Her daddy was in a mood to punish someone, and like as not it would be her or Sammy or her mama. It would be better to let supper pass and hope there was something left over for her to grab on the way to bed. If she didn't show up at the table, and no one missed her, she could avoid a beating.

Crawling to the back side of the house, she hunted for Sammy. Her view was blocked, and she would only be able to see the lower half of his body, but she knew him by his thin legs and shoes. Maybe she should warn him about Gene. If Sammy started asking for things for school, he'd surely get a beating. Gene already wanted Boyd to stop going to classes and to help with the still and the store. At eleven, Billy, too, was getting old enough to work. Sammy was only seven, but no matter what he did, Gene found fault with him.

Peggy rocked back and forth in the damp coolness beneath the house. An idea came to her. The store would be empty during supper time. Mary Jean, who was twelve and too big, had showed her how to slip through the fan blades and get into the store. There were candy bars and crackers and chips. Peggy's hunger returned with the force of a physical blow. She swallowed and began to inch toward the edge of the porch where she could see when Gene went inside for supper. She wouldn't have long. He never took more than ten minutes to eat, and he'd lock the door of the store just to prevent such a theft.

She considered asking Mary Jean or Faye for help but decided against it. If they knew, they'd want some of what she took. Or maybe all of it. That was the problem with warning Sammy or getting help from one of her older sisters. Helping or needing seemed to end up in some kind of punishment. Peggy determined to hide under the house and keep her mouth shut. It just wasn't worth the danger to do anything else.

She'd learned patience in the long days of sitting in the cotton field while her mother worked. She hunkered down on her heels, her head grazing the timbers of the house. The old homes were built up with a two-foot crawl space to allow for cooling in the summer.

It was perfect for Peggy. Dropping into a half sleep, half trance, she waited while the September dusk thickened into a soft, velvety night.

The frogs and crickets whirred and sang and Peggy drifted deeper into the small space inside her that was her only safety. When she heard her mother's voice calling Gene, she was almost reluctant to scuttle to the edge of the porch and initiate her plan. She'd have to climb through the bedroom window and then hurry to the hallway, turn off the fan, get up on a chair and climb through the blades, get into the store, make it back out, and restart the fan. In her dozing state she'd made a small list of what she intended to grab. If she got everything, she'd have to find a good hiding place. From her brothers and sisters, and from the ants and rats.

"Gene!" Inez's voice cut through the darkness, and Peggy was aware of the sound of footsteps above her. Her brothers and sisters had gone inside. She could only wait and see if Gene noticed her absence. No one else would say anything.

The sound of the store door being pulled closed made her tense. She couldn't hear any more footsteps above her in the bedroom, but she had to be certain everyone had gone to the kitchen before she climbed in through the window. Her father's feet and legs passed by.

Peggy darted out from under the opposite side of the house, climbed on top of the fifty-five-gallon drum Gene used to haul sugar to his mash and was in the window in a flash. She could hear the whir of the fan, louder than she'd ever heard it. Sneaking down the hallway that connected home and grocery, she moved a chair into position before she found the switch to the fan and clicked it off. It seemed to take forever for the blades to slow. She imagined her father, already sitting down, his heaping plate being set in front of him by Inez. He would be eating now while the others fixed their plates and found a place to sit. Peggy stared at the fan blades still whirring and saw her father lifting a forkful of food to his mouth. He would be finished soon. She hurried toward the fan, hand extended. When she thought she could safely try, she reached into the blades and slowed them. Sammy had told her never to do such a thing or her hand could be cut off. The metal blade banged against her fingers, slowing. At last she brought it to a halt. Pushing and pulling the blades, she managed to slip between them. In a matter of seconds she was in the shop.

She went first to the Hershey bars, then the beef jerky, grabbing a few plastic sacks filled with the salted peanuts she loved to pour into the neck of an RC. Her small hands were filled, so she crammed some of the contraband into her panties. Her heart was almost making her deaf. She had to get away before Gene caught her stealing from him. He'd tear the hide off her. Clutching at some bubble gum on her way by the counter, she hurried to the fan. With her hands full, she managed to climb up and crawl through the blades. On silent feet, she ran to the fan switch, hit it, and dove through the window. As she hit the ground, she rolled up under the house.

Pulling the booty from her panties, she laid it in front of her. She unwrapped one of the beef sticks and ate the spicy meat as she toted up what she'd gotten. She had three candy bars, five pieces of bubble gun, two bags of peanuts, and two more beef sticks, not counting the one she was eating.

"Peggy!"

She heard Mary Jean's voice and instinctively hunkered over her goodies.

"Peggy, Mama said if you didn't get in here right this minute she was going to tear you up!"

Mary Jean called the whole thing out in one breath.

Peggy eyed the goodies. There wasn't time to hide them and she certainly couldn't take them into the house. She lowered her head to see where the dogs were. They'd eat it all, except the bubble gum, if they found it. The chickens might eat it. They ate anything. Even rocks.

"Peggy Ruth, get your butt in this door or you're in big trouble." Mary Jean still stood on the step, waiting for some sign.

Peggy crawled out from under the house on the opposite side. Running on her bare feet, she hurried to the back door. "I was playing," she said.

"Mama's been lookin' for you." Mary Jean shook her head. They all knew not to aggravate Gene, especially not before he ate. The liquor had had all day to work on him, and he was mean as a snake if he got provoked.

Peggy scooted up the steps. She managed not to even look under the house. "I was playin'. I didn't do anything wrong." Peggy knew defending herself was useless, but she had to try.

She got a plate and hurried to the table, taking the vacant chair that Mary Jean had left. The 'possum was gone, but there were potatoes and biscuits left. Peggy filled her plate and started eating, eyes on the food in front of her. Remarkably, nothing was said by anyone and Gene stood up. His plate was perfectly clean. "Make us some pitchers of iced tea," Gene told Inez. "Send 'em over in 'bout an hour." He walked through the house and let the screened door slam as he headed back to the shop.

"Some men from out of town are coming to play tonight." Boyd was filled with the news his father had confided in him. "There's going to be big money on the table."

"You children are not to leave this house. Not for any reason." Inez looked around her then slapped the table with her palm. "Do you hear me?"

"Yes, ma'am." They answered in unison, but none of them looked at their mother.

Peggy felt a ripple of excitement. If the men were strangers and the stakes were high, there would surely be a fight. Fights brought opportunities for profit. She chanced a look at Faye and saw that her sister was thinking exactly the same thing.

"If I catch a one of you out of your bed, I'm going to beat you until you see Jesus."

"Yes, ma'am," they all answered again. This time Peggy joined in.

"Mary, you and Faye do the dishes. Billy, Boyd, you boys make sure your homework is done."

"Mama, can I . . ."

"No!" Inez swatted at Sammy's head, catching him a glancing blow on the temple. "You know we don't have the money for school things. They shouldn't ask children to take things to school that cost money."

Sammy blinked back his tears. "They didn't ask. It's a science project. I wanted to do it."

"Forget science projects. We have to eat." Inez waved him away. "Take care of Peggy." She remembered Ronald, who had been strangely quiet. "Oh, Lord, I've got that baby with a bad bottom." She hurried from the kitchen and found him in the play pen. His face was red with fever, but he'd given up crying.

Inez unpinned his diaper and lifted him by the feet. In the lamplight she saw the angry, scalded skin. It would take a lot of baking soda to heal that rash. She clucked her tongue and went to gather the things she'd need to care for him before she could drop into bed.

Chapter Six

The house had finally settled into the stillness of nighttime, and Peggy lay in bed and listened for her mother's footsteps going to the bathroom. Her mother's step faltered, and Peggy held her breath.

Since the last beating, Inez was not exactly sick, but not right, either. There were times when it seemed the husk of her mother's body was there but some essential ingredient had evaporated. Inez's hands continued to work the dough to make biscuits or hand-stitch a dress for one of the girls. Sometimes, though, even when she was standing or sitting right in front of Peggy, Inez was strangely gone.

The change frightened Peggy. She was torn by the desire to avoid her mother and her need to protect her. But it was night now, and her father was occupied in the grocery. Busy with setting up for the crap game, Gene had left his family alone.

Mary Jean's regular breathing calmed the night on the left side of the bed. Beside Peggy, Sheila, the youngest of the girls, was sound asleep. A mosquito droned above the bed as Peggy tried to determine if Faye, too, had drifted off to sleep. Thinking of her treasures beneath the house, left there for any animal to raid, Peggy wasn't able to sleep. She had to go outside and get them and then find a place to hide them. Somewhere cool or the chocolate would melt. The Hershey bars would last for a while if she ate only a little each day. Or, she could gobble one down and enjoy the rush of satisfaction that came with completely sating an appetite. Either way, she had to retrieve the goodies first. Easing her feet out from under the worn sheet, she slid off the side of the bed into a standing position. Mary Jean's light breathing continued, a harmony with Sheila's deeper, baby sleep. At last Peggy heard Faye's sigh. Asleep.

Peggy tip-toed to the window and threw a leg over the sill, poised to climb out.

"Where are you going?" Faye sat upright in bed.

Peggy hesitated. She could do a lot of things she wasn't supposed to do, but she'd never been good at fooling Faye.

"You're going to the store!" Faye's voice hardened with excitement. She flung the sheet back and grabbed her shirt where she'd dropped it when she climbed in the bed. "Strangers are comin'. There'll be a fight."

"Shut up or you'll wake them." Peggy had forgotten about the dice game and the men from out of town. Most of the time the games involved only local men. Violence was more likely when strangers visited. And violence meant profit.

"Wait for me." Faye started toward the window.

Peggy let herself go over the sill, dropping to the ground on hands and knees. She scuttled under the house. Her horde of treasures remained just as she'd left them. In the darkness Faye went on to the store, giving Peggy time to put her stash on top of the cage where her father sometimes kept 'coons or dogs or other animals. The cage was empty now. She lined her stolen goods on top of the empty cage, out of reach, until she could do better. Bare feet skimming the ground, she ran toward the glow of a single light bulb that hung from a cord and illuminated the interior of the store. Twenty feet away, Peggy hesitated.

Light spilled out of the front door and the single big window that bore the painted Albritton Grocery sign. The sounds of men filtered into the soft night. The dice game had just begun. Peggy could tell by the excitement, the tone of their voices. There was still camaraderie among the participants, hope of winning, a streak of sobriety. Before the night was over, that would deteriorate to dark suspicion and concerns of being cheated, all fed and twisted by drunkenness. That would be the moment when the fighting started.

Peggy slipped through the open door. Gene caught her eye. He didn't smile or nod, but he didn't order her out. Peggy drifted toward the counter, passing the rack that held the boxes of candy bars where she'd helped herself earlier in the evening. The bubble gum container was nearly full. She looked at the sweets and passed on. Gene might act as if he were paying attention to the dice, but he never failed to see when one of his children tried to sneak a treat. She slipped behind the counter, surprised to find Boyd and Billy waiting.

"Where's Sammy?" She looked around for the brother closest to her age. She wasn't tall enough to see over the counter and shelves, and Sammy could be anywhere in the deep shadows.

"Over by the bread." Billy pointed out his hiding place. "He can get to the table quicker than us, but we're safer back here if they start shooting. Uncle Buddy's here." He nodded toward Gene's brother, who lived a block away with his wife and children.

Peggy sat down. She was tired, but the prospect of money kept her awake.

"Peggy! Faye! Get out to the door and keep watch." Gene motioned to the front door without taking his eyes off a pair of dice being tossed by Judge Walker.

"Damn! Snake eyes!" Judge watched as Vernon Prescott scraped the dice off the cement and began to rattle them in his hand.

The dice clattered against the wall. "Fever in the funk house! Run, whore run!" one of the men whooped.

Peggy edged toward the door, eyeing the action of the game. Three of the men were strangers, and Uncle Buddy watched them as they followed the game. They were slightly better dressed than the dice regulars. They were also cleaner, with an eagerness in the glances they shared that boded trouble. For them or someone else.

"Break out some of the good stuff, Gene," Buddy said.

"Billy! Bring me a jug from under the counter." Gene spoke to his favorite son before he yelled at Peggy. "I told you to get out there and watch for the law. And none of your tricks. We've got guests here tonight, and they wouldn't think much of a girl trying to pull something over on 'em."

Peggy stepped through the door and into the pool of light that fell across the yard. In the shadows, Faye leaned against the side of the grocery. Around them, Basket Street was quiet. There was only the sound of the craps game inside the store. Peggy half listened to the men cajoling the dice, rattling and shaking them before they clattered against the wall and brought out cries of glee or curses.

"Come on Little Joe from Kokomo!" Virgil Upchurch called.

Peggy leaned her head against the cool wall. The night was close, too humid and hot. Moths and roaches fluttered against the lighted window, sometimes making it through the door and into the grocery.

"You think there's going to be a fight?" Faye asked.

"Maybe." Peggy thought about her candy. If she pretended to go to bed, she could sneak away and get a bite of chocolate, but then she might miss a chance at some money. She was tired. Too tired to stand, so she slid down the wall and sat in the dirt, her legs folded under her, Indian-style.

"There's lights comin'." Faye's voice took on an expectant note.

Peggy tensed. Two lights bobbed over the ruts in the road as the vehicle came toward the store. There was no way to tell if it was someone coming late to the game, or if the law had decided to bust up the game and haul whoever they caught off to jail for a night.

"Daddy!" Faye hollered the warning. "Car's coming!"

"Easy boys!" Gene said. "It's just One-Eyed. He said he'd be coming late."

The old car pulled up near the front of the store. The man known as One-Eyed because he'd lost his left eye and wore a glass one got out and walked up to the store.

"Yessir! Yessir! Everything's fine and ya baby's mine!" One of the strangers called as he slammed the dice into the wall.

"Keep a sharp watch, girls," One-Eyed said as he passed between Peggy and Faye and went into the store.

Peggy eased back against the wall. The law coming would be about the best thing. The game would have to break up, and she could get her chocolate and go to bed. She was determined to help Inez pick cotton if she went to the field in the morning. Peggy was deeply troubled by the vagueness in Inez that came and went without warning. It had happened again in the bed of the truck, Inez reaching out to nothing. Inez's convalescence, too, had been different. Usually Inez was up and going a day or so after a beating. Inez never missed a day's work during harvest. She'd been in bed for five days.

Peggy shifted her weight from foot to foot as she recalled what had happened. Even Gene had shown concern. Though he'd refused to take Inez in for medical treatment, he'd spoken with the doctor, who'd given him some new medicine for Inez.

Peggy swatted at a bug. The medicine only seemed to make her mother worse. When Inez took it, she went into a deep sleep where she talked and struggled, repeating phrases that meant nothing to Peggy. Watching Inez twist and pull at the sheet, Peggy felt as if her mother was lost and trying to find her way home. Peggy couldn't think of a way to help her.

"They're too happy," Faye said, as eager as Peggy for the game to be over. Faye did well in school, but the late games took a toll on her alertness the next day. "Did you see any guns?"

Peggy sat up straighter. She'd forgotten to look for guns. "I don't know," she said.

"You better learn to pay more attention. One of the strange men, he had one sort of in the back of his pants." Faye yawned big. "There'll be a fight tonight." Faye swatted at the mosquitoes that feasted on her legs. "Maybe a big pot of money."

Fatigue tugged at Peggy's eyelids. She leaned her head back against the store and tried to make her eyes stay open. If she slept, no one would wake her. The Albritton children were too competitive among themselves. They would not wake her to participate in getting the money, just as she had no intention of sharing her candy with her brothers and sisters. There was never enough of anything for generosity or sharing. Peggy knew if she wanted a few nickels or dimes or quarters, or maybe even a few dollars, she'd have to stay awake and pay attention.

"Got any more of that mash?"

Peggy didn't recognize this man's voice. He was one of the three strangers. She knew most of her father's dice buddies.

"It's five dollars." Gene's voice was pleasant but firm.

"Let's have another jug," the man said.

"Billy! Get us a jug!" Gene called out.

"What are those younguns doing out here?" the stranger asked. "Shouldn't they be in bed somewhere?"

"Their mama's sickly. They're out here to keep the house quiet."

"Don't seem like a place for younguns."

"You want to shoot dice or you want to talk about my younguns." Gene's voice held a threat. Peggy peeked inside to gauge the tension in the room.

"Let's roll," Uncle Buddy said, easing between Gene and the stranger. He held out a pair of dice.

"Give 'em here." The man turned away from Gene and cupped the dice in his fist. "Come on seven! Seven come eleven. Come on seven—you know yo' daddy loves you!" There was the sound of blowing and spitting, and the dice clattered against the baseboard followed by a round of curses.

"Boyd, get us some of that rat cheese and a box of saltines," Gene said. "Sammy, get out of them corners. You're always slinking around like somebody's bastard."

"It's your turn to roll, Gene." Buddy spoke. He scooped up the dice from the floor and handed a pair to his brother.

At the sound of her father's name, Peggy stood up, stumbling on numb feet. She glanced in the doorway to see the men's backs as they knelt or squatted on the floor. Gene took the dice from Uncle Bob's hand. Shaking them in his fist, he called out a nine and threw them against the wall.

"Damn!" Several of the men shouted.

"You've got the touch, Albritton. Those dice roll over for you." It was one of the strangers speaking.

Peggy heard the dark undercurrent in the words and knew the night had truly begun. She'd heard it before, the comments on the Albritton luck, the insinuations of cheating.

"I've had a lot of practice," Gene answered, his voice slick and easy. "Maybe that jug ought to go 'round one more time before I throw again."

There was laughter as the jug passed. Peggy slapped a mosquito on her cheek, the sting part of staying awake. She looked to see that Faye, too, was standing, shifting her weight from foot to foot.

"Put your money up, boys. The dice are fixin' to talk. Seven come eleven!" The dice chattered, and Gene laughed. There was the sound of change being raked over the cement. "You've got to learn to talk to 'em," he said.

A cloud of cigarette smoke hung in the room as Peggy peeked once again. Her feet were tingling where they'd gone to sleep and now were coming awake. Peggy was petite and skinny, with a tumble of unkempt curls. Her size worked to her advantage—she could find a lot of places to hide.

"Roll again, Albritton. Let's see if that strange run of luck you're having's gonna hold. The way I've been figurin' it, you've got a take of more than a hundred dollars there."

"If your luck is runnin' poorly, you can leave."

At the sound of Uncle Buddy's voice, Peggy stomped her feet. Once the fight started, they had to get in quick, snatch the money that would be thrown around the room, and either get down behind the counter or get out the door. Last winter over two hundred dollars had been thrown in the fire during a panic when the gamblers thought the sheriff was coming. Peggy had almost gotten the clump of wrinkled green money. Almost, but not quite. The flames had been faster than she was.

Her favorite moment was when the men jumped up, scattering the pot of greenbacks and change all over the floor. She had the advantage of being small and quick, but the boys were stronger.

"Is it my luck that's poor, or your cheatin' that's good? Let me see them dice."

"Get out." Gene's voice was controlled but hard. "Get out now while you can."

"I want my money back."

"You can't stomach losin', you shouldn't get in a game," Uncle Buddy said in a low, dangerous voice. "Now you boys git. This is a regular game, and we don't have such talk goin' on among ourselves."

The scuffle of feet was the first sign of violence. At the sound of leather soles shifting on the cement, Peggy bolted in through the door, barely edging Faye out of the way. She felt her sister's hands on her hair, but she ignored the tug and ducked as the men all stood up in a rush and money flew in the air.

Out of the corner Sammy scurried forward, along with Boyd. As the men stood and began to push and punch each other, the children scrabbled along the floor, picking up change and dollar bills that had escaped Gene's or Buddy's sweep.

The fighting turned violent. Blows were delivered and absorbed with grunts and curses. Peggy never looked up. There was always someone hurt, someone cut, or bones broken. She had no time to think of the grown-ups. Money was her only objective.

"You motherf—!"

Peggy ducked as one of the men went stumbling past her and crashed into the glass front of the candy counter. Peggy scanned the floor for more money, and when she could find none, she crawled over to the candy. Holding her take in one hand, she used the other to stuff bubble gum into her panties.

"I been cut! I been cut!"

Peggy glanced up to see one of the strangers holding a hand to his face. In the harsh light of the single bulb that hung over the men, blood seeped black between his fingers and dropped to the front of his white shirt. "Shit, Arlan, they cut my face."

"We'll do worse if you don't git while you can," Uncle Buddy promised.

"You cheatin' bastard, you're dead!" The youngest of the strangers pulled the gun from out of his pants. In the sudden hush of the room, the sound of the hammer being pulled back was startling. "Give me my money or you're gonna die."

Gene swallowed and held up his hands. "Don't make a fatal mistake, mister."

"You better take that gun and get out of here," Uncle Buddy said as he eased away from Gene's side. The men shifted slightly, all pulling back from the target. They breathed in huffs and puffs, winded and scared. Virgil broke for the door, throwing himself through it and landing on his stomach in the patch of light on the ground. He made a whoofing sound as he hit and rolled, seeking the darkness of the night.

"Put that gun down," Gene said carefully.

As two others in the room started for the door, the stranger swung around on them, holding them still with the blue steel barrel. "All I want is my money," he said.

Peggy huddled down into the tiniest ball she could make, using the side of the shattered candy counter for flimsy protection. A sliver of glass was embedded in her knee, but she ignored it. Billy had escaped but now he scuttled back behind the counter. Searching the dark corners, Peggy met Sammy's frightened gaze. Faye peeped over the back of the counter.

From behind the wood stove Billy stood up. He lifted the shotgun he'd gotten from the house and aimed it at the stranger. "Drop your gun," he said.

"That's it, son. If he doesn't put the gun down, shoot him." Gene straightened, his stance assuming the lanky grace that was natural to it. "If he makes one false move, blow his ass away."

All adult eyes were turned on the twelve-year-old boy who held the heavy shotgun in wiry arms, the stock larger than his shoulder. Silence ticked softly in the hush.

"Arhrh!" The cry came from a dark corner of the store.

"You cheatin' bastard!"

Vernon Prescott charged across the room. High above his head he held the hatchet Gene used to behead catfish.

The barrel of the shotgun swiveled in Billy's hands, a motion so fluid Peggy followed it as though she had no will of her own. She saw the gun buck and Billy stagger from the discharge. The hatchet jumped from Vernon's hand and went sailing through the front store window. The words "Fresh Fish" shattered, crumbling into diamonds and falling away in the night.

Peggy watched silently as Vernon's hand flapped back on his arm, hanging by a strand of muscle and skin. The blood pumped a split second later, pouring out of the wound and covering his arm as it spilled darkly onto the floor.

The stranger pointed his gun, first at Billy, then at Gene and Uncle Bob Moye, Gene's brother-in-law. Peggy had heard all her life that Uncle Bob had murdered a man down in Florida. She held her breath, waiting.

The strangers formed a tight knot and backed out of the grocery, gun shifting back and forth should anyone think about trying to stop them. As soon as they were out the door, they broke and ran for their car.

Vernon staggered, lurching forward as he stared at his flapping hand. One of the gamblers caught him under the arms while another gripped the bloody wrist tightly, folding the hand back into place as he took the towel Uncle Bob handed him.

"Looks like someone needs a doctor," Uncle Bob said easily.

"Get him out of here right now," Gene said. "Everybody git. The game's over for tonight."

Chapter Seven

"Peggy Albritton, you've gotten off on the wrong foot in this classroom." Mrs. Crow stood up at her desk stationed at the front of the room of the first grade classroom.

Peggy looked away from the petite teacher who was fuming at her and toward the pages of fall leaves the first grade class had colored the day before. Mrs. Crow was petite, but her angry face and sharp tone frightened Peggy, so she focused on the pictures tacked up along the top edge of the chalkboard. Peggy loved to draw and color. She was good at it, too, though Mrs. Crow hadn't said so. It seemed no matter what she did or said in Mrs. Crow's classroom, it was the wrong thing. "Are you going to tell me why you didn't do your printing assignment? Everyone else in class turned in their printed words." Mrs. Crow advanced half the distance to Peggy's wooden desk.

"You don't do your work in school; you don't do your work at home. What do you think you're doing here?"

Peggy looked out the window, ignoring the twenty-odd pairs of eyes that stared at her. Later, during recess, they would point and giggle about her, or run away if she acted as if she wanted to play with them.

"Look at me when I talk to you!"

Mrs. Crow's temper was getting hotter and hotter, and Peggy felt the stares of the other children, heard the giggles they no longer bothered to hide. Though she was small for her age, she was older than most of the other children in first grade. She'd had a few scrapes with several of them, kicking and punching with a viciousness that made even the boys back away from her. Fighting was a survival tactic, not a means of settling hurt feelings. When Peggy fought, it was with everything she had in her, and without regard for the consequences.

"Look at me, girl!" Mrs. Crow's heels clicked against the floor as she approached Peggy's desk. "Look at me when I'm talking to you."

Peggy felt the teacher's fingers dig into her arms and draw her out of the desk. She looked up into Mrs. Crow's small face, red with anger, the mouth set in a grim line. Then her vision blurred as Mrs. Crow shook her until her head snapped back and forth and stars streaked behind her eyes. Finally the teacher thrust her away and pushed back into her desk.

"I don't know why you bother to come to school," Mrs. Crow said as she walked away. "You do everything you can to deliberately defy me."

Titters and giggles swept the room, and Mrs. Crow whirled around.

"Sit down and be quiet!" Mrs. Crow slammed her book on the top of her desk and glared around the classroom. "Just because Peggy can't learn is no reason the rest of you have to act like heathens. Open your readers to page twenty-seven. Anna, read aloud."

"Dick saw Jane run down the hill." Anna read perfectly. It was obvious she practiced at home.

Peggy sat motionless in her desk, her book unopened. She was so tired her eyes burned, and her neck hurt from the shaking she'd just received. The night before, there'd been another argument, another fight. Inez had purchased a china cabinet from a Greenwood furniture shop, putting ten dollars down on it and putting the hundred and ninety dollar balance on credit. She'd saved the money from her job in the cotton fields, and she had worked all afternoon putting the Albrittons' unmatched collection of plates, bowls, cups, and glasses on the shelves. Peggy had not seen her mother so happy in a long time.

Once it was filled, Inez had stood before it, her fingers skimming over the delicate curve of the polished wood, the design carved in the shape of a fan, the way the wood was smooth and cool beneath her fingers.

Peggy didn't fully understand Inez's fixation with the piece of furniture, but she knew that her mother yearned for that cabinet. Inez acted as if the cabinet would work some magic on the Albritton home, if not the family itself.

Though Inez had talked about the cabinet for months as she'd pushed herself to the three-hundred-pound goal, she'd never told Peggy that she intended to buy it. The furniture store had delivered it while Gene was out tending to his still in the woods along the Tallahatchie.

Gene, already drunk, had taken one look at the cabinet and gone into a red-hot rage. First he'd lifted it up, smashing it into the walls and floor. Inez stood helplessly, her fists to her head as if she could stop the noise of the wood splintering. Gene ignored her, turning his full attention to the piece of furniture. He'd stomped and kicked it, beating it with a hammer, cursing and raging until he'd finished it off, smashing every dish in it in the process.

He'd told Inez not to buy the piece of furniture. He'd told her not to put anything on credit at the furniture store. Even knowing that Inez would have to work months in the cotton fields to pay for the cabinet, he'd destroyed it in front of her. Then he had turned on Inez, beating her in much the same order he'd used on the cabinet, except for the hammer. His fists and feet had done enough damage. He didn't need the hammer.

As battered as Inez was, it was the loss of the cabinet which smote her harder than any blow Gene had delivered. Peggy thought a little piece of her mother had died with the destruction of that single piece of furniture.

After one of the boys had carried Inez off to her bedroom, Mary Jean and Faye had cleaned up the broken dishes, picked up the splintered wood to burn in the stove Gene had fashioned from a fifty-five-gallon drum in the grocery store. Peggy had hidden under the house, defiantly eating a candy bar she'd stolen while Gene was rampaging in the house. She'd crammed the entire bar in her mouth, eating it all at once. And she'd stayed awake all night, listening to her mother's soft sobs. Peggy knew it was the cabinet she was crying about, not her swollen face and bruised arms, legs, and ribs.

"Are you going to read, Peggy?"

Peggy lifted her gaze from the unopened book on her desk. She didn't look Mrs. Crow in the eye. She shook her head no. She wasn't certain she could read the lesson. In all the confusion there had been no time to practice, and no one around to help her when she got stuck.

"I suppose reading isn't necessary in the Albritton family." Mrs. Crow pointed to another little boy. "Read, Jim."

Jim read slowly, hesitating before each word, but he made it through the two sentences without a mistake.

"Good work, Jim," Mrs. Crow praised. "Now, Shirley."

Around the room the reading went. Peggy sank back into the nightmare of the night before. The rest of the afternoon passed in a blur. Numbers, printing, singing, reciting little poems. She sat, or stood, as the case required, but she said nothing. Not a sound escaped her mouth. Until at last the bell rang and she was free to go home.

W. C. Williams Elementary School was close enough to Basket Street for the Albritton children to walk. Peggy knew the route, and on the way home she loitered, then ran, slowing again to a crawl as she neared the four-room house and attached grocery. She didn't want to go home, yet she could not stay away. There was nowhere else to go. And no one to see about her mama.

When she arrived, Inez was not home from the fields. Gene was in the store, listening to the radio and talking with one of the Prescott men who had stopped by to visit. On the porch, Becky sat with Ronald in her lap. The sight terrified Peggy. Becky only came when Inez was too sick to take care of the baby.

Becky gazed at Peggy for a long moment. "Your mama's okay. She just couldn't drag this baby out in the fields today. It's hard to believe that little mite of a woman can pull a cotton sack the way she does. Especially not when her eyes are swole shut and she can't open her jaw enough to eat. She ought to give up breedin', but I think she's planted again." Becky shook her head. "Man ought not to beat his wife who's carryin' his child."

Peggy stared at the baby in Becky's lap. Her mama had said he was the last. She said there would be no more babies, but Inez had said that about the little baby boy that died, the one before Ronald. Peggy had never considered that the babies' arrival could be stopped. The babies came, a fact as regular as the cotton crop. If one was a girl, she would be put in the bed with Peggy and her three sisters. A boy would live on the back porch where all the boys slept. It was by far the best place in the summer, when the Delta breezes found their way through the rusted screen to lick at the summer sweat that was a part of August sleeping. During the winter, though, the blankets and tarpaper or plastic that Inez and the boys hung didn't do a lot to keep the cold out. "Could you bring me a glass of water?" Becky asked.

Peggy nodded again. Unless she was cleaning or cooking, Becky wasn't allowed in the house. Even after she cooked a meal, Gene made her sit on the back steps or the front porch to eat it. "Daddy broke all the glasses."

"I jus' use an old Folger's coffee can."

Peggy went inside and found the can that was put aside for Becky's use. She filled it and took it out.

"Straw's skinnin' some fish out in the yard." Becky reached out and pushed Peggy's uncombed hair from her face. "You the toughest of the lot, aren't you? The toughest and the one who hurts the most." She took the water from Peggy's hands.

"Mrs. Crow shook me till I saw stars," Peggy blurted.

Becky's hand brushed her cheek again, light, tender. "That teacher shook you?"

Peggy nodded. "I didn't do my work at home."

66

"Uh-huh." Becky jostled the baby on her knee. "Go on to the back and see if Straw's workin'. He always loafin' around. Go see if he's doin' what he should."

Peggy jumped off the porch and walked around the house, avoiding the kitchen and the place where the china cabinet had so proudly stood.

As Straw skinned and filleted the mess of catfish he'd caught, Peggy watched, nearly dozing in the late afternoon sun. Her brothers and sisters were in and out, but a silence had settled over the house. Peggy could hear the radio playing in the store. Peggy contemplated another raid, but she was too tired to figure out a plan.

At last she heard the truck coming and knew her mother had come home. She ran around to the front yard, compelled by an urge to see her mother, to make sure that she really was okay.

Inez lugged the flour sack that contained her water jugs out of the back of the truck. "Thanks again, Willie," she called before she started walking home. When she got to the front porch, she sat down without reaching for the baby. Her face was swollen, her lip cut and puffy, one eye shadowing a dark bruise.

"Peggy say that teacher shook her today," Becky said.

Inez looked at Peggy, who'd stopped in the yard.

"Did she shake you?" Inez asked.

"She shook me so hard I saw stars," Peggy answered.

"Well, she won't do it again." Inez lifted the sack and went inside to begin supper.

The night passed in a soft calm, the typical lull after an eruption of violence. Exhausted, Peggy ate her biscuit from her hand in the backyard. Since most of the dishes were broken, the children had grabbed what they wanted and gone back out into the late evening twilight. When at last it was time for bed, Peggy crawled in beside her sisters and slept.

It was the next morning before she realized Inez was not going to the cotton fields. Even more peculiar, Becky had arrived again to keep the baby. When Peggy started toward the school, Inez fell into step beside her.

"I'm goin' up there to talk with that teacher of yours," Inez said. "She won't be shakin' no youngun of mine."

Peggy didn't say anything. School was already bad enough. If her mother went and made trouble, it would only be worse.

At the classroom, Peggy slipped into her seat and watched as her mother approached Mrs. Crow. They were both small women, neither weighing more than seventy-five pounds. But Inez was lean muscle and bone.

"Peggy said you shook her," Inez said, getting right to the point.

"Peggy doesn't do her work. She can't keep her attention focused on what's going on in the classroom." Mrs. Crow turned to straighten the books on her desk. "She's never prepared properly for school."

"Did you shake her?" Inez asked.

"I was merely trying to get her attention."

Inez's hands shot out, grabbing the teacher's arms. She shook her with a force that snapped the teacher's head back and forth, a whipping motion that unsettled her thin, light red hair. Inez dropped her hands and stepped back. "Don't you ever touch her again, you hear?" She turned and walked out of the classroom, leaving Peggy at her desk.

Chapter Eight

"Hey! Come see what I broughtcha!"

Gene Albritton's voice rang out through the front yard with the energy and charm that he seldom used for family members.

Hiding from Sheila in a chinaberry tree, Peggy lifted her head to listen. Excitement surged through her. Without regard for the possibility of a broken bone—or being discovered by her annoying younger sister—Peggy sprang from the tree, dropping six feet to the ground where she balanced on her toes and hands until she could dig her feet into the soft dirt and sprint to the front yard.

"Look out!" Gene yelled, laughing, as something whanged the bed of the truck with great force.

Peggy stopped in her tracks. There was something alive in the truck. Something big and alive. And it wasn't one of the tabby catfish that could get up to a hundred pounds or more. It was something else! Something fierce and angry! The big catfish, though they could fight with tremendous force in the water, were usually done in by the time they got to the store, dead, or near death, from lack of oxygen.

Billy and Boyd came out of the house, running up to the truck with a fearlessness that made Peggy hurry over, too. She climbed up on the bumper beside her brothers and peeped in. A large, muscular, green tail struck the tailgate of the truck so hard it nearly shook Peggy in. Billy's hand clutched her shirt, catching her before she toppled in the truck bed with the six-foot alligator.

"Easy there, girl," Gene said. "That gator will have you for supper." He laughed.

"Where'd you get him, Daddy?" Billy asked.

"Tallahatchie River. I eased that boat right up on him and clobbered him in the head. Before he could come to, we tied a rope on his jaws and another around his neck and drug him to shore. I thought you kids might want him for a pet."

Billy, Boyd, and Peggy looked up at their daddy. He grinned down at them then laughed aloud.

Peggy returned her attention to the alligator. She noticed for the first time that a cotton rope held his big jaws shut, and his head was oddly shaped. It took her a moment to realize that a portion of his skull was caved in. He lay motionless in the bed of the truck. Without warning, he stood on his six-inch legs and whirled, sending his tail lashing into the truck with a whack that knocked Peggy to the ground. She climbed back up and held on tighter. As the alligator spun in the truck, Peggy saw the rope dangling from around his neck.

"What are you going to do with him?" Boyd asked.

Mary Jean, Sheila, and Faye had appeared at the front door. They watched from the safety of the house.

"Let's get him out of the truck," Gene answered.

Peggy and the boys backed away as Gene lowered the tailgate and grabbed the rope. With a jerk he pulled the gator to the ground.

The reptile hit hard, stunned for a moment. When it recovered, it swung blindly, using the powerful tail to seek the enemy that threatened.

Shrieking and screaming, the children scattered. Gene drew his feet up on the tail gate and held the end of the rope.

Flip Russell, Edward Hadden, and Breland Ainsworth pulled up at the grocery. Gene hailed them, and they ambled over to check out the excitement in the Albritton front yard.

"You better kill that thing or turn it loose," Flip said as he stopped a safe distance from the alligator. The animal was obviously injured but still had plenty of fight in him.

Gene ignored the suggestion. Pulling the noose tight around the alligator's throat, he drew another piece of rope from the truck. Reaching under the gator's belly, he tightened the rope just behind the front legs. He stood up and looked around the yard. "Who wants to ride the gator?" he asked.

Inez had come to the door, the baby in her arms. "Gene . . ." She let the sentence trail away.

"Come on, Boyd." Gene motioned to the oldest boy.

Boyd hesitated, looking away from his father and at his mother. Inez shook her head no, but she didn't say anything.

"Y'all afraid of an old gator? His mouth is tied. He can't get you." Edward Haddon called out. "Big ole boys almost grown and afraid of a trussed up gator."

Peggy eyed the rope around the animal's jaws. It was frayed, but it would probably hold. Still, the tail looked like it could hurt. The gator was lying perfectly still now, flat down on its stomach. But she'd seen it rise up on its legs. It could move pretty fast. And the skin didn't look like it would be fun to sit on.

"Don't be a sissy," Gene said. He turned to Billy. "What about it, boy? You afraid of a tied up gator? I thought you'd want some fun." He blew a disgusted breath out his nose. "Where's Sammy?"

"I'll ride." Peggy stepped up. She felt everyone staring at her. She'd been in trouble only the night before for dancing around the radio when Gene was trying to listen. She'd only meant to make him laugh, but instead he'd slapped her and sent her into the house. Now he was watching her, his mouth turning up into a smile. "I'll ride him," she repeated with more conviction.

She wore a pair of old shorts and a top that had once belonged to Mary Jean and then Faye. Since the weather was warm her shoes were tucked under the bed.

"Well, Peggy's got all the balls in the family," Gene said, laughing. "Come on up here." He motioned her to his side, and Peggy hurried over. The alligator remained perfectly still, its sides heaving as if it hadn't fully recovered from the hard fall out of the truck.

Peggy stood by her father's leg, the khaki of his pants close enough to touch her cheek. She barely came to his waist. There were only a few days of school left, and she would be going to the second grade. She had not passed her classes, but after a visit to the school by

Inez, the teacher had thought it best to move Peggy along. While the other Albritton children passed without problems, Peggy could not concentrate on the words to learn to read. The numbers jumped around on the blackboard, pushed out of their neat columns whenever a siren passed outside the school window. There had been several fires in the house when Inez was left alone. No real damage had been done, but on one instance, Inez had nearly caught herself on fire. The idea of fire kept Peggy so unsettled she couldn't pay attention, and Gene was constantly berating her for her poor grades. Now, at last, she had gained his approval. He was smiling at her.

Gene swiftly moved away from her, taking two long strides to stand beside the alligator's head. Gene planted a firm foot on the animal's neck, grinding him into the ground. "Climb on," he directed Peggy.

Taking note of the gator's knotty hide, Peggy eased up on top of his back. The animal made an attempt to struggle, lashing its tail in the dirt. Looking behind her, Peggy saw the long patterns left in the dirt. They were beautiful, like tiny waves of sand that rippled in a semi-circle. She fastened her small hand under the rope, gripping it as tight as she could. She had no idea what the gator would do when her father let it go.

"Hold tight," Gene said.

Another car pulled up and Flip called out to Jimmy Hataway and Pete Denley. "Hey! Get over here. One of Gene's younguns is gonna ride a gator."

The two men piled out of the truck and trotted to the bare front yard where Gene, Flip, Edward, Breland, and the other children made a semicircle.

"Go get Molly," Peggy said to Billy. If she was going to ride the alligator, she wanted her cousin Molly to see. Over the past few years, she and Molly had developed a close friendship. As good a friends as they were, Molly would never believe she'd ridden an alligator unless she saw it with her own eyes.

Billy didn't move. "Sammy! Run over to Uncle Buddy's and get Molly," he called to the shadow of a boy lurking at the edge of the porch. "Hurry!"

Sammy took off at a run, cutting through the side yard toward the Dewitt "Buddy" Albritton house, which was half a block away.

The gator shifted, trying to stand. Even through the tightly tied jaws it made a hissing sound that was part desperation and part fury.

"Hang on, Peggy," Gene said. He looked at his friends, his light eyes speculating. "Want to put some money down on how long she can stay with him?"

"Two dollars she won't make a minute." Pete eyed Peggy's thin arms. "Make it three dollars."

Flip laughed. "You don't know Peggy much. She won't let go till thunder knocks him dead or he snaps her hand off. I'll say five dollars that she makes it at least a minute." They turned to Gene and Jimmy.

"I'll put a dollar on her hanging on," Jimmy said. "Who's gone get her when she comes off?"

"Let me and the gator worry about that," Gene said, holding out his hand to collect the bets. "I'll say five dollars she makes two minutes."

Inez stepped out of the door. The baby had begun to fret, but she ignored him. "Gene . . . please . . ." She stopped when he lifted his head to stare at her. The humor had left his face.

Peggy looked at her mother then shifted to her father's angry jaw line, the cold look in his eyes. "Let him go, Daddy. Turn him loose! I'll hang on."

Gene lifted his foot and hopped up on the tailgate of the truck.

"Ride 'em, cowgirl!" Jimmy whooped, slapping his thigh with his hand.

"Hang on, Peggy!" Billy yelled.

"Ride 'em." Boyd slapped the side of the truck to make a noise and get the gator on his feet.

The sound startled the animal and he stood. The sudden motion and the rough hide nearly unseated Peggy. She caught her balance in time and held on as the gator made a dash away from the truck toward the back yard.

The world jounced and jolted as the rope bit into Peggy's hand. She held tight, her forty-six-pound body all lean sinew.

"Go! Go!"

She could hear the shouts and cheers behind her, but her entire focus was on staying with the panicked alligator. She'd meant to count—to be sure she stayed on the full two minutes to prove her daddy's trust in her was justified. But the numbers jumped around in her head the same way they did on the blackboard at school.

The gator cut a sharp left, away from the edge of the house. Peggy looked up in time to see her mother's face. The distant look had returned. Inez stared blankly out into the yard. Lashing with his tail, the gator tried to shake her off, and Peggy's head snapped, jerking her away from her mother.

"Go, Peggy! Go! Twenty-five more seconds!" Jimmy's voice came, raw with excitement. "That'd be my minute."

"Run around there and drive the gator back this way." Gene lifted a stout wooden club, still bloody from the initial bash across the animal's snout. He handed it to Boyd. "Go!" Gene barked when Boyd hesitated. "Since you won't ride it, you can herd it."

With Billy at his side, Boyd moved around the house and came up in front of the alligator. The animal stopped abruptly but remained up on its legs. The tail lashed once then ceased as it waited for Boyd to make a move.

"Kick him in the sides," Boyd directed Peggy. "Get his attention so I can pop him and get him turned."

The hard knobs that ran down the center of the animal's hide were rubbing raw spots on Peggy's bottom. She had no desire to make the gator move, in any direction. If he stood still, she'd finish off her two minutes and get off. She sat as motionless as possible.

"Kick him," Body directed. He took a half step forward, glancing from the alligator to his father.

"No fair!" Pete called. "No fair if the gator don't move. That ain't considered ridin' it. The time don't count!"

"Make him go," Gene agreed.

Boyd stomped his feet and darted at the gator. Before he could land a blow with the club, the gator swung around and caught him at knee level with his tail. Boyd went down on his back, the air whooshing out of him.

Peggy saw no more. The alligator was moving again, running fast toward the south.

"Peggy! What in the hell are you doin'?"

Peggy recognized her cousin's amazed voice and she tried to catch sight of her. The jouncing ride made it impossible to really see anything.

"I'm riding him next!" Molly cried.

"No, me!" Billy said.

"Billy's next," Gene said. "Then Boyd and then Molly."

"Two minutes!" Jimmy called, jumping up and down. "Two minutes, Peggy."

It was all Peggy wanted to hear. Her arm felt as if it had been jerked free from her shoulder. Blood seeped from her palm where she'd gripped the rope so tightly it had cut into her skin. She forced her fingers open and dove to the left, rolling in the soft dirt as fast as she could in the opposite direction of the gator. He was Billy's problem now.

"Peggy!" Inez's voice was filled with panic. "Get up! Get up!"

Still dazed from rolling, Peggy climbed to her knees. She never saw the gator's tail as it slammed into her, the hard muscle knocking her several feet into the sand. She felt blood pouring from her nose but she didn't stop to examine the damage. Scrabbling on hands and knees, she made for the front porch steps and the safety of her mother's arms.

Chapter Nine

Gene kept the alligator, dubbed "the Albritton taxi," chained in the yard when it wasn't being deviled by the children or adults. It was an effective threat to use against any blacks who didn't have cash money for their purchases. The gator also served as a door guard, forcing blacks to ask permission to enter the store. As the days warmed and lengthened, the children grew less afraid of the animal and began to ride it throughout the neighborhood.

The children especially loved riding it over at Verline's church, waiting until the congregation came out of the building and headed for their cars. The open space of the church property gave the gator hope of escape, and it ran fast, sending the congregation in all directions.

Word of the gator was passed on to the Leflore County sheriff and Constable Bill Mays in the form of complaints and hysterical calls from area residents who saw the "Western front" children riding about on a scuttling reptile with its jaws roped shut. Law officers paid a call on Gene, recommending that he take the creature back to the river. Gene, naturally, ignored them.

While the alligator was heating up the summer on Basket Street, racial tensions were beginning to simmer throughout the state, particularly in the Delta area.

In 1954 the U.S. Supreme Court handed down the *Brown versus the Board of Education* ruling, declaring that all schools should be integrated. It was a verdict that white Mississippians did not take seriously, but it was a foretaste of the coming change. The federal court ruling was viewed by many white Mississippi residents as an unnecessary act of aggression from an external force. Mississippi wanted neither change nor interference—especially not that handed down by outsiders.

Negative talk against the actions of the courts and federal institutions was only the beginning. Talk soon turned to action.

On May 7, 1955, Reverend George Lee, a black minister who worked to register voters, was shot twice in the face with a shotgun as he drove along Church Street in a black neighborhood of Belzoni. According to witnesses, Lee's car was pursued by a convertible. The convertible drew abreast of Lee and two shot-gun blasts were fired.

Lee died en route to the hospital, his death ruled accidental. He was shot in the face, and the local sheriff said the lead pellets found in what remained of his mouth were "dental fillings."

The U.S. Supreme Court pressed the integration issue harder in June of 1955, saying that desegregation should "proceed with deliberate speed."

The feeling of persecution by federal agencies combined with a new source of concern. Blacks were beginning to register to vote. They were attempting to integrate schools.

On August 17, at ten o'clock on a Saturday morning, sixty-year-old Lamar Smith, a black farmer who was working to register black voters and who had earlier dared to cast a ballot, was murdered on the lawn of the Lincoln County Courthouse in Brookhaven.

Although it was a busy Saturday, there were no witnesses to the shooting.

The climate in the entire state was such that NAACP field secretary Medgar Evers reported to his superiors that blacks were terrified to come forward with information regarding the violent incidents of the summer. Enrollment in the NAACP dropped at a heady pace. Locally, blacks feared association with the NAACP because of economic, if not physical, reprisals against them.

On a national level, the murders of Lee and Smith had begun to paint a bloody picture of Mississippi, but for the most part, the troubles in Mississippi were only a sound-bite on the national conscience. The nation wasn't paying particular attention—yet.

In the Albritton home, events farther than the front yard held little interest for Peggy. At eight years old, she'd repeated the first grade and was ready to enter the second. The summer was over, though the weather had not cooled—and probably would not until mid-October.

Preoccupied with worries about her mother, Peggy struggled into her school dress and appeared for the first day of school in Mrs. Carruthers's class. Inez insisted that Peggy go to school. Inez had never learned to read and write, and she was determined that none of her children would be illiterate. No matter how much Peggy fought against school, she would go and she would learn.

For her part, Peggy had begun to develop the tough little exterior that showed the world she didn't give a damn. She had learned the hard lesson that a show of weakness brought out the killer instinct in a stronger enemy. When the teachers rebuked or humiliated her, she dared them to do worse. When the children mocked or teased her, she fought them into an attitude of repentance. Students and teachers alike came to determine that she was best left alone with a book, where she could escape into fancy and wait for the release of the bell. The sound of a siren would paralyze her with fear. Unable to leave school, she would sit in her desk and listen, trying to determine if the ambulance, police or fire trucks were headed toward Basket Street to discover some new horror involving Inez. Although Peggy did not confide her fears to anyone, her new teacher sensed that she was not being deliberately obstinate.

To Peggy's amazement, Mrs. Carruthers was a teacher who took an immediate interest in her, and whose gentle encouragement lent a bit of eagerness to Peggy's school day. For the first time in her life, Peggy found approval from an authority figure. When a wailing siren outside the window drew her attention away from the teacher, Mrs. Carruthers would softly call her back.

"Peggy?"

At the sound of her name, Peggy pulled herself out of the nightmare and stared at the slender woman who stood expectantly at the blackboard where the equation two times four had been written.

"Do you know the answer?"

"No, ma'am," Peggy answered. Of all of the work, numbers were the hardest. Memorizing poems and making up stories were the activities in which she excelled—along with coloring the mimeographed pictures of fall leaves, pilgrims and turkeys, Santa and the presents in his sleigh. The multiplication tables were particularly hard, a roller coaster of numbers that increased in measured increments until they careened off the track into an abyss.

"That's okay, Peggy." Mrs. Carruthers's smile was big and especially for her. "We'll work on those later."

The teacher moved on around the room, and Peggy's thoughts went back out the window. The day was so hot that the fan running in the corner was blowing the pictures they'd colored and thumbtacked to the bulletin board. The sheets of paper made a tiny flapping sound, like soft fingers. The air was hot and filled with humidity. If the school day ever got over, Gene had promised to take them fishing. He'd said that the fishing would be best from about six o'clock until the sun set. That would give them time to pack something to eat and drink and get down to one of the rivers or one of the dead lakes where the bass grew up to eight pounds. Even if the bass or trout weren't biting, there would be bream. Or they could fish the river where the channel cat weighed in sometimes at fifty-five pounds. Monster fish with their old men whiskers and liver-spotted skin. That's what she wanted to catch. That way they could sell catfish at the store for the rest of the week and make plenty of money. That would surely make Gene happy.

Across the room, one of the boys stumbled over nine plus nine. Peggy cast a sympathetic glance at him as he blinked and looked down at his scuffed-up shoes, his voice dropping so low that he couldn't be heard. Peggy knew how that felt.

"It's okay, Jimmy. The answer is eighteen. That's a hard one. The nines are always the hardest for some reason," Mrs. Carruthers said. "Just practice tonight with that smart sister of yours, and tomorrow you'll do better."

Peggy didn't have to hear exactly what Mrs. Carruthers was saying to bask in the tone of her voice. There was not a single child in class who caught the rough end of her tongue. At least not yet. But school was only two days old.

"Okay, children, practice, practice, practice. Tomorrow I want you to be perfect." She looked around the room. "And remember, read the first five pages in your book. We have a lot of ground to cover."

The slamming of books was muted by the long ringing of the old school bell. First out of her desk, Peggy almost tripped over a classmate's gangly legs. She didn't slow down. She was out the door like a shot and down the polished wood hallway to the bright August light at the open double doors.

Boyd and Billy and Mary Jean had gone on to the high school, but she could still beat Faye and Sammy home. Sheila would find someone to walk with her. Peggy didn't have time to bother with a little sister. There was fishing to be done, and she knew Gene would leave her if she wasn't ready in time.

Even as she ran through the sticky, hot air that made her skin feel as if a residue of milk clung to her, she didn't understand her own desire to make the fishing trip. No matter how hard she tried, it was never good enough for Gene. If her father was drinking, the trip would be abusive. He would jeer and ridicule her. Or slap and punch her. If he wasn't drinking, he might not even talk to her at all. Sometimes he stopped along the way and picked up buddies. If he took one of his friends along, he wouldn't even notice which of his children had accompanied him. Still, she had to go. The idea of him leaving without her was torment. Maybe this time she would do the one thing that would make him smile at her and tousle her hair.

Huffing into the front yard, she dodged around the alligator that had tried to crawl under the house in the shade. He wasn't looking well, but she didn't have time to inspect him. She yanked her dress over her head, found a pair of shorts and a top and ran out to wait for her daddy at the back of the truck. Billy and Sammy stood there, waiting.

"You goin' too?" Billy asked.

Peggy nodded. Having the boys along could be good and bad. She wasn't sure how she felt about this turn of events. "Where's Mama?"

"Daddy said she was working over at the Stennis plantation today. They're about ready to pick."

"I got enough poles and something to eat," Sammy said, pointing to the back of the truck where the poles rested beside a flour sack. "Daddy said we need to catch some fish. We don't have anything to sell."

"Got the bait?" Peggy asked. Most of the time they used berries or corn.

"We got it," Billy answered. He looked toward the store. They could hear Gene laughing with Melvin Yates and Harrison Vance. The two men had dropped by just as Gene was getting ready to go. Instead, he'd taken them in the grocery and shut the door.

A loud roar of laughter told the children standing at the truck that the men were leaving. Melvin and Harrison stepped out into the sun, still laughing.

"Watch yourself, Gene. She may be little, but she's not goin' to like it."

"I know how to keep my house in order," Gene said, but his smile belied his stern words. "Keep 'em pregnant, barefooted, and in the fields. That cuts down a lot on trouble-makin'."

The men shook their heads, laughing as they walked to their vehicles.

Gene was still smiling when he turned to the truck where Peggy and her two brothers stood at the bumper. "So, all three of you want to go fishin'?"

"Yes, sir." They spoke in unison.

"Climb in the back." He opened the truck door and swung into the driver's seat with a fluid grace.

Her heart thumping with pleasure, Peggy jumped into the back with Sammy and Billy. Her father was in a good mood. He seemed glad they were going fishing with him. Sometimes, when he needed help raising the gill nets, he made them go with him early in the morning before school. Those mornings, especially in the winter when the river was icy and the banks frozen and dangerous, Peggy hated fishing. Today, though, it was going to be an adventure.

They headed north up toward Money and the Tallahatchie, the area where Peggy had spent the first year of her life.

"Maybe we're going to the catfish hole," Billy said. As the second oldest, he knew many of the places Gene caught his fish.

"I don't know. Dead Lake, maybe," Sammy said.

Peggy didn't care. She could already feel the pole bending in her hand as she caught the biggest fish, the most perfect fish, ever. Gene would smile down at her and tell her what a good fisherman she was.

As they came up on a small grocery, Gene slowed and pulled into the loose gravel parking area.

Abandoning her daydream, Peggy looked at the store, then at her brothers. "Why are we stopping?" she asked.

Instead of answering, they stared at her then turned to look at the back of their father's head.

Gene used both hands to smooth his thick, fair hair into place before he got out of the truck. "I'm going to get some cheese and crackers. We need something to eat if we're gonna fish." He slammed the truck door and started toward the little store, his shoes scrunching in the gravel as he walked.

"We got crackers and peanut butter." Peggy pointed to the sack Sammy had prepared. It was too late for Gene to hear her.

"It ain't cheese crackers he's after. Not by a long shot." Billy turned away and spit over the side of the truck onto the dry ground.

"What?" Peggy looked at Billy then Sammy. Even Sammy turned away from her. "What?" she repeated.

"It's Daddy's girlfriend, dummy," Billy said. "Can't you even put two and two together?"

"He can't have no girlfriend. He's married." Peggy felt the words rush out of her chest. They came up so hot they burned her throat. She knew boys and girls talked and courted. But Gene was married. He couldn't have a girlfriend any longer. Whenever he even imagined another man had spoken to Inez in a boyfriend kind of way, he beat her severely.

"Daddy has more than one girlfriend," Billy said. He was angry, too, but he was mad at Peggy.

"Liar!" Peggy's hands clenched into fists. She'd beat his teeth out if he didn't take it all back.

"Dummy!" He grinned. "You're just dumb about everything, Peggy Ruth."

Peggy jumped from the truck like a scalded cat. Her feet spumed gravel as she ran toward the rickety door of the grocery. Just at the side of the store, she brought herself up sharp. Gene wouldn't take it kindly if she rushed in on him. They were never allowed to leave the truck unless he said so. He'd been smiling, happy. If his mood turned black, they'd be at his mercy in a small boat for the rest of the fishing trip. She stopped, frozen with indecision. Finally, she eased forward. She could hear her father's voice. He spoke softly, with a hint of teasing and the easy charm he so seldom directed toward his family.

Cold fury almost suffocated her. As Gene talked, Peggy could hear the smile she craved in his voice. She could easily imagine the lift of an eyebrow that showed he was amused. The woman in the store was getting all the attention she, Peggy, so desperately needed. Creeping to the window, Peggy looked in.

"A woman with your looks deserves to be ridin' high in a big ole Cadillac," Gene said.

Carolyn Bryant's lips were bright red and expertly colored. Her dark hair was carefully done. The illumination from the light bulb made it shimmer. "You're full of it today, Gene. You headed up to the river?"

"Got to get some fish. We've sold everything."

"You do a better business there in Greenwood. Sometimes it seems the whole afternoon goes by without a single car stopping here." Carolyn tidied a block of Doublemint gum on the counter.

"Well, I know how to make an afternoon pass in a pleasurable way. With a woman like you . . ." Gene left it hanging, a tantalizing half-promise.

"You do go on." Carolyn laughed. "Now how much cheese did you want to go with those saltines?"

"Give us a pound."

"You must be planning on catching a mess of fish." Carolyn sliced off the cheese and weighed it. "Either that or you're awful hungry."

"I'm hungry." Gene leaned forward. "I'm really hungry."

Carolyn wrapped the hoop cheese in white paper and pushed it across the counter. "Maybe one day I'll go fishin' with you. No harm in a little bit of fishin'."

"No harm at all." Gene pulled the money out of his pocket. "I'll scout us out a good place. One where the fish are bitin' good."

"You do that." Carolyn rang up the sale. "You do that," she said again as she turned back to the cash register.

Outside the door, Peggy was frozen. Watching the two of them, she couldn't tell if they were boy and girlfriend. Gene had a sassy way of talking to women. Good-looking women. He teased and flattered and hinted at things that made him sound as tempting as a Mounds bar. Just melt in your mouth sweet.

Gene lifted the cheese and crackers and Peggy spun away from the door, hightailing it back to the truck. She vaulted into the bed, sat down, and didn't look at either of her brothers. She finally glanced up when she heard Gene's footsteps on the gravel. He was grinning to himself. She looked at Sammy and Billy, expecting to see their grin of pleasure at her stupidity. Instead, she saw only blank faces.

Peggy stood. "I'm gonna tell Mama." She glared at her father.

The smile left his face. "You get her stirred up, I'll just have to beat her back into actin' like a wife. You want to see her bleedin', go ahead." He opened the door and swung into the truck.

She felt her brothers' hands grab and pull her into the back of the truck as Gene pressed the gas pedal and spun out. Only Billy and Sammy saved her from cracking her head against the tailgate.

"You better shut up, Peggy." Billy flipped her onto her stomach and twisted her arm behind her back as Gene put the truck on the main road. "Don't go startin' trouble."

"Let me up." Peggy was white hot with fury. If Billy let her go, she'd tear his ears off, gouge out his eyes, snap his arms at the shoulders.

He pressed harder, his knee now on her back in the rocking truck. "I'll let you up if you promise to keep your yap shut."

"I'm gonna kill you." Peggy tasted the grit on the bed of the truck. Her wiry body hummed with hatred, for Billy, for Sammy, but mostly for her father.

"Get that piece of rope, Sammy," Billy ordered. "If she can't shut up, we'll just tie her and leave her in the back of the truck while we fish."

"I don't know . . ." Sammy didn't move. "Peggy, say you'll shut up."

The fury left her as suddenly as it came. If they tied her, Gene wouldn't make them let her go. She'd spend the evening trussed like a hog, them laughing about it. She let her body go limp, unresisting.

Billy moved his knee from her back, allowing her lungs to expand fully.

She drew a breath, and when she didn't struggle, she felt him release her arm. Easing it down beside her, she gave the pain a minute to subside before she pushed herself up into a sitting position.

"It won't do any good to start trouble," Sammy said, watching her from a safe distance.

Peggy scooted to the side of the truck where she leaned against it. She looked away from her brothers and toward the thick growth of trees that signaled they were close to the river. Billy and Sammy were right. Starting trouble would only make it worse. Gene would do whatever he wanted.

Chapter Ten

Peggy tipped the bucket of hot, soapy water into one of the empty wash trays that normally held the fish. The soap bubbles picked up the remnants of blood and gained a pinkish tinge as she sloshed the water to every corner. Faye and Sheila hated cleaning the wash trays, but it was a chore Peggy didn't mind so much. If she'd had her way, she would have preferred to work in the large vegetable garden where Gene raised the produce he sold in the store. Inez often worked the vegetables, sneaking a few things when she could for supper.

From beneath her bangs Peggy glanced up at her father. Gene sat with his feet propped on the counter, chair tipped back a little, as he listened to Patsy Cline on the local Greenwood radio station, WABG.

The brown RCA radio normally stayed in the house where Inez could listen to the swap shop or Brother Robert Hall on the early morning gospel show, but Gene had moved it out to the grocery for a day or two. He listened to the music, but he seemed to be waiting to hear something else, turning up the volume whenever a news report came on.

Peggy scrubbed the wash tray with a cloth, lifted it up, and carried it out to dump the water. As she started toward the door, a shiny black Ford pulled up at the store. Gene dropped his feet to the floor and stood. The appearance of a new-looking car usually put a smile on Gene's face, but he was not smiling.

Peggy glanced to the corner to make sure the broom was in its place, just in case her daddy asked for a show. Peggy had found her true calling in singing the rockabilly songs of a new singer, Elvis Presley. There was something about the singer and his songs that Peggy felt to the soles of her feet. She used the broom as a microphone and a dance partner.

"Git to the house."

Gene's unexpected order brought Peggy's head around.

"Move!" He pointed to the front door. "Now!"

Peggy put the tray down and scurried through the doorway, wondering what had put her daddy in a foul mood. Before he'd been counting the day's take, and they'd made money. Gene had sold the fifty pounds of fish they'd caught out of the Tallahatchie a few days before. It had gone fast. Everyone, black and white, had been hosting fish fries in the last days of the summer. Now Straw was in the back yard cleaning a mess of fish Gene had brought home earlier that morning. And she'd heard Inez and Gene talking about a carpentry job for a rich woman in Greenwood. Her daddy was known as a fine craftsman, when he chose to work. All in all, things sounded pretty good.

As she took her time leaving, she glanced through the window and saw the granite face that usually meant trouble. Ducking fast, she got out of his line of vision.

Instead of going into the house, Peggy took a stance by the edge of the front porch. She watched as two men got out of a shiny new car. They wore white shirts, the long sleeves rolled against the heat. Their black suit pants were dusty around the cuffs, harsh creases pressed into them all whichaways from riding in the hot car.

Yankees. They were as easy to spot as pigs at a church picnic.

They weren't the first to stop by the store in the past several days. Peggy knew a black boy had been murdered, and now the Greenwood area was "crawlin' with nosey reporters and damn nigger-lovin' Yankees."

She glanced at the spot where the gator used to reside beneath the willow tree. Too bad the law and the conservation men had come to take him away. They'd said they were going to set him free so he could have a good life, but her daddy had said that they would kill him, that his busted head made him unfit to live.

"Mr. Albritton?"

Edging closer to the side of the store, she peeked out to watch the two Yankees. She'd never really heard one talk, up close, and they sounded hard and mean. One of them held a big camera and the other a notepad. It occurred to her that they might put her daddy in the newspaper. The thrill made her want to jump forward, but balancing out the anticipation was fear. She'd been warned enough about Yankees and newspaper reporters. Still, if they could see her dance, they might take her picture. She had a talent for dance. Even in school they called her Peg-leg-shake-a-leg. She inched closer. She could perfectly imitate the white boy singer who sounded black and jittered across the stage, gyrating and shaking. When she really put on a show, she'd even wet her hair and slick it back like he wore his. Terrified of being discovered but unable to resist, she inched closer.

"You boys here to buy some fish?" Gene met them at the door. His smile was in place, but even from a distance Peggy could see that it wasn't real.

"We're here to ask a few questions." The man with the notepad did all the talking. He introduced himself and the man with him.

Peggy caught only the word Chicago. She knew it was somewhere in the middle of the country, a big city with belching smokestacks and buildings so tall they blocked out the sun. All in all, a very unpleasant place to live.

"Some folks up the road said you used to live at Money, that maybe you'd have some information about that Negro boy who was murdered."

"I heard that nigger got what he deserved." Gene lounged against the doorway. "I heard he made advances toward Mrs. Bryant."

"Well, we heard a lot of things." The reporter tapped the notepad in his hand. "We heard that maybe you knew something about who abducted Emmett Till. We heard maybe it was some of your friends. Maybe even some of your relatives."

Gene's pose didn't change, but Peggy knew he had gone stretched-wire taut. She saw it in the jut of his hip.

"You boys want a cool RC Cola?" Gene asked. "Looks like you're not adjusted to the Mississippi climate." His gaze traveled to their long shirt sleeves and their rumpled black pants. One side of his mouth lifted in a grin. "It's hard to tolerate a place when you come down to visit not knowin' nothin' about it."

"We'll take an RC" The man signaled the one holding the camera to move toward the store.

"You know it's too bad you didn't make it here a few weeks before. I had an old gator I caught. My younguns would ride it around like a pony. Now that would have made a good picture for your newspaper."

The reporter cast a look at the cameraman. "Yeah, it sure would have." They disappeared inside the store.

Peggy eased toward the front door where she could hear better. She'd heard talk at the store that a Negro teenager had been taken from a relative's house, beaten, shot, and dumped off the Tallahatchie Bridge into the river. They'd found his body, and the big funeral had created a lot of interest from outsiders. "You know Carolyn Bryant from up around Money?" the reporter asked.

"Sure do." Gene's voice was sociable. "Stopped by that store a number of times on fishin' trips. Mrs. Bryant is a very nice woman."

The man with the notebook was tilting back an RC so cold the condensation from the bottle dribbled on his white shirt. He put it down. "So you don't know anything about what happened to Emmett Till?"

"Who?"

"The Negro."

"I heard the boy drowned."

"Right, with a seventy-pound cotton fan barb-wired around his neck."

"There's no tellin' what crazy stunt a nigger will try to pull." Gene leaned on his hands on the counter. "There ain't no news up in Chicago for you boys to write about? You got to come all this way just to make up lies and trouble?"

"There's a lot of interest in what's going on here in Mississippi." The man flipped his notebook shut. He swirled the remains of his soft drink in the bottle. "Yeah, folks are mighty interested in what's going on down here."

"I'd say the same thing that's goin' on up North, except we aren't so interested in hidin' it."

"Not hardly." The man finished his drink and put the bottle on the counter. "Not hardly."

"Maybe you just can't see it when it's right at home."

"Thanks for the sodas. We'll be around, if you think of anything you want to tell us."

Peggy backed away from the door. She felt someone behind her and nearly jumped out of her skin. Whirling, she came face to face with her mother.

"Reporters?" Inez looked at the shiny car, then the two men who came out of the store. She put a hand to her breast and took a tiny step forward. She halted as soon as Gene came to the doorway. He shot her a look that dared her to say or do anything.

"I want to tell them," she whispered, but only loud enough for Peggy to hear.

"Tell them what?" Peggy put a steadying hand on her mother's arm. Sometimes Inez acted as if she were lost. When she did that, folks made fun of her. Peggy tightened her grip. She didn't want her mother to do something embarrassing in front of the strangers. Gene would never forgive her if she did something stupid in front of Yankees.

"I want to tell them about . . . that boy. I know . . ." She drifted off as she caught Gene's warning glare.

The men got in their car and backed into Basket Street. Gene stood in the doorway, waving to them as if they were long-lost relatives departing after a joyful visit. Abruptly, Inez turned out from beneath Peggy's hand. "I got to make some biscuits," she said. "It's time for supper."

PEGGY INCHED TOWARD the far side of the bed, listening in the stillness of the house for the argument that had broken out nightly since the reporters had visited. Her sister's body was too hot, too close for the stifling September night. Outside the open window, the night was abnormally still. The crickets and the frogs were doing their job, sawing away at the darkness with their blend of rhythm and blues. The old hoot owl that Boyd had been trying to get for two weeks was outside, questioning the night. Peggy didn't like the "who-who-whoooo!" Inez told her the owl brought death.

Absent was the sound of cars coming and going, of men talking and laughing. In the past week or so, the dice games had been abandoned.

Unable to sleep, Peggy twisted on the bed. Mrs. Carruthers had given her a special assignment. She was supposed to tell a story after lunch. Her very own story. She didn't have to write it down; she could simply stand up in front of the class and tell it. Mrs. Carruthers had said she was a gifted storyteller, but Peggy suffered ten degrees of hell at the thought of standing in front of the class.

Anticipation made her squirm. More than anything, she wanted to see her classmates listening to her, eager to hear what happened next. As much as she wanted the limelight, she dreaded the possibility of messing up. She had tried to piece her story together. It was a good one if she didn't get anxious and forget like she always did.

She flipped to her stomach and dangled her hand off the bed. Mary Jean, Faye, and Sheila were breathing softly, inhaling and exhaling with a regularity that finally lulled Peggy into relaxing. If she matched her breathing with them, she could feel the nervous hum begin to leave her legs and arms. She closed her eyes.

She heard the approach of the first car. As she listened, it pulled into the front yard beside the grocery. So, the games were on again. She let her eyes drift shut, comforted by the return of routine. Too tired to get out of bed in the hopes of a fight and money tossed about the floor, she let go of consciousness, only to be tugged back to wakefulness at the sound of another vehicle. Then another, maybe two. They were coming fast.

She heard her father. "Where's Buddy?"

The tension in Gene's voice drove the thought of sleep from her brain. She sat up, swinging her legs out of bed as she came fully awake. Her first thought was of her mother. Standing, she listened to the quiet of the house around her. Only the sleep-soft murmurs of her sisters could be heard. On the screened porch her brothers made not a sound.

Tiptoeing out of the room, Peggy headed toward the front door. Something was happening. The boards of the porch were still warm beneath her feet as she stepped into the night. Yellow light glowed from the store, and the tall shadow of a man shifted across the open doorway. Peggy's skin rippled with a cool chill. She thought of her bed even as she stepped off the porch and into the dirt. This gathering of men had none of the raucous laughter of a dice game, none of the high spirits that she'd come to expect on a hot evening.

Hard laughter slid through the open door, a blade cutting the night.

Wearing only her panties, Peggy glided across the lawn, a small shadow among the bigger ones cast by the trees and cars. Peeping through the open door, she saw the men. Instead of kneeling, their backs to the door as they gambled, they stood in a semicircle beneath the bare bulb illuminating the store. Virgil Prescott held a newspaper.

Peggy wasn't surprised to see the Prescotts, though they had threatened to kill Billy and Gene. The feud over Vernon's blasted wrist had been patched over in the spring. Vernon had admitted that he couldn't hold a grudge against Billy for nearly shooting off his hand, not when Vernon had intended to chop Gene in the skull with a hatchet. They had all agreed that it was the right thing for a boy to defend his father.

"Who-ee!" Virgil Upchurch passed the newspaper to the next man as he shook his head. "That's one dead nigger."

The men nodded. The newspaper made the rounds slowly.

"Whatever would they have an open casket for? Half his head is missing." Buddy held the newspaper, staring at it, absorbed. "Looks like a big funeral."

"Those reporters still around?" Gene spoke into the void of silence that followed the passage of the newspaper. No one had an answer. He reached behind him and pulled up a photograph.

"That'll teach them uppity Northern niggers to come down here and try something with our women."

Peggy wasn't sure who was speaking. The men's voices were different, their faces covered by the photograph that moved from hand to hand, the blank white side always facing the door.

"What happened to his head?"

Uncle Bob pointed to the picture. "That's swelling, from the beating, and that's where he was shot. 'Course being in the river for several days, the fish and the snapping turtles did a little work on him. We weren't lucky enough for a gator to snag him."

"I heard that an alligator can drag a body down to its hole in the bank and that sometimes they keep them there for months," Uncle Buddy said. "I told Gene if that gator he had got one of the younguns we might never know."

Gene laughed. "I wasn't too worried. Inez would just pop out another one."

The men all laughed. Some of the tension had eased from the room.

"Well, that's one nigger that won't be whistlin' no more," Bob said, gathering up the picture and the newspaper. "Now all we have to do is keep our mouths shut. The Yankees and the reporters will all go home and this'll blow over."

"Just like all the rest," Virgil said.

"That's right." Gene walked behind the counter. "I think this deserves a drink." He leaned down and pulled up a jug. With a quick, efficient movement he unscrewed the cap and lifted the jug to his mouth.

Pressed against the doorway, Peggy watched her father's throat work. The men were not going to throw the dice. They'd come, oddly enough, because of the newspaper and the photograph.

Gene passed the jug. It followed the same order that the picture had taken, from hand to hand, mouth to mouth. "The first drink is free," he said.

"What about Inez?" Uncle Bob wiped his mouth with his sleeve.

"What about her?" Gene's voice went deadly.

"What does she know? Did she hear all of it?" There was an argument waiting in his questions. When the jug came back to him, he passed it without drinking.

"What if she did?" Gene shrugged. "Forget it, Bob. What does it matter? Inez don't have a memory. She forgets what day of the week it is."

"There's already trouble about this." Bob straightened up. "This ain't just our business, Gene. Folks are asking questions. Outside folks."

The other men turned to stare at Bob. Finally, he shrugged, too, and lifted the jug to his mouth as it came back around.

Suddenly compelled to check on her mother, Peggy backed away from the door. Three nights before, Inez and Gene had had a terrible fight. Inez had fought back like a wild thing. She'd climbed on Gene's back and ridden him around the bedroom, punching and screaming, the name Emmett Till falling out of her garbled cries and curses. Gene had beaten her until she was unconscious, and then ordered the children to put her in a tub of cold water. He had pulled her from the water, his fingers twisting in the wet material of her dress, and told her if she ever spoke the name Emmett Till again, she would pay a terrible price. Emmett Till, the murdered Negro. Emmett Till, the boy the men were talking about. Fear seemed to swell inside Peggy's small ribs. She sucked at air, but nothing seemed to go inside her. She had to get away before they saw her.

Crouching low, she started backing up, ready to abandon the night and the men who seemed to thrive on violence.

"Peggy!"

Her father's hand clamped down on her bare shoulder, the long fingers digging in for a good grip.

"Ow-w-w-!" Peggy fought against the punishing grip, but her father lifted her into the store.

"Get in here!" He grasped her hair for a better grip. "What are you doing out there in the dark?"

"She was tryin' to steal some candy." Uncle Bob grinned at her. He held the pictures in his hand. "Or maybe she was trying to poke her nose in business that don't belong to her."

"I heard y'all laughin'." Peggy tried to glare up at her father, but his hold on her hair was so tight she couldn't lift her head. "I came to see what you were laughin' at."

"You want to see what we were laughin' about?" Bob asked very politely.

"Yes, sir." Peggy tried not to squirm against her father's fingers tearing at her hair. She stood tall and still.

"Turn her loose, Gene," Bob said softly.

Tears stung her eyes at the sudden cessation of pain. Gene's fingers were still on her head, but he had quit pulling. She would not cry. It was a battle of wills with her father. While the other children cowered and obeyed, she refused. To do so would be to betray Inez. She looked straight ahead.

"What about it, boys? Should we show Peg-a-leg what we're lookin' at?" Gene asked.

Laughter rippled with expectancy. Peggy tried to look out the door, but Gene's hand tightened in her snarled hair. The sudden jerk made her wince and almost drop to her knees.

"Give it to her, Bob," Gene directed.

"Take a good look, girl. This is what happens to niggers who come to Mississippi and try to make trouble," Charlie Lee said. He thrust the photograph into her hands.

She took it at the corners, aware that her small fingertips might smudge the surface if she touched it. At first she didn't understand what she saw. The image in the photo was not like anything she'd ever seen before. There were eyes and . . . she realized that it was a Negro boy. An almost man. Barbed wire was wrapped around his throat, cutting into the tender flesh. His face was beaten beyond recognition, and the side of his head was missing.

The picture slipped from her hands and coasted, back and forth forever, to the floor.

"Pick it up," Gene ordered her, his voice so soft that Peggy felt the instant spur of fear.

She bent down and retrieved the picture, careful not to look at it again. Afraid to move, she shifted slightly toward the door, waiting for a moment of weakness, of diversion when she could break free and escape.

"She looks spooked," Uncle Bob said, laughing. "I believe that took some of the sass out of that girl."

Gene nodded at Peggy. "Go to bed."

Before anyone could stop her, Peggy flew out the door and ran full tilt across the yard. She had to get away from the men. No matter where she went, she had to get away. Without thinking, she ran straight for the bed where Mary Jean, Faye, and Sheila slept on, oblivious that their world had changed forever.

Chapter Eleven

Peggy pulled the sheet free of the clothes pins and dropped it over her head. "Whooooo!" She lifted her arms beneath the white material and advanced toward little Ronald Eugene. "I'm gone getcha," she moaned.

Three-year-old Ronald, the baby, stood his ground for a moment, then stumbled and fell as he set up a wail.

"I'm gonna getcha!" Peggy trailed the end of the sheet over his back as he scrambled up and ran straight into his oldest sister's arms.

"Mama's gonna get you," Mary Jean said from the back steps, "if you get that clean sheet in the dirt." She tucked the young boy against her hip and jiggled him in a gesture that spoke of second nature.

"I could be a ghost." Peggy pulled her sheet forward, the material ruffling her strawberry tresses as it finally came over her head and tumbled into her arms. "We could cut a couple of little eye holes, and I could trick-or-treat as a ghost. Lots of kids are goin' as ghosts, and no one would know me."

"Cut holes in Mama's sheet and you won't be worried about trick-or-treat." Mary Jean was no longer interested in Halloween costumes. In the next month she would be fifteen, and boys were taking notice of her charms. She took the steps two at a time and snatched the sheet from Peggy's hands. "Get the rest of the clothes off the line."

Peggy ignored her. There was always plenty of work to do, but she wasn't going to let Mary Jean boss her around. "Molly's going as an Injun." She was envious that she hadn't thought of that idea first. "If I could get a gun, I could go as a cowboy." It was a game she and Molly played with great vigor and enthusiasm. Usually, though, they were both cowboys and the Indians were imaginary, or some of their brothers.

"You'd better worry about your spelling and forget foolishness."
A frown of concern touched Mary Jean's features. "Mama's not in
any shape to be worried about Halloween costumes, you hear? You
can just forget it this year."

Peggy pretended not to hear as she skipped across the yard to
the path where she might catch a glimpse of her cousin coming over
to play. She and her cousin Molly Albritton had become solid
friends. Molly's home situation, living with Peggy's Uncle Buddy
and Aunt Josie, wasn't much better than hers. Maybe even worse.
But Molly had spunk and spirit, and she was always ready for
adventure.

As if she'd imagined her, Peggy caught sight of her cousin's
brown head bobbing around the bare branches of a sycamore tree.
Her red sweater was a pinpoint of vivid color against the landscape,
which was rapidly taking on the winter grays and browns.

"Molly!" Peggy called out to her as she started to run. She
halted as she saw that her cousin was carrying something resembling
a short fishing pole.

Molly held up the slender wooden stick. "A spear. Let's go get
us some rabbits for supper."

Peggy needed no second invitation. She heard Mary Jean calling her back into the yard, but she sprinted away. Mary Jean could
get the clothes in and help Inez with supper. Peggy wanted no part
of the house or her mother's shuffling walk about the kitchen as she
tried to accommodate the new bruises from the night before. It
seemed that in the past few months, Gene and Inez had fought
nearly every night. More and more often, Inez smelled of the same
raw liquor that Gene did. And she had started fighting back with a
viciousness Peggy found frightening. But Inez's small fists hardly left
an impression on Gene; they only served to make him angrier, to
make the beatings more severe.

And if Gene wasn't beating on Inez, then someone else was fussing and cussing her. Lately, it seemed like all of the Albritton family

felt they had a right to punch on Inez whenever she opened her mouth. Gene's sister, Nellie Moye, found fault with everything Inez did. Even Peggy had learned to use aggression against her mother to silence her when Inez provoked Gene to a fury that might be deadly. Remorse gnawed at Peggy for those times, but it seemed she could not stop herself. She could not understand why Inez would not shut up, why she drank and argued and fought. Sometimes, the pressure of trying to keep her mother from being beaten to death made Peggy want to end it all, with whatever means necessary.

"Hey, Peg-a-leg, you okay?" Molly asked. When Peggy nodded, Molly looked around to make sure no one else could hear. "Let's go to the secret hollow."

Peggy took the left-hand fork in the narrow trail. Within ten minutes, the two young girls were deep in the thick woods that marked the eastern boundary of the Basket Street area. There were plantations, shacks, and houses along the highways, but between the roads and the rivers, there were plenty of woods. Walking single file, they ambled eastward, heading for the blackberry thicket they'd picked last May. The thick, shoulder-high briars were used as protective barriers by the rabbits to guard their warrens.

"You flush 'em out, and I'll spear 'em," Molly said.

"You can spear the first one, then it's my turn." Peggy had no intention of doing all the leg work and letting Molly take the glory.

"Okay," Molly agreed. She took her stance at the edge of the thick briars as Peggy waded in, ignoring the thorns that hooked her clothes and hands as she stomped around, determined to drive the rabbits from safety and into their supper pot.

Molly held the spear poised, ready, for as long as her arm held out. First it began to wobble, then she lowered the tip she'd sharpened with an ax to the ground. "You're bleeding," she said.

Peggy held up her bare hands. The thorns had snicked her in five dozen places, and there were tiny pin-pricks of blood. Three long tears on her right arm bled freely. She stopped and began to pull the thorns from her skin. "I don't think there are any rabbits here," she said.

"Maybe they smell the blood on you and so they won't come out. Or maybe they're hibernating." Molly leaned on her spear. "Lots of animals sleep through the winter. Maybe rabbits do, too."

Peggy prodded the briars with her shoe. There was nothing there, not even an old snake. "Boyd and Billy get rabbits when they hunt, even in winter."

"They have a gun," Molly pointed out. "If we had a gun, we could find the rabbit hole and shoot into it. That would wake 'em up and make 'em run out. Then we could get them too."

Peggy stepped out of the briars, moving carefully as she came to stand beside her friend.

"I think we could live in the woods," Molly said.

By mutual unspoken consent they moved toward a wild walnut tree that made a perfect place to sit. As they took a seat, their backs against the trunk, two crows roosting in the tree let out a burst of angry caws. The afternoon was growing chill, and though Molly had thought to wear a sweater, Peggy had not. She leaned against her cousin.

"If we could learn to catch some food, we'd never have to go home," Molly said. "We could just stay out here." She leaned her head back against the rough bark of the tree. "Right here in these woods where it's easy."

Peggy didn't bother to look at Molly. She'd seen the mark on her neck. The routine violence in her cousin's home was the same, only different. "If we can't catch a rabbit, we can walk to the river and get some fish. I know we can catch some fish. I've had plenty of practice at that." Gene and the boys wouldn't let her shoot a gun, but she'd learned to be a crafty fisherman.

"Maybe we could build a raft." Molly sat up. "We could, Peggy. I know we could. We could float on down . . . Well, we could float down to New Orleans and get a job and make some money and then take the train back to Memphis." She turned so that she could see her cousin. "I'll bet that Elvis Presley is playing in some of those clubs around Memphis. You know that's where he went to high school. He still lives there with his mama and daddy, when he isn't goin' around on Louisiana Hayride and them other tours." Molly rolled her eyes dramatically. "We could stroll down the streets of town and just walk right into one of those clubs and see Elvis live."

Peggy couldn't help the pleasure she got from that idea. "He's on the road down in Texas. Mary Jean read where the Louisiana Hayride tour was goin'." Another thought gave new hope. "But he was born in Tupelo. Maybe he'll come sing in Greenwood."

"How do you keep up with him? He's no big star." Molly wiggled into a more comfortable position, pulling a walnut from beneath her thigh. "Everybody says he sings nigger music."

"Mary Jean and Faye hear about him at school." Peggy shrugged. "They like him."

"Well I do, too. But I'm not a fool for him, like you. You spend the whole afternoon waitin' on one of his songs to come on the radio."

"One day I'm gonna marry him and just go away."

Molly picked up her home-made spear. "Marryin' ain't no cure-all for problems. 'Specially not to some crazy singin' man. Just 'cause he can sing don't mean he won't hit you."

Peggy squinted her eyes shut tight. She felt Molly's elbow in her ribs.

"If we're always best friends, we won't let nobody beat on us. Right?"

"Right." Peggy opened her eyes. She was safe in the woods, safe with her cousin and best friend. They had a little more time before the sun went down, before they would have to go home.

"Maybe Elvis will come to Greenwood and you'll marry him and I can go with you." Molly took off one side of her sweater and offered it to Peggy so they could wrap up close together. With the sun setting, the woods were turning cold. "I wish we could spend the night here."

"We didn't bring any blankets." Peggy didn't want to go back, but she knew they would have to. Soon. "Have you got your costume ready?"

"Yeah!" Molly's voice picked up enthusiasm. "It's great. Mama took a potato sack and made me an Indian dress, and I made a bow from a willow stick and some string. We're gonna braid my hair, and I'm making a headband. What are you going as?"

"Maybe a pirate." An eye-patch wouldn't be hard to make. And she could borrow one of the knives used to butcher the fish for a sword. Still . . . "Maybe a ghost."

"You'd better make up your mind. Halloween is tomorrow night. You won't get no candy if you don't have a good costume."

"I'll be ready." Peggy slipped her arm out of the sweater. "We'd better go back. Mama will have supper ready."

Molly stood, picking up her spear. She looked at it in the light that had grown dusky. "I need to make some arrows, too."

Peggy started toward home. Molly had her costume almost made, and she hadn't even begun to think of anything good. Mary Jean wouldn't help her. Not after she'd run off and left all the clothes on the line. Faye was busy. Boyd and Billy were too old to trick-or-treat. That left Sheila, Sammy, and Ronald, and they'd be wanting costumes, too. Ronald was a baby, but he'd still want to go house to house, holding out a paper bag for pieces of candy to be dropped in like gold.

"Maybe Aunt Inez can come up with something good for a costume," Molly said. She nudged Peggy with her spear. "You can use this if it helps."

Peggy shook her head. She couldn't count on her mother. Not now. Something bad was wrong with Inez. She'd almost quit eating, and when she wasn't cooking or working, she sat at the table or on the porch and stared down the road, as if she expected to see Satan spitting fireballs as he came toward them.

"What's wrong with Aunt Inez?" Molly asked. "She acts funny. I think Uncle Gene musta beat somethin' loose in her head."

"He did not!" Peggy turned, the anger instant. "Take that back."

Molly held the spear in front of her in a gesture of defense. "I didn't mean nothin'. It's just that she's always lookin' down the road, and she was talkin' to herself yesterday."

"She's all right." Peggy could see the corner of her house, white against the grayness of the surrounding trees. The house needed painting in the worst way, but from a distance it didn't look so bad. "Mama's all right."

"Okay." Molly came to the point in the path where she had to turn away to go home. When she glanced toward Peggy's house, her eyes widened. "Look at Inez. She's digging a hole in the front yard."

"I gotta go." Peggy's chest was suddenly touched with sharp pain. Without saying goodbye, she ran toward her mother, jumping the fifty-five-gallon drum Gene was turning into a wood stove for one of his friends. Inez was digging a hole in the front yard. She used the shovel as if she'd never seen such a tool before.

"Mama!" Peggy skidded to a halt. She took in the cedar tree that lay on its side, bare roots stretched out along the ground. "What're ya doin'?"

"Faye told me you dug up this tree in the woods." Inez pointed the shovel at the cedar.

"I did. I was going to plant it. I thought if we put it in the yard, we'd always have a Christmas tree."

"Well, that's what I'm doin'." Inez jumped on the shovel and rode it halfway into the packed dirt. She was too light to force it any deeper. "I thought it would be nice, right here by the edge of the house."

Peggy had hated it at school the Christmas before when all the children talked about their tree decorations. "We can put lights and ornaments out here."

Inez scooped up some dirt and moved it to the side. "We have to plant it first. Leaving it lying in the yard, roots sticking up at the sun and no water, that ain't no way to keep a tree alive. I thought I'd taught you better than that. You got to care for plants, Peggy. Growin' things is hard work."

Peggy pressed her lips together. She did know better. The large vegetable garden where Gene got produce to sell at the grocery was evidence of Inez's green thumb and hard work. And no matter how long and hard Inez worked in the fields, she insisted on a few flowers in the yard. She could make anything grow. "Daddy said I couldn't plant it. He said the weather was too hot and the sap was up, that it would die anyway."

Inez lifted loose dirt out of the hole and then jumped back on the shovel. It went down about three inches. "Gene thinks he knows everything. But I know what I know." She stopped and stared at Peggy, her gaze suddenly intense. "I know, Peggy Ruth. I know and I can't keep it to myself." Her fingers released the shovel and it fell beside her, the tip kicking up a tiny spray of dirt. "I have to tell," she said. "I can't live with not telling. Can you understand?"

Her mother's eyes, burning in her thin face, made Peggy sick with worry. Instead of answering, she retrieved the shovel. She set the point in the ground and jumped. The blade slid smoothly in. She pulled back and lifted the rich brown earth.

Inez touched her shoulder, forcing Peggy to look up. "Your daddy don't know half of what he thinks he knows, and what he does know could send him to prison."

The mention of prison didn't slow Peggy down. It wasn't hard to imagine Gene behind bars. He'd come close a time or two with his bootlegging and gambling, but he'd managed to stay out of a cell. He always managed to get by, and Peggy knew this time would be no different.

"Mama, put the tree in the hole."

"Peggy, you have to take care of this tree." Inez stooped and carefully pushed the roots into the soft dirt. "You water it and make sure it grows so we can have us a Christmas tree, like you said."

"Yes, ma'am." Peggy stared down at the top of her mother's head as she knelt beside the hole. Inez was not old, not really old, but she looked old. Her hands, worn and sun-darkened, pushed the dirt over the roots.

"Anything will grow if you take care of it. Remember that."

"I will, Mama." Peggy swallowed hard. Her mother was talking scary.

Inez stood, her gaze almost level with her eight-year-old daughter's. "I've got to tell. I can't live with it. Gene's tried to beat it out of me, but he can't. Peggy, when you hear the name Emmett Till, you can say your mother told the truth. You remember, the truth is a terrible master and one that must be served. Now I got supper to cook. Put the shovel up, pour a little water on the roots, and come inside."

"Mama, just don't say anything." Peggy grabbed at her arm. "Why can't you just shut up? You keep on, and Daddy's gonna kill you." Anger almost choked her.

Inez's smile was ghostly in the dying light. She pulled free of her daughter's hand and slowly walked into the house, taking each step first with her left leg, then her right to accommodate her bruised hip.

"Just shut up!" Peggy felt the words swell like lumps of biscuit dough. "Why can't you just shut up?"

Inez entered the house, the screen door slamming behind her.

Chapter Twelve

Peggy squatted in a dark corner of the bedroom, the sheet in her hands and the scissors beside her foot. On the other side of the wall, she heard a body hit the wood, hard.

Inez's words came out in winded huffs. "Where . . . you . . . been?"

"None of your damn business. It ain't your place to question my comin's and goin's. If you want to keep your crazy head asittin' on your shoulders, you'd better remember it." Gene's answer was an invitation to fight.

There was a sound, like strangling, and Peggy hunkered into her knees and buried her face in the sheet.

Inez's question came from deep in her throat. "You been with her, ain't you?"

"Which her?" Gene's voice held a taut. "Damn you!" he shouted as something smashed into the wall. "That's the last thing you'll throw at me, you crazy bitch. We'll see who wants to slap and fight."

Inez's scream seemed to saw through the wooden wall and enter Peggy's heart. She curled tighter, unable to force herself to go into her parents' bedroom and try to intervene.

There was the sound of fist against flesh and a few muffled cries.

Peggy could imagine her mother, pinned face down on the bed, as her father knelt on her with one knee and punched at her head. She'd seen it before.

At last the slapping, kicking, and punching ended. Gene's footsteps went out the front and across the porch as the screen door slammed. In a moment he was back on the porch. "You damn idiots can't remember to turn off a light." The sound of breaking glass, then darkness fell outside the front door.

His uneven gait returned into the house, and Peggy looked up to see him standing in the doorway of the girls' bedroom. "I told you and told you to keep them lights off. You think power bills don't have to be paid?" He limped across the floor, one shoe in his hand. With a swing he busted out the light, throwing the room into darkness. "Burn those lights now, damn you." He went to the kitchen and there was a long, hissing sound before the smell of burning urine filled the house. More glass broke, and the kitchen went black. The back door slammed and he was gone.

Inez's ragged breathing in the next room was the only sound in the house. Each breath sounded painful, like maybe the last.

Peggy hugged the sheet into her abdomen and pressed her face hard into it so that no one would hear her cries. Inez was going to die. Her mother was in the next room dying, and she was too afraid to go in there and help.

Peggy whispered into the damp sheet. "Mama." Her hands came over her ears, trying to block out the breathing. "Mama." For a moment there was silence, just the hot feel of her own humid breath caught in the folds of the sheet. Nearly suffocated, she was forced to lift her face to the ugly tear of her mother's breathing. Peggy cried soundlessly into the sheet.

MRS. CARRUTHERS'S HAND touched Peggy's shoulder lightly, drawing her attention away from the window.

"Peggy, you better be sick or else you better start paying attention."

Peggy rubbed her eyes. They itched madly, and the lids, pink and swollen, felt like they had sand under them. "I'm not sick."

"You're not paying attention." Mrs. Carruthers's voice was soft, so the other children could not hear. "You have to listen to what I say or you'll get behind. If you're sick . . ."

"I'm not sick." Peggy picked up her pencil. "I can listen." She did not want to be sent home sick. At home was the bed where her mother lay beneath a sheet and blanket, a lump hardly bigger than Sheila. This time Inez was dying, and Peggy did not want to go home and listen to the breathing, the sound that had continued, ragged and torn, through the night and into the morning as she dressed hurriedly for school and fled out the front door. "I'm not sick," she repeated, even though Mrs. Carruthers had walked back to the front of the class and once again picked up her chalk.

When the final bell rang at last, Peggy took her time gathering her sweater and spelling book. The children around her were eager to get home, eager to hurry into their Halloween costumes and get their painted sacks to hold out for pieces of candy. They had been talking all day about which houses to go to, who gave the best candy. The very best were the shiny silver kisses or the packages of candy-coated peanuts. Some houses gave apples and oranges, but the chocolate or caramel candies were the ones the children craved.

Distracted, Peggy had listened to the talk. Halloween had been pushed aside by worry and fear. Now it was time to confront both emotions. It was time to go home. As she started toward the door, Mrs. Carruthers stepped in front of her.

"Your eyes look funny, Peggy. Maybe you're getting pink eye." There was speculation in her tone as she lifted Peggy's face so she could examine it more closely. "Have you been crying?"

"No, ma'am." Peggy swallowed the truth. "I don't never cry."

"You're too tough to cry, aren't you?" Mrs. Carruthers's tone was sad. "Well, if that's pinkeye, we need medicine or every child in school will have it. Will your folks get you to the doctor?"

"Yes, ma'am." Peggy stepped back, pulling free of the teacher's hand. Normally she would have basked in the attention, but there was too much to hide, too many secrets she couldn't tell.

"Have fun trick-or-treating," Mrs. Carruthers said, releasing her.

Peggy walked out the door and into the long hallway that seemed to gleam with the afternoon sun hitting the varnished wood. At the very end of the hall, a silhouette against the sun, was a girl.

"Sizzzzzzz!" Molly hissed. "Hurry!"

Peggy kept her same slow place. Molly might want to go home, but she didn't.

"Have you got your costume?" Molly asked as she fell into step beside Peggy at the doorway. "Hurry. We want to get ahead of the other kids, or they'll get all the good candy."

Molly skipped ahead, but when Peggy didn't follow, she stopped and waited. "What's wrong?"

"It's Mama." Peggy could talk to Molly, if no one else.

"Uncle Gene beat her?"

"Yeah." Peggy felt the tears that she could never allow anyone else to see. "Bad."

"Mama said she was talkin' crazy, sayin' things she'd best keep her mouth shut about." She put a hand on Peggy's shoulder. "She'll be okay." Molly got in front of Peggy and walked backwards. "I thought you could go as a hobo tonight. We could paint your face, and you could kid around. People like that, and they'll give us more candy."

Peggy looked down at her feet. The left foot, then the right, moving in a steady rhythm, taking her home, even though she didn't want to go.

"Good grief," Molly said in exasperation. "It ain't the first time Uncle Gene nearly killed her. She'll get okay. She always does."

They were at the corner where Molly went home. She halted impatiently. "Are you going tonight or not?"

"I'm going. I'll get a costume."

"I'll come by for you so we can go together. Some of the boys were saying they were going to the cemetery to look for ghosts. That sounds like fun."

The idea of ghost-hunting caught Peggy's fancy, and for a moment the weight of gloom lifted. "Yeah, that sounds like fun."

"Good." Molly nodded, her face suddenly eager. "We'll sneak up on them and scare the be-Jesus out of them."

"We could hide behind a tombstone and wait." Peggy could see the whole thing unfolding. If they jumped out at just the right time, the boys would hightail it out of the cemetery, and she and Molly would be left laughing out loud.

"Okay." Molly gave a quick wave as she scampered off toward home and her Indian costume.

Peggy walked the short distance to Basket Street, feeling better. She could borrow some pants from Gene or the boys and stuff pillows in them to make herself look old and fat. A hobo was a good idea.

At the edge of the yard she stood for a moment. The house was quiet. If she stepped inside, would she hear that horrible rasping, that terrible struggle to stay alive? Maybe Inez had gotten better. She took the steps fast and hurried inside, stopping first in her parents' bedroom. The spread and sheets were rumpled and stained with blood, but the bed was empty.

"Mama?" The word seemed to hang in the afternoon sunlight that came in through the window. "Mama?" It was like an eerie echo.

Faye came to the door. Her eyes were red with weeping. "She's not here."

"She's dead."

Faye shook her head. "Not dead."

"In the hospital?" Peggy felt her hopes rise. But the look on Faye's face dashed them. "Where is she?"

"Whitfield."

The fear that touched Peggy was worse than when she'd thought her mother dead. "Whitfield?" She repeated the word as if she'd never heard it before, but it was a familiar word. A dreaded place.

"The crazy house." Faye's anger was combined with tears. "Our mother's gone to the insane asylum."

"How?" Peggy looked at the bed. Inez had not gotten up and walked to the insane asylum. Whitfield was down close to Jackson, a good two hundred miles away. Inez wouldn't go to Whitfield, a place where only the worst of community crazies went, folks who were so bad off they walked up and down the streets, clothes soaked in urine and feces, talking to themselves or sometimes sitting in a ditch rocking and screaming. "Who took her?"

"The sheriff."

Peggy had seen the sleek patrol car glide by the school. It had turned toward the east, but the siren had not been going, or the lights. Of all the times she'd worried for Inez when the police went by, this time she hadn't. She'd been too busy watching for the ambulance or the hearse. Now it had been the sheriff who'd come and taken her mother away.

"We'll get her back." Peggy felt trapped. "We'll figure out a way to get her back. I should have stayed home with her." A sudden thought occurred. "Where was Daddy? He wouldn't let anybody take Mama. Not even the sheriff. He's always saying how Mama belongs to him and can't nobody interfere."

Faye gave a bitter snort. "He called the sheriff." She turned away. "She's at Whitfield, and she's staying until she can act better. That's what Daddy says."

Peggy watched her sister walk away. She was left alone with the empty bed. There was the sound of someone in the kitchen. Someone cooking. At the thought of Becky, Peggy started toward the kitchen. Becky would tell her what to do, what she had to do to save her mama.

"Beck—" She stopped at the sight of her father standing at the stove. He was stirring something in a large black skillet. "What're you doing?"

Gene turned to her, one side of his face raked with four straight lines. The wounds were deep. "Makin' supper. Your mama had to go get some treatment. She's more than half a bubble off."

"When's she comin' back?"

"When she can act decent." He opened the oven door and pulled out a pan of flat biscuits. "When she learns to obey her husband and quit talkin' crazy talk."

"Mama ain't crazy!" Peggy clenched her fists. She wanted to pick up the pan of hot gravy and fling it in her father's face.

"You're actin' a bit too much like your mama for my taste. Maybe you're crazy, too." Gene poured the gravy over the biscuits. Peggy watched the thick gelatinous lumps slide out of the pan and felt her stomach flop.

Gene didn't look up from pouring the gravy as he spoke. "Maybe I shoulda sent you off with her, get some treatment for you." He held the empty skillet and stared at her. "Whitfield might just be the place for you and your mother. Two of a kind. When they finish with her she'll learn to do what she's told. Maybe they could teach you the same."

"They better not hurt her."

Gene's jaw tensed. "Mary Jean needs help with the laundry."

"To hell with you and that laundry." Peggy gripped the door frame to keep her legs from buckling. Inez had washed her mouth out with soap for saying "God dang it." She was afraid, but she wasn't backing away. "I hope you burn in hell," she added. "I hope you burn to a black crisp."

Gene's laughter bounced against the kitchen wall. "You better hope I don't get my hands on you, or I'll make you sorry of the day you fell out of your mother in the cotton field dirt." His light eyes were cold with anger.

"One day I'll kill you." Peggy backed away as she talked. "Just wait. One day I will."

Gene grinned as he put the skillet back on top of the stove. "Tell your brothers that supper's ready. Better come while it's hot."

Chapter Thirteen

"Peggy, you aren't gonna pass school this year, so you stay with your mama." Gene tipped his hat back and gave her a stare that conveyed he meant business.

"No." Peggy had no great love of school, but Inez was too difficult, and scary. She'd been home from Whitfield for months, but she still wasn't right. Whatever they'd done to her had left her vacant and confused. "Mama leaves the stove goin'. She's gone burn down the house."

"That's exactly why you're gonna stay and watch her." Gene rubbed his hand over his jaw, checking to see if the day's stubble was too bristly.

"I'm goin' to school." Ever since Inez had come back from Whitfield, Peggy had been saddled with the care of her.

"You stay with Inez." Gene's voice was oiled steel.

"I got a test today. It's the end-of-the-year tests. Let Sheila or Faye or Mary Jean stay with her. They're all doin' good in school."

"They take their studies to heart. You ain't never gonna get out of school. Mind your ma, or you'll wish you did. I got to get out on the river and get us some fish. Without your ma workin', things are hard." Gene headed for the grocery store where Peggy knew he'd pack some cheese and crackers, a jug of moonshine, and whatever else he needed, depending on who was fishing with him. He'd stopped taking Peggy and the boys. Peggy had accepted the fact that he had a girlfriend. Sometimes he brought home fish to sell. Sometimes he came home drunk and spoiling for a fight. Inez was still his favorite target, though now he focused his rage on his children, especially Sammy, with more frequency.

From the front door, Peggy watched him load the old truck with poles, bait, and his lunch before he climbed in and took off. Chances were he'd go up around Money. He said the fishing was better there. It all depended on what kind of fish he was going after, Peggy thought bitterly as she stepped back in the house to check on her mother.

Inez stood at the sink washing the breakfast dishes. The morning sun struck the amber of her medicine bottle, and the tumbler half full of the burnished moonshine she had begun to drink without any attempt to hide it from her children.

Standing in the doorway, Peggy watched her mother at the sink, struck by the child-like quality of her narrow body.

Inez turned to her suddenly. "Peggy, you want me to make you something special? How about a chocolate cake? Or that caramel cake you love? Or that rich pound cake? We'll make it for your birthday." Her eyes widened. "A dozen eggs, two cups of sugar, a pound of butter, flour . . ." Her voice trailed away as her gaze shifted around the kitchen. "And vanilla flavoring. I know there's some here somewhere."

Peggy was unable to move. "Not today, Mama." She went to her and took her hand, leading her to the table. "My birthday was two months ago."

"Did we have a cake? When I was a girl, my mama always baked me a fresh pound cake with a whole pound of butter and a dozen eggs in it. It would just melt on your tongue." Inez rocked slightly in the chair, a gentle motion.

"Maybe we should get Grandma to come see us?" Peggy had been trying to think of a way to get in touch with her grandparents since Inez had been committed. She knew only that they lived near Clarksdale. She wasn't sure of their last name, even, and Gene had laughed when she had asked. He'd never tell her now that he knew she wanted to know. "Mama, can you remember how to call Ma?"

Inez got up from the table and returned to the sink. "Don't get Mom and Pop." She put her hands to her head, trails of soap catching in her disordered hair. "They'll kill Gene."

"I know," Peggy mumbled.

"I think I'll take a nap." Inez shuffled out of the kitchen, hands still wet from the dishwater.

"It's not even eight o'clock." Peggy fought against the fury that wanted to turn her inside out. She followed Inez to the bedroom where Inez sat on the side of the bed and then fell back onto the pillow. "It's mornin', Mama. Can't you stay up a while?"

"I'm sick." Inez pulled the sheet over her face even though the May morning had already turned hot. "Leave me alone."

Returning to the kitchen, Peggy eyed the medicine bottle. Gene had said if Inez acted funny, to give her a pill. Instead Peggy went to the sink and finished washing dishes. The day was quiet except for the squabbling of two mockingbirds and the busy clucking of three hens searching the yard for food. Drying her hands on her skirt, Peggy went to the back door and looked out. A small patch of pansies and several roses, protected from the hens by pieces of rabbit wire linked together to form a fence, were blooming with a vivid courage that was suddenly too painful to look at. She almost backed away, but instead she went out into the sun and walked over to the plants.

Her mother had seeded them and planted them, a moment of peace and promise in a year of hopelessness. The doctors at Whitfield had said her mother had epilepsy. It was a disease that could make her have seizures, foam at the mouth, and swallow her own tongue. If she had a seizure and no one helped her, she could die. Peggy knew it was her job to protect her mother. If a seizure started, she would have to stick a spoon in her mouth and press down hard to keep Inez from swallowing her tongue. The idea frightened Peggy, but she'd been left to see, if necessary, that it got done.

She knelt in the dirt and reached across the fence to the flowers. Her fingertips grazed the soft petals of a red rose before she stood up, turned, and ran back up the steps and into her parents' bedroom. "Mama! Mama! Come look at the pretty flowers." She pulled the sheet back and roused Inez up and out of bed. Leading her mother by the hand, she took her into the yard. "See the flowers we planted. They all came up."

"They're so happy looking." Inez smiled.

Leaning over the short fence, Peggy used her thumbnail to snap off the lush head of a rose. Inez's eyes brightened at the sight. Peggy handed it to her, and then helped her work it through the top buttonhole of her dress.

"That looks pretty, Mama." Peggy took her mother's hand and held it. "Want to see the Christmas tree? Daddy said it would die, but I watered it just a little every day, and it lived. We can decorate it when Christmas comes again."

Inez tightened her grip on Peggy's hand and leaned to whisper in her daughter's ear. "I haven't forgotten."

The taste of rusty iron filled the back of Peggy's mouth. "Don't talk about that." She jerked free of her mother.

"What they don't want me to say. I haven't forgotten. About the colored boy . . ."

Peggy grabbed the sleeve of her mother's dress and jerked hard. "Shut up!" She tightened her grip. "You just shut up!" With all the fury she possessed, she shook her mother by the dress. "Don't say that stuff any more!"

Inez turned her head and gave Peggy a glancing look. "I know," she whispered. "I know the truth. Tell the truth, Peggy. You have to tell the truth."

The image captured in the photograph slammed into Peggy with a force more powerful than a physical punch. She could remember the humid night air, the feel of her father's fingers burning into her shoulder, the mouths opened in laughter and eyes slanted with cruel amusement.

"You need more of your medicine." Peggy released her mother's dress and ran into the house. In a moment she was back with the bottles of Dilantin and Phenobarbital. She flipped off the cap of one bottle and grabbed a pill between two dirty fingers. Before Inez could dodge away, Peggy pushed the pill to her mother's lips. Her command was terse. "Swallow it!"

She hurried to the back door and returned with a cup of water. "Drink!"

Inez swallowed the liquid, her attention once again on the flowers.

"The red ones are my favorites." Her hand strayed up to the buttonhole where the flower bobbed against her thin throat. "You're a good girl, Peggy. My best girl."

"Oh, Mama." Peggy blinked against the sun, which had grown too bright. "I'm sorry." She took her mother's hand and gently led her back to the steps. "You can't be talking about that. They'll send you back to Whitfield. Forget it all. Forget it."

"Where's Mary Jean and Billy? They said they were going to bring me some fish. We need to get supper going; it's time for Gene to get home."

"I'll take care of it," Peggy said. It was not even nine o'clock. "Maybe I'll make us a cake." The idea had tremendous appeal. Gene was gone from the store, and even if Billy was in there taking care of things, Peggy had great faith in her ability to steal some butter, eggs, and sugar without him catching on. Once the cake was made, it would be too late to do anything about it. Except eat it. Peggy could already imagine the smile Inez would give her when she tasted a real cake made with fresh butter and eggs. The recipe that Inez recited was cherished, handed down from her mother. Inez had committed it to memory since she couldn't read.

"Mama, you take a nap, and I'm gonna make you a surprise."

"Nap and surprise." Inez slurred the words. She followed Peggy through the kitchen and into the bedroom where she sat down on the bed.

"Rest, Mama." Peggy slipped off her mother's shoes and eased her back on the bed. "You rest while I make a surprise."

Inez obediently closed her eyes, her hands folded across her stomach. Peggy stared at her mother, willing her to sleep and forget.

When Inez's breathing was even, Peggy slipped out of the room and made a bee-line for the grocery. The front door was locked, but Peggy knew how to slip in. There was a back window that she could slither through. Once inside, she gathered the items for a cake, snagging a fistful of bubble gum and a few candy bars on principle. There weren't many opportunities to turn the tables on her father, and she took every one she could.

The window was more difficult to manage with her stolen goods, but Peggy made it through and stopped in the yard long enough to hunt for eggs. There were plenty of chickens, but since they didn't have a hen house they roosted and nested anywhere they could find relative safety. The egg hunt took nearly half an hour, but she had a dozen perfect, fresh eggs when she went back in the house.

Pausing in the kitchen, Peggy listened for her mother. The house was silent and she found a mixing bowl and began to accumulate the ingredients for the cake. Although Inez had always been a good cook, she seldom baked for her children. Her fried peach pies had been sold to help buy pews for the Baptist church Inez had once attended. Gene did not like Inez baking for the good of the church and had finally stopped it. He did not allow her to use the staples or produce in the store for the family. Even the berries gathered in the woods or the apples and peaches stolen by the children from a neighbor's orchard were used for jams and jellies that could be stored. A cobbler or cake was a rare treat, but not so rare that Peggy couldn't remember the recipe. She'd heard Inez recite it a million times, remembering the happier days of baking with her own ma. Peggy mixed the butter and sugar, added the flour, and picked up an egg to crack.

Tapping the egg on the edge of the bowl, she felt the shell crack and caught a powerful whiff of something burning. A little afraid to look, she peered into the yellow mixture to see the perfect yoke of a fresh egg. Bending lower, she sniffed. Nothing. When she lifted her head, the acrid smell of burning came to her again.

Peggy jerked open the oven door, certain that some pan of biscuits or plate of leftovers had been stored inside and forgotten. The oven was empty.

A soft moan came from another part of the house, and Peggy dropped the bowl clattering to the table as she rushed into the bedroom where Inez sat in the middle of the bed, smoke billowing from the mattress.

"Mama!" Peggy leaped forward, knocking Inez away from the fire. She jerked the quilt that Inez had worked so hard to make off the bed and threw it into a corner. There were no flames, but the heavy ticking and cotton stuffed mattress billowed clouds of white smoke.

"Get back!" Peggy screamed at her mother as she grabbed the edge of the mattress and pulled it to the floor where she could stomp on the fire.

In only a moment the embers were extinguished. Only the acrid smell of burning cotton remained.

Peggy sucked down air and felt her heartbeat calming. When she could speak without screaming, she looked at her mother. Inez sat on the floor beside the window, chin tucked, gaze on a pattern of sunlight on the wooden floor boards.

"Mama, you almost burned the house down."

"They told me to."

"Who told you to?" Peggy felt a tickle rush over her body. Ever since Whitfield, sometimes Inez acted as if she might be talking to someone who wasn't there. Peggy looked around the room. "There's no one here."

"Out there." Inez pointed to the window. "The convicts. They were working on the road, and they came up to the window and told me to do that. They gave me the matches." She held up the book of matches that showed a Greenwood club where B. B. King played the blues.

"No convicts gave you those." Peggy snatched the matches from her mother's hand. She stared at the club's name. Once, when she'd gone with Gene to sell fish, she'd seen B. B. King on the street in Indianola, but no one in the Albritton family had ever been in the club where he performed. Only Negroes went to that club. Fingering the matches, Peggy looked out the window, almost afraid of what she'd see. But the road was empty.

Far in the distance was a steady clanging sound. Like metal on gravel. Like a shovel digging in the road.

"They were wearing black stripes." Inez hunkered down on the floor, casting a glance at the window. "I heard their chains rattlin' as they came to the window. It was a chain gang. And this big nigger man, scars all over his face, he gave me the matches and told me to burn the house down."

Peggy didn't believe her mother, but she eased away from the window. In the hush that had fallen over the room, she thought she heard the sound of a chain rattling just outside the window.

"They had a demon with them." Inez sprang from the floor onto the box springs of the bed and drew her feet up into her chest. "He's up under the bed. He said he was waiting on a little girl to get. Waiting with the chain gang."

"Stop it, Mama." Peggy stooped over, heart pounding, as she sighted under the bed. The hardwood floor showed only a few dust bunnies and a pair of Inez's shoes. "There's nothing there."

The hands that closed around her shoulders were surprisingly strong. Peggy tried to struggle free, but Inez held her in a tight grip.

"I saw the demon. He's got you now. He's inside you." Inez's face twisted as she shook Peggy hard. "Cough them demons up. Cough them out and be rid of them."

Peggy twisted sharply, terror giving her the strength to finally break her mother's grip. Head down, she ran at Inez, barreling her back onto the bed. "Mama!" Peggy held her mother down, thumping up and down on her shoulders. "Mama!" Hysteria built in her. The woman she held bore no resemblance to her mother.

"It's the demon of certain damnation." Inez struggled for a moment and then went limp. "Someone better watch out the window for those convicts. They'll be back." She picked up a pillow and placed it over her head. "I'll hide, and they won't find me, but they'll get you."

Peggy sat back on her heels. The fear passed, and she was left with the bitter taste of regret at the back of her mouth. "They won't come back, Mama. I won't let them." She went to the window and looked out onto Basket Street. The dirt road was as empty as the May morning. "I won't let them come back," she said softly.

Reaching up to the wall, she worked a flap of wallpaper loose then tugged it down. Her hands shook as she reached for the matches. She had to get someone to come and help her before the chain gang came back. The convicts often cleaned the ditches up and down the road, and Inez must have seen something to get so worked up.

Peggy drew a match across the cover. When the flame sparked, she held it to the wall paper she'd dropped onto the still smoldering mattress. As the flames licked the papers and began to burn hot, she went to the bed and held her mother while they waited for someone to come and help them.

The fire brought only the police and firemen—authority figures who had no sympathy for a woman and a child who were so careless they started a fire. Though Peggy tried to get help for her mother, nothing changed on Basket Street. There was no one, it seemed, who cared enough to intervene.

Chapter Fourteen

In the summer of 1957, Inez Albritton gave birth to her last child, Michael. He was a healthy baby, but Inez's physical condition had greatly deteriorated. Carrying and birthing ten babies, the years of hard work, the abuse, and her childhood illnesses topped off by epilepsy and her more recent addiction to alcohol took a toll on her petite frame. Her drinking had increased, as had Gene's, and throughout the pregnancy they fought nightly, vicious rounds of slugs and curses that ended only when Inez was totally subjugated by Gene's superior strength.

While Mary Jean, Boyd, Billy, Faye, Sammy, and Sheila clung to school as an escape, Peggy could not concentrate on learning. She had been passed by Mrs. Carruthers, but Mrs. Wheeler had not passed her and in the summer of 1957, she was set to repeat the third grade when school started. She was falling further and further behind her classmates, but there was nothing she could do to change it.

After the baby's birth, Inez remained in the hospital. Inez's doctor broke the news to her that she would have to have a hysterectomy. Her recovery was slow, and little Michael arrived at Basket Street several days before his mother was released.

"Now you girls tend this baby," Gene said as he placed the blanket-wrapped infant in Faye's arms.

Faye looked up in alarm. "We don't want to tend a baby. We got our own summer jobs." She looked to Mary Jean and Sheila for support.

"Take turns." Gene was already out the door, headed for the dusty car that had just pulled up at the grocery. Faye was left holding the infant, who began to cry, a lone whimper that became a full scream of hunger.

"I guess we can make do till Mama gets home," Faye said. The boys, too, were working part-time or else helping Gene with the fishing, bootlegging, and the store.

Splitting shifts, the girls took turns with Michael, but it seemed nothing they did could completely make the infant comfortable. Five days passed, and the baby's temperament seemed to worsen. Faye and Mary Jean tried the remedies they knew for colic, but Michael fussed and fretted, his small body beset by twinges and flushes.

Exhausted with trying to keep up with the lives they were developing outside the Albritton home, take care of the younger children, cook, and tend the baby, the older girls dropped into bed with a hope of sleep. Sheila, too young for a summer job, was taking care of the infant.

As Peggy got ready for bed, she heard Sheila settle into the old rocker in front of the stove. Michael was a cold-natured baby, and it seemed only the warmth of the stove and contact with one of his sisters would quiet him. Gene, drunk and in an ugly mood, had gone to bed with orders that he'd better not be awakened by a crying baby.

Peggy woke to the sounds of wild and hysterical screaming. At first she thought it was her mother, dying. But as she rushed from the bed she knew it was Sheila's voice. She heard her brothers, rushing across the bare floorboards of the front room, their excited yells and the sound of stomping. Peggy ran forward, terrified to look and too afraid not to. At the door of the living room, she froze. Sheila stood in a circle of burning quilt, the flames licking up her calves as she held Michael out of their reach.

Billy, Boyd, and Sammy snatched the quilt from their sister and rolled it tightly, stomping to extinguish the flames before they caught the wooden house on fire. Behind her, Peggy heard the panicked sounds of her sisters, watching and unable to help.

Peggy gripped the doorframe and stood helpless. Sheila's screams had stopped, and she stood, holding the baby, looking down at her burned leg. The silence was more frightening than any noise would have been. At last Michael began to cry, breaking the paralysis that held Peggy in its grip.

Boyd cussed as he stomped the quilt again and again, long after the fire had been extinguished.

"Sheila!" Sammy pointed to her foot. The burns were obvious.

"My leg." Sheila was still numb from shock. She looked down at her foot as if it belonged to someone else.

Mary Jean took the baby and walked outside to sooth his crying. She came back in to make a bottle while the boys tended to Sheila's burns.

"I think she needs a doctor," Boyd said. "She should go to the hospital."

Where the fire had brought no tears, huge drops slid down Sheila's face at the mention of the hospital. The shock was wearing off.

"Put some tea leaves on it," Faye suggested. "Tea helps a burn. Do we have any tea?" She went to the kitchen to look.

Gene appeared in the doorway, his hair tousled and his face rumpled from sleep. "What the hell's goin' on here?" he asked.

"Sheila burned her foot." Peggy gave the report. "She needs to go to the hospital." She knew by looking that the burn was severe. The skin had gone white, then red and it was raising up and splitting.

Gene stooped to inspect Sheila's foot, ignoring her tears and whimpers.

"That's not so bad. Get some of the salve we use for cuts and smear some on it. It'll be fine."

"It's burnin', Daddy." Sheila could hardly talk she was trying so hard not to cry.

"Well, hell, it burns because you burnt it." Gene stood up. "Now stop all this commotion and get back to bed. All of you. Faye, you or Peggy shut that baby up." He turned back to the bedroom.

The hinges of the screen door creaked. Peggy turned with the rest of the children to stare at the wasted apparition that stood half on the porch and half in the room. The air hissed out of her lungs in fright.

The woman who stood there looked something like her mother. The hair was unkempt and flying about her head, and the loose gown she wore flapped around her ankles.

"Mama?" Mary Jean said, drawing back and shielding the baby.

"Where's my baby?" Inez asked, stepping into the room, one hand clutched at her abdomen. Eyes wild, she looked around until she spotted the bundle in Faye's arms. "Michael!" She reached out toward the infant, stumbling as she entered the room. "Give me my baby. I knew something was wrong!" She was crying.

"Inez, what in the hell are you doin' out of the hospital?" Gene's voice held equal amounts of amazement and anger. "They didn't let you out of there at midnight. How'd you get home?" He looked down at her bare feet and saw the answer. She'd walked.

At the look on Gene's face, Peggy stepped to her mother's side.

"I dreamed somethin' was wrong here," Inez said. She spoke to the top of the baby's head as she kissed him softly. "My baby was in danger. He was suffering and burning up with fever. I saw it in a dream and I had to get home. I had to get away from that place and get to my baby." She looked around her, counting the children as her gaze shifted across the room. "You're here. All of you."

"My leg." Sheila pointed to the burn. "I burned my leg bad."

"My Lord." Inez hurried toward Sheila, the baby still in her arms. "You'd best go to the hospital with that," she said as if she hadn't just escaped from the place. "Gene, better get us a car. Sheila's leg is burned somethin' awful."

Gene walked slowly across the room to Inez. His hand shot out quicker than a snake could strike, and grabbed her arm in a punishing grip. "You crazy bitch, you're suppose to be in the hospital. And you're goin' back there right now. Sheila ain't hurt. Now you go get in the car, and I'll take you back where you belong. The last thing we need is your guts fallin' out all over the floor right here in front of the children." He pushed her toward the door, slapping the back of her head hard. "Peggy, get that baby from her and hush it up." He went back to the bedroom to find his pants.

INEZ REMAINED HOSPITALIZED until her surgery had healed sufficiently. But her mental condition did not improve. She was thirty-five, and the hysterectomy dealt her a terrible blow. Her entire life had revolved around her ability to bear children, her role as wife and mother. Now she felt useless. What tiny scrap of self-worth Gene's fists had not beaten out of her, the doctor's scalpel had taken.

There is no record of how Inez's parents were notified of her circumstances, but Ben and Mary Early arrived in Greenwood determined to take their daughter and grandchildren home.

The summer heat lingered in the house, seeming to dwell in the center of each room and radiate outward to the corners. Ben Early sat at the kitchen table, his wife across from him, as Inez stood at the stove. Her posture was more stooped than normal, a concession to the surgery and her broken spirit.

"Your mama and me can't take it any more," Ben said softly. "We just can't take it. That man has beat you and beat you, and we've had to sit by, unable to stop it. I'm tellin' you, Inez, you come home with us now, or I'm gone have to kill him."

Inez fumbled with the knife, narrowly missing her finger as she diced an onion for the fried balls of cornmeal and egg mixture called hush puppies.

Slipping into the doorway, baby on her hip, Peggy listened. Someone had to stay with Inez to make sure she didn't accidentally hurt herself, and the brunt of that job had fallen on her. Mary Jean was deeply in love and whispering about running away. Faye was working. There was no one else to take care of the baby. Inez did not always remember he was there.

From her vantage point just outside the room, Peggy listened to her grandparents. For a brief moment she wondered if Grandpa Early would really kill her daddy. More than anything she wanted Gene gone, to simply vanish so that he could no longer torment Inez or threaten them with violence. He drank heavily, and daily, and did not come home until he was drunk and furious. His step on the porch was enough to stop all chatter in the house. Coming through the door, his rage as tangible as a weapon, he would lash out at Inez for no reason. Anyone caught in the path of his blast got peppered with abuse. Sammy, in particular, seemed to catch the full force of his awful fury. Gene's unsupported suspicion that Sammy was the child of a Jewish merchant in town had grown into an obsession— even though Inez had not lived in Greenwood when Sammy was conceived. She'd only encountered the businessman in passing on the sidewalk, but Gene had latched onto Inez's imagined infidelity and Sammy's imagined parentage with the grip of a pit bull.

Michael began to cry, and Peggy jostled him, aware that her grandfather's gaze had settled upon her and the baby. His eyes were sad, as if he might cry.

Mary kept her focus on her daughter. "Inez, did you hear your daddy? Are you comin' home?"

Peggy waited for Inez to answer, watched as she dumped the onion into the cornmeal and reached for a handful of flour. Inez looked like an old woman. Older than her own ma. Pregnant with Michael, she had been rounded and sometimes happy. Now she was like a dried up old stick, not moving when the wind blew hard against her, just dry and brittle.

"You can't live like this," Mary Early whispered. "We can't let you live like this. Not any more. We've had enough. The children have had enough."

Inez cracked the egg into the bowl of cornmeal. On the stove the pan of grease began to pop and sizzle. There was no fish to cook. Gene had been drinking for several days, and the shelves in the grocery were nearly bare. The only thing he seemed to have a steady supply of was the moonshine which had at last caught the interest of some men who could be nothing other than federal revenue agents.

"We'll get a lawyer, and you can file for divorce. You can live with us in Clarksdale until you're legally rid of him." Mary was making her plans in the air.

At last Inez looked at her parents. "Where are the children goin' to live? Where will they go to school?"

For the first time, hope entered Benjamin's voice. "You can get the house, Inez. And the store. You can make a livin' at it. Or you can sell it and find something at home in Clarksdale, away from this hell."

"No man has a right to beat a woman the way Gene beats you." Mary Early sat taller in her chair, her jaw rigid. "I've wished him dead many a time, and if you don't get away from him, your daddy's gonna wind up killin' him. Do you want to see your daddy in prison?"

"No, ma'am." Inez turned away from the sizzling grease and went to the table to sit down. "I'm just so tired."

Mary reached across the table and touched her daughter's forehead. "Come home, Inez. Get your children and come on home."

Inez leaned into her mother's palm, resting, for a moment, against the steadiness of her gentle hand. "Okay," she whispered. "I'll file for divorce."

Slipping into the room, Peggy went to the stove and turned off the fire beneath the grease. She moved fast, her mind spinning, ready to act before Inez could change her mind. "I'll get the baby and his things," she said. She hurried to begin packing.

She heard her grandmother's footsteps behind her as she pulled diapers, dirty and clean, together in a bundle.

"Peggy, slow down a minute. I want to tell you somethin'."

Ma Early's level voice stopped Peggy's mad packing quicker than a slap. Michael on her hip, she faced her granny.

"Pa and me don't have much, but whatever we have, you children and your ma are welcome to it. It's not gonna be easy, but we'll make do."

"Yes, ma'am." Peggy glanced at the stack of clothes. There was a lot to get done so they could leave before Gene got back and stopped them. There wasn't time for talking about how things were going to be. Things would be the way they were, but it couldn't be worse then the present.

"When your ma was a little girl, just bigger than a baby, she got real sick. We thought she was gonna die." Mary Early rubbed the large knuckles of her right hand.

Peggy noticed that her skin was so thin it looked like wax paper. "We'd better go." She glanced out the window, worried that Gene would drive up.

"You need to hear this. It'll help some, when your patience gets thin." Mary pushed a strand of gray hair back from her face and then went to worrying her hands together. "Inez was real sick. Her fevers were so hot that she had fits. The doctor said she had spinal meningitis and there was nothin' they could do for her. Just wait, put her in cold water to bring the fevers down. And wait some more. That's what we had to do. And she got better." Mary worked her thumb over the knuckle of her forefinger, pressing the skin white. "She got better, but she didn't ever get completely right. She's like a child. And you just have to remember that, Peggy. I'm countin' on you to remember that." She left the room abruptly, calling over her shoulder. "Get all the baby's things. If I have my way, he'll never come back here."

WITH THE HELP of her parents, Inez hired a lawyer and filed for divorce on the grounds of cruelty and inhumane treatment. Even after moving back to Clarksdale, Inez's mental condition did not improve. Depression and despondency set in, seemingly relieved only by Gene's regular appearances, and his suddenly charming attempts to win her back. Ben and Mary watched in horror as Inez slowly let Gene back into her life.

Tormented by her hysterectomy, Inez found Gene's desire for her, his promises of a better life and better treatment, irresistible. She was the mother of his children, and she had a duty to him. It was the code she was raised to uphold, no matter what the men in the courthouse said. Gene was also in trouble with the law; the revenue agents were hot after him. Most importantly, in Inez's mind, Gene needed her.

Though she was legally separated and in the process of a divorce, she and the children were back in Greenwood as the '57-'58 school year approached.

Mary Jean eloped with Wayne Miller, an event that resulted in a multi-vehicle car chase through the Carroll County hills. Gene, Uncle Bob, and several of Mary Jean's brothers and sisters all hotly pursued the fleeing couple in an attempt to stop the marriage. Mary Jean and Wayne prevailed, and the couple set up housekeeping on the Basket Street property in a small house in the back.

Gene had not returned to live at home, but he was running the store, and Inez seemed to be getting back on her feet mentally. Both Inez and Gene had slacked off the whiskey, and Gene produced money for school shoes and for food. An unusual peace settled over 2021 Basket Street.

In the last days of warm weather, Peggy played with her cousin Molly, talked about Elvis and daydreamed, and helped tend the baby.

Gene's bootlegging flourished, and his sudden generosity with money for necessities eased the entire family situation. For Peggy, the faint hope that things might be okay had taken root and begun to grow.

Gene and one of his buddies had gotten up early on a hot morning, determined to get out on the river and resupply the grocery with fresh fish. The big end-of-summer fish fries at all the churches, black and white, were coming up, and Gene knew he could make good money on whatever fish he could catch. For most of the past year his focus had been bootlegging, but with the increased demand, fish was a good commodity, and less risky. Several times he'd found strange men asking questions about him in the area. Men who were likely federal agents out to put him in prison. A fish market without fish was a dead give-away.

"Hurry up, Virgil!" Gene complained as he checked his fishing tackle.

Inez appeared on the porch with a brown sack cradled in her arms. "I made some lunch for you both," she said, extending the bag to him. She looked over her shoulder into the dawn shadows of the front door. "Peggy, bring that baby so he can wave bye to his daddy."

Peggy appeared at the door, easing open the screen and stepping up beside Inez with Michael in her arms. She obediently lifted his little fist and waved goodbye with it.

"Well, thank you, Inez. You'd make a man a good wife," Gene teased her. "How come you're not married?"

Inez laughed out loud with pleasure. "As if you didn't know."

"When we sell this fish, I'm gonna take some of the money and buy you a dress." Gene let his gaze rove from her shoulders down to her toes and back up again, lingering just long enough to bring a flush to her cheeks. "Some of them pure silk stockin's, too."

Inez pushed the bag into his arms. "Go on with you, Gene. Bring home some fish before you go spendin' your money."

Chucking her under the chin, Gene slid behind the wheel. Virgil opened the passenger door and climbed in. "Quit flirtin' and get on the road," he said. "It's going to be ten degrees of hell out on that water, and I don't aim to spend the coolest part of the mornin' sittin' here listenin' to you try to win back a woman who spat out nearly a dozen kids for you."

Gene cranked the truck, the motor not quite drowning out his laugh. On the porch, Peggy could clearly hear their conversation.

"What's got you in such a mean mood?" Gene asked. "Wife holdin' out on you?"

"Go to hell," Virgil answered, his eyes narrowed with anger. "At least I don't have to kiss up to some half-wit to keep her from takin' everything I own."

Gene's face darkened then cleared. "If you don't come back from the river, I'll be sure and tell your wife how much you loved her."

The truck roared out of the yard.

"Gene asked me to tend the store," Inez said softly, not looking at Peggy.

Peggy turned to her mother, mouth open. Gene never let anyone tend the store without him, except maybe Billy. He'd been too afraid Inez or the children would steal food or candy. "He give you a key?"

Inez dangled the key in the air. "I'm goin' over there now."

"I'll come."

"No." Inez turned to her. "I want to do it alone. Stay with Michael."

"But Mama . . ."

Inez clenched her fists. "Alone. I want to do it alone."

Peggy took a step back. "Yes, ma'am."

Inez turned away abruptly and went to the grocery.

For an hour Peggy sat on the porch, rocking Michael. Mary Jean was busy in her own house, and Faye had a job, as did Billy and Boyd. Sometimes the boys worked with Gene.

The morning passed. Peggy played in the dirt, using the baby as a pretend captive as she played cowboys and Indians in the front yard.

In the house the radio played the popular songs of Buddy Holly, the television star Ricky Nelson, and Pat Boone, and, of course, Elvis. "Teddy Bear" was the greatest.

Peggy knew from listening to her sisters that another singer, Wildman Jerry Lee Lewis, had Mississippi Delta roots and was burning up the piano with a brand of honky tonk music that shared a seed of something rebellious with her idol, Elvis. There was also a black man breaking onto the white airwaves with a strange tune called "Blueberry Hill" that seemed to combine the best of any summer. Fats Domino. Peggy loved his name. It made her want to laugh and do the "camel walk." There wasn't a dance step she couldn't master in a matter of minutes.

When Inez did not return to the house for lunch, Peggy went in to feed the baby and find something for herself. Standing in the house, silent except for the radio, Peggy blinked back an unexpected rush of tears and wished to be back in her grandparents' home. The Earlys were old and not in good financial shape, but for those brief summer weeks, the burden of protecting Inez had been lifted from her shoulders and assumed by Ma and Pa Early. Life had been so much better without Gene, even with her mother's black depressions.

While Michael slept on a pallet on the floor, Peggy used her school notebook to draw pictures and make up a story. The land of fantasy and imagination was her only haven. Though she hadn't passed Mrs. Wheeler's class, she had earned first place in a school writing contest with a short story about a frog that could sing like Elvis Presley, and she toyed with drawing pictures of the handsomest frog ever seen.

She did not trust the truce that lay between her parents. She'd heard her uncles talking about the divorce and how Inez would get everything if Gene didn't do something to stop it.

"Peggy, open the door."

Inez called from the porch, and Peggy rushed up from the table to push open the screen. Inez stood, arms loaded with staples.

"Let's make something good," Inez said. She walked into the kitchen where she dropped the supplies on the kitchen table.

"Daddy's goin' to be mad," Peggy warned. She could already hear him, see the fury in his face. Inez had taken flour, lard, bacon, sweet potatoes. It was going to be a terrible fight.

"He said he was bringing us some fish to fry up for supper. I thought we'd make something to go with it. Like a regular family." Inez's face was lit with a smile.

Peggy side-stepped out of the kitchen. "I'll check on the baby." She felt her own anger at her mother. How could Inez be so stupid? How could she believe for a second that things would not blow up?

She heard the car coming before she saw it, a sleek blue sedan that stopped at the grocery. The car wasn't new, but it was washed and clean. Two men, wearing the khaki pants and white, starched shirts that marked them as other than field laborers or professionals, got out. They walked to the store and rattled the handle.

Walking out on to the porch, Peggy called out to them, "Store's closed."

"Well, that's a fine howdy-do," one of the men said, grinning. "Where's Gene?"

"Gone fishin'."

"Then where's Bob?" The same man asked.

"Gone, too." Peggy eyed the men. They didn't look like the type who would be on a first name basis with her daddy or her uncle. There was something sharp about the men, a crispness that didn't go with their friendly manner.

"Can someone open the store and sell us something?" the man who'd been driving asked.

"Store's just about empty," Peggy said. "Daddy's gone to catch some fish to sell. Hardly nothin' else in there."

"We need a few supplies," the man persisted.

"Store's closed." Peggy didn't like the men. They smiled, but it was only a stretching of their lips.

"Get your mama, girl." Even the little bit of softness had left the man's voice.

Inez appeared in the doorway.

The man's voice went suddenly polite. "Can you open the store, please ma'am?"

Inez eyed the men and the car. They had money. "Okay." She fished in her apron pocket for the key and brushed past Peggy as she crossed the porch.

"Mama . . ."

"Watch the baby." Inez walked to the front door and opened it. The men followed her inside.

Instead of going in the house, Peggy followed them to the store. Lingering outside, she listened as the men made their way around the store, picking up small items, putting them back, talking softly together, finally settling on a box of crackers and some sardines.

"That it?" Inez eyed the purchases at the counter with a sudden wariness.

"Gene said we could get us somethin' to drink." The man laughed.

"There's some cold drinks." Inez nodded toward the cooler. "Nickel each."

"We were hopin' for somethin' to put a little fire in our blood." Both men laughed.

"Well, you came to the wrong place." Inez had a peculiar note in her voice. "You men revenuers?"

They answered with laughter, too loud and too harsh.

"We're friends of Gene and Bob," the driver finally said. "They told us to tell you to sell us some of Gene's mash. We've heard it's the best in the county, and we want a sample of it. Might be we could place some bigger orders later on."

Inez looked from one to the other. She pressed her lips together and grasped the edge of the counter to still the nervousness in her hands. "You know anything about a Negro boy murdered up here a couple of years ago?"

The men were halted for a moment. "Yeah, we know about that," the driver finally answered.

Inez was breathing shallow. "I know about it, too."

"The whole world knows about it. That boy was murdered, and the guilty men got off scot-free and then confessed in a magazine. We didn't come here to talk about the past. We're just thirsty men. Now tell the truth; you got somethin' good to sell some thirsty men?"

Inez's voice flattened. "We don't have no mash to sell."

Peggy slipped into the grocery and moved to stand beside Inez at the counter. She felt her mother's leg move, pushing the jugs of moonshine up deeper into the hidden space of the counter. There was hardly anything in the store except the illegal whiskey.

"Bob Moye said you would give us a hard time." The man who'd been the passenger patted his friend's shoulder, talking to him as if Inez wasn't there. "Ole Bob said she wouldn't want to sell it to us. He said she was smart and afraid of the law."

"Mama said we don't have nothin'. The store's closed." Peggy glared at the men, who simply ignored her.

"Gene's gonna be mad at you if he hears he missed a sale. We've got cash money." The man drew out a thick roll of money. The top bill was a fifty.

Inez eyed the money and swallowed. "Gene's not here. I can sell you the crackers and sardines." She rang up the purchases on the cash register. "That'll be fifty-five cents," she said, proud that she'd finally learned to work the register correctly. "You think you got business with Gene or Bob Moye, you come back when they're here." She took the money for the crackers and sardines and gave them change. "Now I'm closin' the store," she said, pointing to the door.

The men took their purchase and walked out. There was no longer any talk or laughter between them. A few seconds later there was the sound of the car cranking to life and then it sped past the store and down the road.

"Revenuers," Peggy said. "Sure as heck, revenuers."

"I know." Inez leaned against the counter. "I had something I needed to tell them." She sagged slightly.

"Don't talk to no revenuers or lawmen, Mama." Peggy took her by the arm and started toward the door. "They never listen. They never do anything. Except make things worse."

"Not always, Peggy. Mr. Bill Mays has helped us before."

"If you do talk to the revenuers, you should tell them about Daddy and nothing else," Peggy insisted.

"Let's close up." Inez and Peggy moved to the door. Inez had just turned the key when the rumble of Gene's old truck drifted ahead of the cloud of dust that marked his impending arrival.

"Revenuers were here," Peggy informed him as soon as the truck came to a stop. She liked the impact the words had on her father. For a split second, he showed his fear. Revenuers couldn't always be bought off, like most of the local law. If the feds caught him, there was a chance he'd do hard time. "Mama said we didn't have no whiskey." As much as Peggy enjoyed wielding the tool that made Gene's eyes go hollow, she knew there would be a price if her father became too upset.

"What else did she say?"

Peggy heard the rattle in his question. Snake rattle. "She didn't say nothin' else. Just that we didn't have any moonshine and the store was closed."

Gene gazed down at his daughter. "Go to the house."

"Did you get any fish?" Peggy caught at her father's hand. "Let's look at the fish. I'll bet the customers will be lined out the door."

Gene shook free of his daughter's grasp and used the same hand to slap her away from him. "Go inside."

Inez started around him, but he grabbed her arm. "What else did you say, Inez?"

"Nothin'." Something in her eyes had snapped to life. "I didn't say nothin' 'cause they wouldn't listen."

"Shit a mile," Bob whispered, his voice a buzz like a swarm of bees.

Gene dropped Inez's shoulder as if she'd suddenly gone sizzling hot. He went to the truck and pulled out a jug of bootleg. "Get inside. Both of you," he said, tilting the jug up and swallowing before he handed it to his brother-in-law. "Let's go, Bob." Gene motioned for Bob to get back in the truck. Without unloading the fish, Gene drove out Highway 7 toward Greenwood.

THE ROCKING CHAIR was hard and Peggy's neck ached from the awkward position of trying to sleep sitting straight up. There had been no sign of Gene. Her fear was that he would return and take up the issue of what Inez had tried to tell the revenuers. That her parents were still legally divorced seemed not to matter. Gene was still the man of the house.

Checking the clock, Peggy found that it was nearly five A.M. She forced herself out of the chair and walked to the bedroom where her sisters slept. Pushing against Sheila, she made a space for herself and crept beneath the sheet, falling immediately into a deep sleep.

She awoke to glass breaking and a sound like an enraged bull. It took only seconds for Gene's voice to register in an oath. Inez's shriek of fury followed.

"Get up," Faye said, shaking all of her sisters. "Get up." The weak light of dawn illuminated her worried face.

Peggy and Sheila slipped to the floor and began dressing. It seemed the walls would collapse about them. Glass broke again, and Inez's voice mourned the loss of something of value to her. From sorrow she went straight to a howling attack, a sound made more fearsome by its primal intent.

"We're going to school," Faye said in a cold, iron voice. She grabbed Peggy's arm in a tight grip. "You can't do anything here except make Daddy worse. We'll go on to school, and maybe they'll quit before they kill each other."

While the fight raged on, Peggy and her brothers and sisters walked to school. Faye had bundled up clothes for the children too young for school and left them with newly married Mary Jean.

"Peggy, you stay in school," Faye warned her. "Don't go home. You'll only make it worse. You set Daddy off, even when you don't mean to. You get up in his face, and he'll take it out on Mama. Just stay away."

Peggy tried, but the day was an endless torture. The minutes stretched long and hot, the sound of a fly buzzing in the open window seemed to last forever. Finally, she could stand it no longer and slipped away from the school grounds during the final recess. The study of history and the Choctaw Indians was over for the day. She would miss only math, and it was a subject she didn't have much regard for anyway.

Gene's car was parked in front of the grocery store, and the front door of the house was open when she walked into the yard. Stepping inside, she inched toward the bedroom, expecting to find the small lump of Inez in bed. Though the sheets were rumpled, there was no sign of her mother. Peggy's pulse increased and a knot gripped her stomach. Inez was not in the kitchen or the bathroom.

She was not in the house.

Walking to the store, Peggy listened to her father laughing with two men who stood at the counter as he passed a jug to them. She recognized them as the men who'd come to buy moonshine from Inez. The revenuers.

"Daddy!" She burst into the store. "Daddy, don't . . ."

His hand slammed down on the counter. "Don't be interrupting me when I'm talkin'."

"Where's Mama?" The revenuers were forgotten.

Gene looked at the men as if he'd been waiting to answer this question. "The law had to come and take your ma down to Whitfield. She's crazy as a Betsy bug."

Peggy stepped back, stumbling into the metal racks that held the peanuts and fried pork rinds. "No." She looked from her father to the men. "Mama's okay. She was okay. She didn't need to go to Whitfield."

"Like hell she didn't. She was makin' things up in her head and tryin' to hurt me and herself."

"I want to go with her."

Gene shook his head so that the two men were included in his tolerance of his child. "You're 'bout crazy enough to go, Peggy, but you ain't goin'. Now get in the house and take care of that baby. Becky couldn't come today and tend him, and Mary Jean had things to do. He's probably hungry."

"I'm goin' up there to Whitfield to take care of Mama." Peggy set her feet solid into the wood of the floor. Tears burned behind her eyes, fire in her head. "I'm goin' and you can't stop me."

"You're goin' in that house and if you give me one more lip full of sass, you're gonna be sorry of the day you were born."

Peggy saw his hand go under the counter. He could be reaching for his gun, the stick of wood he kept there for a club, or the fly-swatter he used to kill the bottle flies or punish his kids. She didn't wait to find out which.

"You're gonna burn in hell," she yelled as she ran out of the store and toward the house.

Chapter Fifteen

Standing at the sink, Peggy heard Ronald's Indian yell that signaled something big happening. Tired from tending to baby Michael and trying to concoct a scheme that would get her to Whitfield to help her mother, Peggy almost ignored the commotion in the yard.

Her curiosity finally won out and she walked to the front porch. The dust boiled out behind the spanking new 1957 Cadillac as it tore down Basket Street and spun to a halt in front of the Albritton porch. Peggy ran to the kitchen and jammed the pot she'd been drying under the sink. As she ran back to the front door, she avoided looking in her parents' bedroom where Inez should have been lying on the quilt-covered bed. Her daddy had refused to tell her when Inez was coming home.

"Starley!" Peggy yelled as she pushed open the screen door and ran toward her friend.

"Peggy!" Starley jumped up and down beside the open car door.

Peggy flew across the porch and danced into the yard, clasping Starley's hands as the two girls giggled and hugged. Peggy hadn't made new friends. She was two grades behind the other children, and though she liked her new teacher, Mrs. Metcalf, she was lonely and tormented during classes. Seeing Starley was a tremendous relief.

"Get your clothes," Starley said. "Hurry!"

"Where we going?" Peggy didn't really care. All she wanted was to flee the house. For a brief moment, escape seemed the only logical answer to her woes. If she could just get in the car with Sister Verline and Starley, maybe they could drive her to a new life.

Verline opened the driver's door and got out, one foot still in the car as she leaned on the roof. "Would you ask Gene to come to the door?" she called to Peggy.

"He's not here." She hesitated. "He might not be back until real late."

Starley eased around Peggy and peeped through the screen door. It was late September, but the days were still hot enough to leave doors and windows open.

"Mama's down at the Hadden place." Peggy lied without a twitch.

Verline got back in the car. "Pack some things, Peggy. We're goin' to take a trip. A long trip, and you can stay the night at our house."

"Hurry!" Starley jumped up and down with excitement. "You won't believe where Mama's takin' us. The one place in the whole world you want to go most. To see the one person in the universe you love the most. The coolest . . ."

Peggy's eyes got so big it felt as if her eyebrows would touch her hairline. "Elvis!" There was no second alternative.

"Yes!" Starley jumped around the front of the car. "Mama said she'd take us to the fair in Tupelo. Elvis is performing there. It's the biggest thing happening. Last year they made it Elvis Presley Day in Tupelo!"

Peggy started to run in the house, then turned around. "What should I wear?" While at the Earleys', Inez had made Peggy several new dresses, her hand stitching slow but well done.

"A sundress. Something cool. It's going to be hotter than blue blazes, and we want to go on all the rides, too."

Peggy sprinted into the house, bumping the wall as she tore into her bedroom and flung open the drawers. Clutching shorts and dresses, she held each up and tossed them aside. At last she picked a yellow sundress. It was perfect. She got a sack from the kitchen and shoved her things into it. She rushed out the back to take Michael to her sister's house. In less than five minutes she was back in the front yard and ready to go.

"We have to ask Gene," Verline called from inside the car. "I can't take you off without his say-so."

"It's okay," Peggy said. She clamped down on the worry that made her heart beat too fast. Gene would never let her go. Never. She had to figure out how to get away. "I'll tell one of the boys." She darted into the back yard.

Boyd stood beside an old hickory stump, a blood-drenched ax in his hand. The body of a huge loggerhead lay on one side of the stump, its head on the other. Gene had caught the turtle the day before.

"I'm going to Tupelo with Sister Verline Ellis to see Elvis," Peggy announced, watching as Boyd hefted the hundred-pound turtle closer to the stump.

"Sure." Boyd brought the ax down on the turtle's leg, severing it. He tossed the leg into a pan of water that turned pink with blood. Turtle legs were good seasoning. Gene would sell it to the Negroes to cook with rice. "One thing about you, Peggy. You ain't much for books, but you've got an imagination."

"I am so going." Peggy was panting with excitement. "I got to tell . . . Daddy. Do you think he'll let me go?"

"I expect not," Boyd said, not missing a stroke in the dismemberment of the turtle. "You better not run off without telling him." Breathing hard, Boyd put the ax head down in the dirt and leaned on it for a moment as he took in Peggy and her sack of clothes.

"Daddy's not here, and Sister Verline is ready to go." A sense of panic set in. "It's Elvis, Boyd."

Boyd lifted the ax, then hesitated. "Go on," he said. "I'll tell Daddy."

The rush of gratitude made Peggy start forward. She stopped after a step. "Thanks, Boyd."

"Go on," he said, waving her away as he tightened his grip on the wooden handle.

"I'll be back tomorrow night." Peggy's feet skimmed the ground as she hurried to the Cadillac and climbed into the big front seat beside Starley. The new car smell was like heaven as she settled against the soft, buttery leather.

"Ready, girls?" Verline asked. She cut the wheel sharply and spun out of the yard.

"Yes, ma'am," Peggy said. She'd never been so ready for anything in her life.

For the first hour of the drive, the rows of cotton flashed past the Cadillac window, a vista that Peggy knew so well it required no notice. She and Starley made a list of the songs the Cool Cat would sing.

"He'll do all the songs off the new record," Peggy said confidently. "He better sing 'Hound Dog' and 'Love Me Tender.' Those are my favorites."

"Peggy can dance just like Elvis," Starley said.

"Especially when I wet my hair and comb it back. I'm gonna dye it black, too."

"Not on this trip, you're not," Verline warned. "I'm not takin' you home with soot-black hair. Besides, there won't be time for no dye job. I hear the crowds get pretty wild. Ole Ed Sullivan thought he was going to have a stampede in the audience. It's a good thing he had that accident and couldn't be there to see Elvis. I'm afraid he'da stroked out right there on national television." Verline chuckled to herself at the memory. "Nothin' like seein' a Mississippi hillbilly boy shake up those show biz snots."

"You like Elvis?" Peggy wasn't certain what Verline's purpose in seeing a rock 'n' roller might be.

"The boy's got the spirit," Verline conceded. "He sets my toes to tappin', and I have to admit, I can't keep my eyes off his hips when they wiggle."

"Mama!" Starley giggled as she jabbed Peggy in the ribs. "Mama's just sayin' that."

"Anyway, I thought you girls would enjoy seein' him. One day he's gonna be really big, a major star, and you can tell everyone you saw him when he got welcomed back to his hometown at the livestock fair. This is history in the makin', girls. And we're gonna be a part of it."

When the flatness of the Delta gave way to truck farms, pine forests, and the beginning rumble of the Appalachian Mountains, Peggy kept glancing out the window. She'd never been out of the Delta. For her the world was flat, rows of cotton, green or brown or white, extending until the heat devils blistered the horizon. Highway 45 North rode the gentle swells of land unlike any Peggy had seen. The rich Delta soil had been left behind, and the shallower, less fertile soil of the northeast corner of the state had been put into pasture for the herds of red Herefords and black angus.

Verline reached over and clicked on the radio, searching the staticky dial for the call letters of Tupelo's stations.

"The folks at the Mississippi/Alabama State Fair and Livestock Show are expecting over twelve thousand teenagers wanting to see Elvis Presley," the deejay reported.

"And one old preacher-woman," Verline commented. She pressed the gas pedal a little harder. "We want to make the show early and get our seats," she said.

The deejay continued talking, his voice building with excitement. "Tupelo residents and visitors are urged not to park along the downtown streets," he said. "We want the way clear for Elvis when he starts out toward the fairgrounds. Elvis Presley, right here in Tupelo. By the way, folks, in case you don't remember, Elvis's appearance on the *Ed Sullivan Show* gathered an astounding eighty-two percent of the viewing population. There's been some talk around Tupelo that Mr. Sullivan wasn't really injured in a car accident at all, but that he simply couldn't face Elvis since he'd made the statement that Elvis Presley would never appear on his show. Anybody out there got any real facts on the matter? While you're calling in, I'm going give you the Cool Cat himself, with 'Don't Be Cruel.' "

The music spun through the car, licking Peggy like hot little tastes of fire.

"We're not goin' home right after the show. We're stayin' to ride the rides, aren't we?" Starley's mouth opened in complaint.

"You can ride the rides," Verline said wearily. "I made you a promise."

"Even if we don't get to ride, Elvis will be the best," Peggy reassured her.

"How can you be so certain?"

"Elvis wouldn't disappoint his fans. And this is his homecoming. All those folks are waiting to see him, and he's not the kind of guy who would let everybody down."

Verline laughed out loud. "You surely sound as if you've known him all your life."

"She reads everything about him. Everything!" Starley said. "One day she's goin' to marry him."

Verline never slowed as she whipped through the outskirts of Tupelo. Still speeding at sixty-five, she looked long and hard at Peggy. "Miss Peggy Ruth Albritton is a very determined young lady. If she decides to marry Elvis, she just may do it."

Starley's squeal made all three glance up. "Look!"

"The Ferris wheel." Peggy wondered if she was really awake.

Verline slid the Caddy into a parking space and signaled the girls out. "Quit gawkin' and get movin'," she said, shooing them out the passenger door.

Almost as soon as her feet touched the dirt parking lot, Peggy could taste the sweetness of the air. Cotton candy, candied apples, the sizzle of burgers and fries in the small, portable stands all mixed and mingled with the sweat of livestock into a heady and rarified blend.

"I can't wait," Starley whispered. "It's too exciting!"

Peggy's eyes went directly to the Ferris wheel, which spun though the blue September sky until it stopped, seats rocking. Teenage girls shrilled their delight as they clutched the arms of boyfriends. Beside the Ferris wheel were a number of other rides, some swarmed by little children no bigger than Peggy's younger brothers.

It was the noise that Peggy registered last. Even as the rides spun through the afternoon heat, they pinged and whirred. Calliope music issued from one wheezing old sled ride that seemed a favorite of the under-five kids. And everywhere children were screaming. Screaming with pleasure and mock fear, yelling out their delight in the day and the once-a-year-only thrills of the state fair.

Peggy bit her bottom lip. The Tupelo fair and livestock show was everything she had hoped for.

"Hold on there, girls," Verline said as she grabbed their shoulders. "The show starts in an hour."

Peggy froze. As much as she wanted to dash over to the Ferris wheel and climb right on, she didn't want to miss Elvis.

"We can ride after the show," Verline explained. "We'd better find a seat. It's going to be packed."

"Can we get up close?" Peggy asked. She had never dared to believe that one day she would hear the tall, dark-haired singer who danced as if electricity sizzled through him.

"You got it bad for that boy," Verline said, patting her shoulder.

"Mary Jean read in some magazine that Elvis didn't live in Memphis until he was in high school. Mary Jean said he's even played a few clubs around Greenwood." Peggy had memorized every tidbit of fact or fiction Mary Jean found in her star magazines.

"Well, he's got a lot of mamas all distressed," Verline said, herding the girls toward the man selling tickets to the stage area. "Land's sake, folks act like a boy shakin' his leg is Satan at work."

"I've heard Elvis on the radio lots lately," Peggy said. "The radio man said he was the most famous Mississippi talent."

"That or the plague," Verline said, pulling the money for the tickets out of her purse. "Three," she said to the attendant.

"The real show don't start for a hour," the man said, handing the ticket stubs back.

"We came to see Elvis." Peggy took her stub. She intended to keep it forever.

The man pushed his hat back a little and looked down at her. "Elvis, huh?"

"Elvis Presley." Peggy spoke precisely.

"Now if it was Porter Wagner, I might agree with you. That Presley boy's a mite too close to nigra music for my taste." He waved them into the area, which was beginning to fill with teenage girls, their voices an octave too shrill and their bodies already jerky and hot.

"Let's find a place where we can see," Verline said, directing them toward the hot metal seats.

Enthralled with watching the arena fill, Peggy hardly noticed the sun and the heat. Verline found an old program and fanned herself, one eye on the stage and one on the girls.

"Why do you like Elvis so?" she asked Peggy.

The question brought the singer vividly to Peggy's mind. He sang good, but so did a lot of other, more popular singers. He danced in a way that made her feel alive. But it was something more than that. Something in his dark eyes that said no matter how much fun he was having on the outside, inside he knew he'd pay a price for it. There was always a price.

"He's handsome," Peggy half-answered. "And I like his songs. I like 'em, and sometimes he seems like he . . . needs someone to think just about him."

"Peggy's in love with him," Starley said. "She dances in the store for the Negroes."

"I do," Peggy admitted.

Verline smoothed Peggy's hair with a gentle hand. "Well, maybe toward the end of the show, we'll put you up on stage."

"Really?" Peggy's heart leaped. No matter that the thought terrified her, she would do it. She could do it. To dance on stage with Elvis Presley would be the high point of her life. She'd never do anything better. Never. Maybe he would even give her a job dancing like him, right up on the stage beside him.

Verline laughed. "Probably not, but it does make an interesting picture," she said.

"One day, maybe," Peggy said. "Maybe I'll get a chance to dance with Elvis."

"Maybe you will." Verline's face was suddenly sad. "Peggy, honey, they won't let anyone on stage with him here. But you never can tell what's going to happen in the future. Just trust in the Lord and wait and see."

The sun burned down on the tops of their heads, and Starley and Peggy took turns standing over Verline to shield her from the worst of it. But they quickly became absorbed in the thousands of girls who'd come to hear Elvis perform. The sight was awe-inspiring, and also depressing for Peggy. Out of the billions of girls who obviously loved him, he would never notice her. Never in a million years. She studied their dresses and their painted fingernails and lipstick, the black and white rock 'n' roll shoes. Some had ponytails and full skirts, others wore shifts and sandals. They clustered in groups of three or more, and their gazes never left the stage.

"Look!" Starley's finger pointed to the stage. Out from the wings stepped a slender young man with baggy pants, a gold lamé jacket over a navy blue shirt with a big collar and open at the throat. His dark hair glistened in the sun. A guitar was slung over his neck, and several other young men took up their places at drums and bass.

"Hi, my name's Elvis Presley. My band and I want to play a few songs for you."

Peggy felt as if she were caught in a pocket of air so heavy, so dense that she would not live beyond the moment. Somehow, it didn't matter. She did not hear the girls screaming and shrilling. She never saw their tears and the way they reached out to him across the distance of the audience, knowing that he could not touch them but unable to stop themselves from reaching.

For Peggy there was only the black-haired young man in the glittery gold jacket wearing a shirt made by his mama. As he danced and sang across the stage, Peggy connected with his energy, with the rebellious antics that dared her to care about him. And when he finally slowed long enough to strum the guitar for the opening measures of "Love me Tender," she had already decided in her own heart, that her tenderness would go only to him, forever.

Chapter Sixteen

Attending the Elvis performance was the only good event of the years 1955-57. The trip to Tupelo, orchestrated by a kind woman with a generous heart, was the event that Peggy clung to during "the storm years." She had seen Elvis, live. She had connected and in the process had made a vow that she would love him always. Elvis was her future, but Inez was her present. Something had to be done about her mother.

In her determination to join her mother in Whitfield, Peggy concocted a scheme with the help of Faye and a neighbor boy, Thomas Turner. Armed with a broom stick and a five-pound cloth sack of flour, Peggy managed to wedge herself onto the top shelf that Gene had built over the bathtub.

When Gene entered the bathroom, Peggy swung the broom stick with all her might. The blow struck Gene on the side of the head. He went down hard, and Peggy aimed the sack of flour at his head.

Her intentions were not necessarily to kill him, but to attack him. The reasoning among Faye, Peggy, and Thomas was that if Inez had been sent to Whitfield for striking at Gene, then Peggy's punishment would also be incarceration in the mental institution. Once there, she would be able to take care of her mother.

The plan did not succeed.

Gene was furious, but his injuries weren't serious. Peggy was severely beaten. No matter how she fought and ranted, she was not sent to Whitfield.

Institutionalization did not negate Inez's court-decreed possession of the house on Basket Street. She was a mental patient, and she was also the legal owner of the house. That was the fact Gene intended to remedy.

On October 17, 1957—two days after the divorce was officially granted—Gene borrowed his brother's green and white Ford Fairlane and went to Whitfield to visit Inez. He no longer had any legal right to participate in her treatment, but the asylum authorities had no knowledge of the divorce. Gene had been Inez's husband during her 1955 commitment. When he signed the papers for her release, Inez was turned over to him.

Gene promised Inez he would take her to her parents in Clarksdale. On the way, he convinced her to remarry him. They were united in holy matrimony that same day in Bolivar County, only an hour from the Earlys' home in Clarksdale. Inez never returned to her parents. She went straight to Greenwood with Gene and resumed the life she'd led since her marriage at fifteen. The only change in her life was that she could no longer bear Gene's children.

For Peggy, the school year was torment. She attended school irregularly, staying home to take care of the baby because Inez was rarely up to the care of an infant. Though Mrs. Metcalf was kind, and interested in Peggy, there was little she could do for the child who attended erratically.

Gene was tried for bootlegging and given a three-year suspended sentence and put on probation.

Though the fighting between Gene and Inez waned a bit, the drinking grew heavier. Gene and Inez were often drunk by the time the children arrived home from school. Peggy and her older brothers and sisters had the care of the younger children and the running of the household. Faye was following in her big sister's footsteps toward freedom, and both Billy and Boyd were showing signs of independence. Members of the Presbyterian church in town stepped in and made arrangements for Billy to be removed from the Albritton household and sent to a religious and educational institution in the small town of French Camp.

The Albritton household was beginning to shift and change as the oldest children made preparations to leave. The daily worry about Inez continued to fall on Peggy. She was also the lightning rod that drew Gene's wrath. Her stubborn protection of Inez resulted in all-out assaults against liquor. Peggy could find the bottles hidden around the house that none of the other children could locate. She would pour out the amber whiskey, watching it soak into the rich Delta soil. Knowing her actions were futile, that Gene would simply unlock the store and get another jug, she did it anyway. And when she was caught, she took the beating that was her punishment.

Billy's success at French Camp Academy prompted another attempt by church authorities, with assistance from the local welfare department, to remove more of the Albritton children from the day-to-day trauma of the home. Peggy and Sheila were selected to attend the academy that served as a foster home for orphans, problem children, or children from abusive families.

Though Inez had fought like a tiger against the child welfare authorities to keep her children at home, she was at last worn down. With the hope of a better future for Peggy and Sheila, she gave her consent.

It was a sunny day when the car that would take the girls to the church school pulled into the Albritton yard. The tall man who got out of the car came up to the porch slowly, as if he were taking the measure of the house and neighborhood. Peggy and Sheila waited on the porch, watching his every move. The one lesson that Peggy had learned well was that no one in authority could be taken at face value.

"Are you girls ready?" he asked.

"Peggy doesn't want to go." Sheila viewed the trip as an adventure, a chance to escape the hell of the household. A chance to show that she was braver than her older sister.

"You're going to find French Camp to be a place where you can make lots of new friends," the tall, thin man said. His voice was soft, gentle, with none of the hardness Peggy so often heard from the men who hung around the store. "My name is Mr. Hamilton, and I want to make sure you and your sister get a good start."

Peggy cast a glance at Inez, who stood by the front door, her hand on the screen.

"What will we do?" Sheila spoke with a hint of excitement.

"Well, you'll live with several other girls and an adult who acts like a temporary parent, just while you're there." Mr. Hamilton touched one of Sheila's golden curls. "You can go to school, just like you do here in Greenwood, and all of the boys and girls who live in the academy help out with the chores. You do chores at home, don't you?"

"Yes, sir." Sheila smiled.

"It won't be so different, except that you'll have lots of other children to play with, and there are all kinds of animals."

"Horses?" Peggy couldn't help asking.

"Yes, Peggy, there are horses and cows and goats and chickens."

"Can we ride the horses?" Peggy took a tentative step across the peeling paint of the porch. "Really?" Everything the man said sounded wonderful. Except the school part. But if she stayed in Greenwood, she'd have to go to school anyway. "Sometimes Mr. Chaney lets us ride his palomino."

"All of the children are allowed to ride. Of course if you ride the horses, you have to help take care of them."

"I can do that." Peggy imagined the feel of the horse's muzzle against her hand. She'd ridden a few times and been in the barn where the horse was kept. She loved the sound the horse made when he ate. A niggle of excitement made her bite her bottom lip. "Where will we live?"

"All of the girls live in dormitories with a bed for each of you. You'll have ten other girls living with you, all about your age, and then one of our young volunteer ladies will be there to look out for you. They'll help you with your homework and any problems you might have."

The strangest sensation crowded into Peggy's chest. She had a sense of someone looking over her shoulder, someone nice like Mrs. Metcalfe, with a finger to trace along the book and explain how the words went together. Inez had never been able to help her with her homework. Peggy glanced at her mother in the doorway and the feeling died in her chest. "Mama?"

"Your mother knows this is the best thing for you, Peggy." Mr. Hamilton's hand touched her face, turning her away from her mother to look into his eyes. "You can learn your schooling at French Camp, learn skills so that you can get a job. Your mama knows this is the best. She wants the best for her children because she loves you."

Peggy felt something tough begin to tear inside her ribs. "What about Mama?" She looked at the screen, but Inez had disappeared.

"Your brother is up at French Camp. He'll help look out for you and your sister. Without two more mouths to feed here at home, things will be better for your mother. Mary Jean can help her with the younger children and your mother can rest more. She's sick, Peggy. She needs to rest."

"I want to go." Sheila had made up her mind.

"Good. Now wait here." Mr. Hamilton went to his car and returned with two boxes. "I brought you something pretty to wear so you'd feel special when we get there." He opened the boxes and took out two store-bought dresses. He handed a red and white striped one to Peggy.

"This is mine?" Peggy hardly believed it. Most of her clothes had been made by Inez. Her mother could sew pretty good, but not like this beautiful red and white dress that looked like summer and a candy stick mixed together.

"Go put on your dresses, and we'll get your things. We have a little drive ahead of us and we need to get going."

The dress was crisp, the red and white stripes snapping like fire-crackers. Peggy took it and followed Sheila into the bedroom. Automatically she began to put it on. Sheila finished dressing first and began putting her clothes together. While Peggy fumbled with her sash, Sheila gathered Peggy's things, too.

Finally dressed, Peggy stared at the jumbled pile of her belongings. The dress made her feel like Cinderella, but the stack of clothes made her slightly sick. "I don't know . . ." She started out of the room to go and see about her mother.

"Peggy!" Sheila's voice was a hiss. "We can come home if we don't like it. Let's see what it's like. Billy didn't come back. It must be good."

Peggy looked out the window into the front yard. She couldn't even imagine a place called French Camp.

Sheila had tied her clothes in a bundle and pushed them into her arms. "I'm going. You can stay here and listen to them fight for the rest of your life. I don't want to be here any more." She marched out the door and to the porch where Mr. Hamilton patiently waited.

Peggy found her mother resting on the bed. The smell of whiskey was fresh in the room. "Mama?"

"You go, Peggy." Inez didn't sit up. "They say it's a good place. You remember what I taught you. Keep your manners, and make Sheila behave."

"You come with us, Mama?" Peggy went to the side of the bed.

"It's for children, Peggy."

"But you could work there." The hard thing in Peggy's chest tore a little more, a silent ripping that hurt like fire.

Inez raised up on her elbows and looked into her daughter's face. "Go on, girl. This is for the best."

"What if I don't like it?"

"You can come home."

"What if I get in trouble like I do in school?"

"Tell the truth, Peggy. Whatever you do, just tell the truth." She gave a soft snort of laughter. "Tell the truth if anyone will listen to you." Inez looked away from Peggy and reached for the glass jar on the table. The amber liquid sloshed against the side but didn't spill. "If I could have . . ." She took a swallow. "I taught you and Sheila to work hard. You do that and everything will be fine. Mind your manners. Tell the truth and remember that kindness kills. If somebody tries to be mean and hard with you, don't go tryin' to fight 'em. I know you, Peggy Ruth, and you want to lash back. Don't do it. Kindness kills. Remember that." She took another swallow and put the glass back on the bedside table.

"Mama, I don't want to leave you here."

Inez's hand moved out toward her daughter. She stroked Peggy's tangled hair. "Try to find something better than this, Peggy. Go on, now. They're waiting. Go." The last word was final.

Still clutching her clothes to the bodice of her new dress, Peggy walked out onto the porch. Mr. Hamilton and Sheila were already in the car, waiting. It seemed to take forever for Peggy's feet to carry her across the worn and familiar boards of the porch, down the steps and across the dusty yard where she'd once ridden the captured alligator.

The car door swung open and she crawled in beside Sheila. Before she could say a word, the car was speeding down Basket Street toward First Avenue and the highway that would take her out of the Delta for the second time in her life.

Chapter Seventeen

The large room was filled with two rows of individual beds, a fact that Peggy found immediately unsettling. Never in her life had she slept alone in a bed.

She and Sheila were put in the same house with Mrs. Pilgrim, a woman who met them with smiles and said she would help with any problems they might have. Mrs. Pilgrim succeeded in giving Sheila a welcoming hug. Something inside Peggy did not allow her to relax in the embrace. She held herself stiff and rigid, and the woman turned to Sheila, commenting on her golden curls and winning a smile from the nine-year-old.

"Breakfast is served at seven, and then school begins," the woman was speaking, looking at a sheet of paper. "So, it seems you're both in the third grade, is that right?" She forced her tone up at the end.

"Yes, ma'am," Sheila answered when Peggy remained mute.

Peggy eyed the single beds again, neatly made with clean, white sheets. Several of the beds had stuffed dolls or animals on them, and a few had open books.

"You'll each be assigned a bed. Cleanliness is next to Godliness. Each morning your bed will be neatly made. The sheets will be pulled tight enough to bounce a coin." She looked from one to the other, her tone gentling slightly as she continued. "Discipline is part of life, and it's better for you to know the rules from the beginning."

Peggy saw Sheila's lower lip begin to tremble, and she poked her in the ribs with her elbow.

Mrs. Pilgrim continued as if she hadn't seen the interaction between the sisters. "The cook here makes a wonderful breakfast and lunch, but I suppose it's supper you're interested in now. Why don't we go over and see what the cook has made?"

Peggy didn't resist but fell into step as they left the long, narrow building and walked across the grounds toward the cafeteria. The land was not Delta. There were big trees and hills that rolled gently, and Mr. Hamilton had told them on the drive that the Natchez Trace, a famous highway that had been used to settle the lower portion of the state, was near the school. He had also told Peggy that he would see about getting her a pair of glasses. The teachers at W. C. Williams had told him that they suspected she had a vision problem.

In the distance the lowing of some cows caught Peggy's attention.

"The barns are over there," Mrs. Pilgrim assured her. "Tomorrow you can go and check out the cows and horses, maybe pick the one you'd like to ride. Mr. Hamilton said you were very interested in horses. Of course, there's work in the barns, too. The cows have to be milked and the barn cleaned."

Peggy didn't answer, not even when Sheila slugged her in the back.

"Peggy thinks she's a cowgirl," Sheila said. "She and my cousin Molly are always playing cowboys and Indians and pretending they have horses and such. Peggy thinks she's Annie Oakley." Sheila almost skipped beside the woman. "Peggy can't pass school, but she can make up a pack of lies and pass them off as a story."

"Imagination is sometimes a gift," the woman said. "Maybe when Peggy is more comfortable here she'll honor us with one of her tales. I'm sure the other children would be delighted to hear a real storyteller."

"Liar is more like it." Sheila dodged the blow that Peggy started to deliver.

Mrs. Pilgrim's hand grasped Peggy's forearm. "Now, none of that here. As you'll learn, there's a system for taking care of things between the children." She dropped Peggy's arm and turned to Sheila. "In the future, be more careful of the accusations you make about your sister. Words can hurt, even when the pain isn't intentional." She increased her pace so that Peggy and Sheila had to step long and fast to keep up.

Peggy glared at Sheila, but there was no time to do anything about it. The smell of something delicious wafted from the long cafeteria, mingled with the sounds of plates and cutlery on a table.

"What's that smell?" Sheila asked.

"I believe chicken pot pie is on the menu for tonight. Nothing is wasted here, but we're fortunate to have some wonderful cooks. Some of the children even work in the cafeteria."

Peggy swallowed. The smell was enough to make the saliva rush into her mouth.

As they stepped into the line, Mrs. Pilgrim caught their attention. "You can eat as much as you like, but you must eat whatever you put on your plate. As I said, the good Lord frowns on wastefulness."

"Yes, ma'am," Peggy and Sheila chorused in unison as they grabbed plates and held them out for the steaming pie that contained chunks of carrots, peas, potatoes, and chicken.

"French Camp ain't gonna be half bad," Sheila whispered to Peggy as they made their way down the line for fresh rolls and milk. "Look at the food."

Peggy could hardly answer because her mouth was watering so. Even as she lifted her tray, she was struck by a thought so cruel that she almost dropped her food. What would Inez be eating for supper? If the older children went out, as was their wont, who would make sure that Inez had a bite of something to eat?

"Sheila?" Peggy called after her sister's back. Sheila was out to find a place to sit.

"Hurry!" Sheila hissed back at her. Her attention returned to the tables and she saw a likely spot beside a girl who was looking at them with open interest. She made for it, trusting that Peggy would follow.

"God dog-it," Peggy whispered aloud. "We're never gonna get home now." She slid into the seat beside her sister.

"Hi, my name is Ruth Lee," the girl said. "It's not so bad here, but I want to go home."

FRENCH CAMP ACADEMY was a school for students from first grade to high school seniors, and it was the center of the institution. The teachers were volunteers, men and women who wanted to do something of importance, to help young people who needed foster care for a number of reasons, some of them disciplinary in nature.

The days were busy. Peggy attended school and worked through the list of chores assigned to her. The daily routine, established to be soothing to troubled children, only wore on Peggy. As long as the days were, it was the nights when fear and anxiety swept through the open window on dark wings. Twisted images and torn bits of the past surfaced, waking her from sleep and leaving her too worried about her mother to even talk to her sister about it. Where Sheila's tears of homesickness began to lessen, Peggy's increased to the point that Sheila was tired of listening to her.

The dreams became so vivid that even the tempting food offered by the cooks in the cafeteria did not attract Peggy's interest. Several of the grown-ups talked to her about being homesick and how it would pass. They assured her that she would adjust to the camp. Peggy's feisty nature surfaced during the day, and she threw herself into the activities. But at night, the demons swarmed. She plotted ways to get into the office. She had to call Inez and tell her to find someone to come and get her and Sheila.

It was not that French Camp, the academy, and the small community that had sprung up around the home, was not a good place.

For Peggy, worry over Inez would not allow her to yield to the many things she enjoyed about the school. If she gave in to liking French Camp, she would be abandoning Inez. There was no one else to help her mother.

One night as Sheila buried her head in her pillow and tried not to listen to her sister's complaints, Peggy slipped into her bed. "I know how we can get home," Peggy said. She'd been thinking about it for several nights. The only way she could imagine was if there was an accident.

"How?" Sheila asked.

"I'll slam the window on your leg. They'll have to send you home if your leg is broken, and I'll have to go to take care of you."

"No!"

"It'll work," Peggy insisted. "Mama needs us to get home. We've been gone a long time. We need to be sure she's okay."

Sheila picked up her pillow and held it. "I don't know, Peggy . . ." It didn't sound like the best idea she'd ever heard.

"It'll work. And it'll be over in just a second. The doctor can put a cast on it and fix it just like new. It won't be too bad."

"Maybe I could slam the window on your leg," Sheila suggested.

"You're not strong enough."

"I don't know . . ."

"Hush! Just do it." Peggy helped Sheila position herself so that her shin was right where the heavy window would come down. "Now when you go to sleep, I'll pull the window down."

As soon as Sheila's breathing was light and regular, Peggy brought the window down. Instead of crashing down on the leg, the window jammed, grazing Sheila's shin.

"Dang it!" Peggy said.

"It's not gonna work." Sheila made an attempt to withdraw her leg.

163

"Grit your teeth," Peggy advised as she brought the window down with all of her might.

Sheila's howl of pain woke everyone in the dormitory. Mrs. Pilgrim flew out of her private room and to the source of the scream. She pulled Sheila to her and held her while taking in the evidence of what had occurred.

After an examination by the academy nurse who affirmed that Sheila's leg was only badly bruised, everyone went back to their beds.

The next morning, Peggy and Sheila were asked to remain behind. Mrs. Pilgrim studied both girls. "Sheila, I thought you were happy here." She didn't give them a chance to talk. "It might be better for Peggy to go to another dormitory. She should have gone to the junior dorm, but we thought she might adjust better if we allowed the two of you to stay together. That was, perhaps, a mistake. Peggy, get your things. You'll be moving up the hill."

"I have to get home to my mama. Just let me go home, please!" Peggy felt her throat closing with tears. A big part of her wanted to stay in French Camp. She had found her horse, and she was doing better in her studies. More importantly, there were grown-ups who made the decisions. While she chafed at the authority, there was also a sense of freedom in the loss of control. For the first time that she could remember, she could think about her studies and look forward to the end of the school day when she might hurry to the barn to begin her chores. Simple chores that were easily finished under a grown-up's supervision.

She had made a friend. Ruth Lee had become her constant companion whenever they could make their paths cross. Staying wasn't so bad, but it was the worry about Inez that was killing her.

"I'm sorry, Peggy, going home isn't an option. Now get your things."

The new dormitory was the same as the old, except Peggy had Ruth as a constant companion, and she worried about her little sister. She saw Sheila and knew she was doing okay, but the separation was hard on both of them. It didn't take Peggy long to plan another escape attempt. This time Ruth Lee joined her—in running away. Peggy's plan was to get to Inez in Greenwood. Inez would figure a way to get Sheila out of French Camp.

Peggy and Ruth were caught several miles down the road and returned to French Camp. Members of the academy had been out, scouring the roadways for them, worried sick. They were returned to the dormitories until the morning. After breakfast, Ruth was sent to school, and Peggy and Sheila were called into the director's office.

"Are you sure you want to go home?" she asked.

"We have to go," Peggy answered before Sheila could back out. "Mama needs us."

"Go to your classes," the director said, dismissing them.

Peggy and Sheila went to get their books. Peggy walked down the hill to the young children's dorm with Sheila. They'd collected books, paper and pencils and were walking back up the hill when Sheila stopped. She pointed into the distance. "Look, Peggy."

Peggy turned to see what her sister was watching. A cloud of red dust spiraled down the road, a small tornado seeming to be headed straight for French Camp. It took a moment for Peggy to make out that the head of the cloud was something pink. A big, pink car. It topped the rise of a gentle hill, front fender distorted by the heat of the road. In a second, though, Peggy knew it.

A big, pink Cadillac.

"Sister Verline!" Peggy cried, running out of the house and toward the road. "It's Sister Verline! Mama sent her to get us!"

Sheila stood motionless as Peggy ran to meet the car.

Chapter Eighteen

Riding in Verline's pink Cadillac, Peggy and Sheila returned to Greenwood. What they left behind was the possibility of a stable future and a chance to have a few years of childhood. Billy, four years older, chose to remain at French Camp and eventually graduated. Without Peggy's influence, Sheila might have chosen to remain. But Peggy's obsession with getting back to Inez influenced Sheila to leave. French Camp Academy was voluntary, a foster home of choice. Peggy's struggle against adapting, her endless worry about her mother, convinced the school administrators that Peggy would be better off at home, and they made no effort to keep her.

In the days that followed her return to 2012 Basket Street, Peggy thought of her brief stay at French Camp as a dream. The cool sheets of her single bed, the regular meals, the peaceful sound of crickets chirring in the quiet night outside the dormitory remained as strange shapes and patterns which she sometimes thought about, a phenomenon that made her wonder what it might have been like to live that way on a regular basis. She did not really miss it because it had never belonged to her.

The last months of the fifties developed the familiar rhythm of the days that had gone before—re-runs of family scenes. Drinking, fighting, gambling, men gathering at dusk in the grocery store, and Inez slowly slipping away into her own world of medication and alcohol.

Peggy began to take a more direct and confrontational stance with her father. Channeling her energies into protecting her mother and attacking her father caused Peggy's school progress to slip even more. Already several years behind her peers, she remained in a state of academic and emotional limbo, unable to move out of childhood and yet assuming the burden of the protective adult.

Though Peggy seemed to be in the center of a static landscape, all around her the world was changing. Uncle Buddy Albritton died of bleeding ulcers, and Molly's mother, Aunt Josie, began to try to rebuild her life. It was not the first tragic loss in Molly's life. Her younger brother, David, who'd been born with severe physical problems, had also died. The economics of the situation were such that Josie needed to marry to provide income for the family. Single women were not allowed credit, and in a world where society expected a woman to marry and produce children, even a widow felt the pressure to remarry. The world of business was a man's world, and a woman needed a man to tend to such affairs.

Both Molly and Peggy turned instinctively toward driving any new male influence out of the Josie Albritton household. Josie's attempts at dating were thwarted on every front. The adolescent girls found great satisfaction in deviling Josie's suitors. They would hide on the roof of the house and plaster a gentleman caller with rotten tomatoes or attempt to sabotage the dates by hiding in the suitor's car.

The two girls also found comfort in their imaginations. Even though they were twelve, nearly thirteen, they loved to play cowboys and Indians, with Peggy always playing the gun-toting, justice-seeking Annie Oakley. With the woods around Basket Street still thick, they galloped through the overgrown branch heads, the stands of timber, and the edges of cotton fields, seeking criminals, tracking renegades, and dispensing justice.

Like all serious cowboys, they needed a horse to ride.

The owner of the local drug store in town, B. C. Chaney, often allowed different Albritton children to ride his palomino gelding on a nice afternoon. Peggy and Faye tried, whenever possible, to steal the horse from the boys when it was their turn to ride. In one such episode, Faye rode the horse through the backyard and Peggy was left hanging by the neck on the clothesline. Though she was frightened, she wasn't seriously injured.

Mary Jean was married. Boyd had joined the Navy, and Billy was at French Camp. After a brush with trouble, Faye was sent to Columbia Training Center, and Sammy was looking for work outside of Greenwood. Even Sheila, a year younger than Peggy, was inclined to pay attention to curling her hair and making sure her clothes were neatly pressed and her school work done. Her interest was on the future rather than running wild through back yards, fields, and woods.

Peggy clung stubbornly to her tomboy ways. In her experience, men and boys were not to be trusted. She preferred the reliable company of Molly. Her own father remained a source of constant fear, anxiety, and torture, and Peggy viewed him as the reason for her mother's drinking problem. As the older siblings left, and Peggy was left alone with the burden of caring for Inez, she began to daydream about killing her father. If Gene were dead, Peggy felt she could get rid of the liquor and finally get her mother on the right track.

With each passing day and each glass of whiskey, Inez grew more and more unstable. Peggy was helpless to stop the slow deterioration.

Around her, the social fabric of Greenwood was also unraveling. Racial tensions in the town, which is the county seat of Leflore County, were steadily building. The talk in the Albritton grocery was often derogatory, violent, and aimed at blacks in general and a few in particular. The anger washed over Peggy as she moved between the house and the store, now doing many of the chores that Inez had once done to keep the family together. Peggy was too busy to listen to the growing outrage shared by Gene and his pals. The anger and ugly threats directed toward the Negroes were a constant in the life of the men who hung out at the fish market. Whenever the talk turned more violent, more vicious, angrier, Peggy didn't pay attention; her concern was Inez.

She attended school less and less often. When she did go, she found integration to be a constant subject of gossip. Mimicking their parents, students spouted threats and warnings about what they would do if Negroes ever tried to come into their classrooms. The idea of integration forced by the federal government angered some parents to the point that school authorities were preparing for the worst. Anonymous tracts calling for citizens to arm themselves against the threat of integration were being distributed in the Delta town, a scene that was repeated again and again throughout the state.

Violence erupted all over Mississippi, small skirmishes of angry whites and blacks, one side determined to cling to the past and the other determined to force change.

Peggy heard the talk and went on about her business. Her focus was narrow, centered entirely on her immediate problems. The idea of Negroes sitting beside her in a classroom, compared to the reality of her mother's drunken rages and seizures, the necessity of forcing a spoon into her mother's convulsing throat to keep her from swallowing her tongue, wasn't worth thinking about. She could not imagine what harm it would do to allow black children to attend school. She could not imagine why they would want to.

Mrs. Watson, Peggy's fourth grade teacher, had made an effort to have Peggy placed in special classes, but Inez had thrown a fit at the school and, once again, help for Peggy was not pursued. She was passed to fifth grade, which she repeated, and finally made it to her concluding year of grammar school.

She completed the sixth grade in the spring of '62. She was fifteen years old and still more interested in using her free time to play cowboys and Indians with Molly than date. The only male who'd ever really struck her fancy was Elvis. The hip-swiveling rocker was safely out of reach.

IN THE LATE summer of 1962, as Peggy prepared to enter the seventh grade, James Meredith announced his plans to enter the all-white University of Mississippi. Ole Miss at Oxford was the elite state university, home of networking fraternities and sororities where the sons and daughters of good families cemented their future connections, social and economic. Oxford was also the home of William Faulkner and the state's premiere law school. Ole Miss had a history as deep in the Southern soil as any institution in existence.

Meredith's stated intention to integrate was nothing less than a declaration of war. Ole Miss, a bastion of Southern manhood and magnoliaism, was under attack. Many factions of Mississippi society, even those long at odds with each other, united against the common enemy, the aggressive black. In Leflore County, where the black population was 64 percent, the voting black resident was greatly feared.

Until the threat of integration, white society was rigidly stratified. The rich and poor met only in commerce, or as employer and employee. For all practical purposes, rich and poor lived completely apart. These worlds shared common themes, though the wealthy would never acknowledge such a link. The rich also possessed the political power to keep their secrets private. Violence and alcoholism threaded through the Delta like the slow yellow rivers, touching the families of all backgrounds.

On the surface, Gene Albritton shared very little with Byron De La Beckwith. They lived on separate sides of the tracks, but both shared a fondness for alcohol and beating their wives. The violence at 2012 Basket Street was duplicated in the Beckwith household, except Beckwith, or De La, pronounced "deelay" by many, and his wife, Willie, often resorted to gunfights to settle their marital disputes.

Beckwith was fond of pointing out that he came from the planter class of the Delta, the pinnacle of Delta society. He was actually born in California, but his mother was a Yerger, a well-established Delta family from Glen Oak Plantation near Greenwood. Byron D. Beckwith was a businessman who pioneered the use of irrigation in the Central Valley of California. At the age of five, De La returned to Greenwood with his mother upon the death of his father. It was in Greenwood that the young boy met his first black person, and it was in the Delta that his attitude toward blacks developed.

Several years later, when De La's mother died, he fell under the supervision of two uncles. Stints in private and military schools proved unsuccessful, and he eventually graduated from Greenwood High School. When his grades at the Mississippi State University in Starkville were not any better than his high school academics, he entered the Marines. It was at the Naval Air Station in Millington, near Memphis, Tennessee, that he met the beautiful Mary Louise Williams, known as Willie. With two bad marriages behind her, Willie had enlisted as a WAVE. De La and Willie found they immediately had one thing in common; they both liked to drink. After drinking, they argued.

That cycle, begun during courtship in the 1940s, continued throughout their three marriages, escalating with the passing years. They were married in 1945, and their only child, Byron De La Beckwith III, was born in 1946. For another fourteen years the drinking and fighting continued, mixed with De La's increasing prominence in segregationist and white supremacist activities and the growing collection of firearms.

Like Inez, Willie stayed in the house while her bruises and black eyes healed. Although an ocean of class difference separated Willie and Inez, they shared a fact of life—the law did not protect them when their husbands beat, threatened, abused, and tortured them. Although Mary Louise Williams had married into a respected planter family, she had no more protection than Inez, who healed behind the closed door of her home on "the Western front."

It was common knowledge that the Beckwith marriage was built on abuse and alcoholism, but the law did not intervene—at least not on Willie's behalf. On several occasions, Willie, like Inez, was picked up and "held" in jail until she "cooled down." In Inez's case, trips to the local jail sometimes ended in Whitfield.

As the racial tensions increased in Greenwood, so did the violence in the Beckwith home. Willie Beckwith filed for divorce in June 1960, dropped the suit, then refiled in September of that same year. The divorce was granted. Four months later Willie remarried De La on Feb. 14, 1961, and they left the Delta behind, starting a new life in Natchez.

De La's uncle, Will, died in May 1961, precipitating the Beckwiths' return to Greenwood. Beckwith fell back in with his old friends, and the pattern of drinking, violence, and segregationist activity was quickly reestablished.

On August 1, 1962, Willie Beckwith had her husband removed from their home and placed under a peace bond. Willie filed for divorce again in September, citing physical and mental cruelty. While Beckwith's marriage was coming apart, his state was under attack.

James Meredith attempted to enroll at Ole Miss on September 20, 1962. Three efforts failed, and rioting broke out across the state. On the fourth attempt to install Meredith in Baxter Hall on the oak-lined campus, the Mississippi National Guard, which had been federalized, U.S. marshals, and the highway patrol finally prevailed. Meredith was installed in a dorm room. But two Mississippians were dead, and the animosity felt by many state residents toward the federal government was running high. In the minds of many Mississippians, even those who did not view integration as evil, the use of federal force was clearly an act of aggression. The federal boot-heel, felt so keenly during the years of Reconstruction, was deeply despised, and members of the White Citizen's Council and the Ku Klux Klan fed those hostilities.

Listening to her schoolmates repeat the vows of segregation they heard at home, Peggy felt only pity for the Negro children she knew. They often traded at the Albritton store, accepting the bad fish and verbal taunts as their due. None had ever expressed a desire to attend the white schools. They seemed as trapped as she felt. As a member of the "poor white trash" class, Peggy had felt the lash of prejudice herself. She knew the cruelty of labels such as "crazy," "poor," and ironically enough, "nigger-lover." The Albritton family, because Gene traded and often drank with Negroes, was thought by Greenwood's middle class to be socializing with Negroes. It was an accusation that could never be leveled at De La.

But there was a pattern of behavior shared by both the Beckwiths and Albrittons—the penchant to marry, divorce and re-marry. Willie Beckwith divorced De La on October 9, 1962. They were remarried October 30 that same year, for the third time.

Separated by a distance of less than two miles, Beckwith dealt with his marital problems and his increasing fury at the imposed integration while Peggy attempted to keep her mother afloat and finish the seventh grade.

In the pressure cooker summer of 1963, Peggy took a job as a waitress at Charmaines, a busy lunch cafe, to earn money for school clothes. Thrust into the heart of downtown Greenwood and one of the busiest lunch places in town, Peggy served plate lunches and sandwiches to Greenwood's leading businessmen, to those who vocally protested integration and to the quieter men who did not.

Chapter Nineteen

The summer heat was stifling, but Peggy picked up the tray of sandwich platters and quick-stepped to the table where four Greenwood businessmen leaned toward the center of the table, their voices low and terse.

"It's gonna get worse," one of the men said. "The whole state's goin' up in flames. I don't understand why those folks up North don't mind their own business and leave ours alone. They come down here and we're the ones seein' our towns burnin' and our neighbors hurt."

"Damn outside agitators," another of the men spoke angrily even as he ducked his head.

"Well, it's out of our hands now. It's gone beyond reason. Both sides won't be happy now until somebody's dead."

"Damnation." The short, heavy set man spoke on a sigh.

"Club sandwich with fries?" Peggy held the heavy tray balanced on one hand and the sandwich plate in the other.

"That's mine," the thin, balding man said as he leaned back from the conversation to allow Peggy room to put the plate on the table. "Thank you, little lady."

"You're welcome." Peggy gave him a smile. She liked working the lunch crowd in Charmaines. From eleven until two, the cafe was hopping with Greenwood businessmen. They were almost invariably pleasant, easy to serve, and always remembered to tip. The money for her school clothes was growing, quarter by quarter. With the completion of seventh grade, Peggy had suddenly blossomed. As a sixteen-year-old, her appearance had become acutely important to her.

"Hey, Blondie, how about some catsup?" one of the men called.

"You got it," Peggy replied, dodging a customer as he dropped a dollar on the table and started to rise. She snagged a catsup bottle and whirled back to the man who requested it. The customers in the cafe had a host of nicknames for her from Babe Ruth to Boney Maroney, and she liked them all.

"It's a pleasure to see a young lady so full of life with such a big smile," the man said.

"Thank you, sir," Peggy answered, her smile notching up a little brighter. She spun away to pick up her next order for the two gentlemen at the counter. The rich odor of fried chicken wafting up to her, she delivered the plates with a flourish. "There you are, gentlemen," she said. "Anything else?"

"How about some sweet tea?"

"Two?"

The men nodded.

"Comin' right up." She hustled over to fill the glasses with ice and sweetened tea, making sure a big lemon wedge clung to each glass and long teaspoons rested on clean napkins. She set the frosty glasses on the counter. "How's the chicken?"

"Good. Like always." The men wiped their mouths. The one with the dark tie smiled. "You sure get around fast for such a little girl."

"Let me know if you need anything." She walked to another table, refilling iced tea glasses and making sure the customers had salt, pepper, hot sauce, and plenty of catsup.

She wheeled into the kitchen, running smack into the cafe's owner. "Peggy, slow down. You're going to catch on fire and burn to ashes," Mrs. Damguard said, laughing. "I've never seen so much cheerful energy."

"I like havin' my own job," Peggy said. She nodded to the cook, a middle-age black woman known as Nigger Mary.

Mary pointed her spatula at a steaming plate of pork chops.

"I got you 'nother order ready."

Peggy picked up the platter and hurried out the kitchen door to deliver it. The cafe was filled, not an empty seat to be had. The talk buzzed all around her, fragments of chatter.

"Dang that De La. He'd better mind his own business . . ."

"We can't afford any more fires in Greenwood . . ."

"My son has just been accepted in the law school . . ."

"Can you believe the price on that Impala? I told Cilla it would be a steal . . ."

The conversations merged and blended, words floating, some whispered and some called out. Peggy heard it all but retained none of it. In her mind the quarters were mounting up. There was one little black and brown dress with big buttons on it that she wanted in the worst way. She and Molly had admired it more than once, and it was perfect for her, a size two. At eighty-two pounds, trim and fit from the last of her tomboy days, she could wear any outfit in the entire town, but it was the button dress that had stolen her heart. As long as she focused on earning the money for the dress, she didn't have to think about what might be happening at 2012 Basket Street.

"Peggy Sue! How 'bout some salt in this here shaker?"

She recognized the voice of one of her regular customers. "Sure thing, Mr. Smith." She picked up a full shaker on her way by the counter and traded it with the businessman for the empty one. "My name ain't Sue," she told him.

"I thought that famous song was written just for you," he teased. "Somebody told me Buddy Holly had been a regular customer here just so you could wait on him."

"I might of waited on Buddy Holly, but if anybody ever writes a song about me, I want it to be Elvis," Peggy said.

The man laughed. "I'll bet if he could see you waitin' tables here, you'd be immortalized in song. Somethin' about a little blond streak of lightnin'."

Peggy laughed out loud at the pleasure of the thought. She hurried back to the counter to check the two fried chicken men and refill their tea glasses.

The lunch rush ended at two, and Peggy was taking off her apron when Mrs. Damguard asked her to work a longer shift. One of the other waitresses had a sick child. Always glad for extra hours and the chance to make a little more money, Peggy agreed.

The afternoon turned slow, and Peggy took a seat at the counter and ordered a piece of the homemade lemon meringue pie with a cup of fresh coffee. There was nothing so tartly sweet as the cool lemon custard combined with the perfectly whipped and baked meringue. For the first time in her life she had money to indulge herself, even if it was just a piece of pie. The freedom, the independence, was so totally delicious that sometimes it made Peggy's skin prickle with guilt. Then she'd think about Inez.

The situation at home had become a quagmire for Peggy. Gene was drinking heavily and working more carpentry jobs. The money he made went for liquor. Inez had reached full-blown alcoholism. It seemed they stayed apart during the day to recharge their supply of anger with which to attack each other at night. They drank and fought to the point that Peggy could only hope they would kill themselves and finally free her of the horror of walking home each evening, dreading to discover the corpse of one or the other.

Faye had married, without the drama of Mary Jean's elopement chase, and Sammy was courting a girl named Cissy who would, in short order, become his bride; he wasn't home often. For all intents and purposes, Peggy was the head of the household—the oldest child at home. Though Gene had never allowed her to drive before, when he got drunk enough to risk a DWI, he needed someone to chauffeur him down to the juke joints and clubs where he bought and sold bond or bootleg, depending on whether he'd had the time and initiative to tend his stills.

"You look like a hound dog somebody just kicked," another waitress said as she sat down beside Peggy and lit a cigarette. "Your boyfriend done you wrong?"

Peggy shook her head. She'd learned never to discuss what was happening at home. Never. No matter who asked or why, the things that went on in the Albritton household were deadly secrets.

"Men are dogs," the woman said, exhaling a big puff of smoke. "My old man grabbed me by the throat last night." She reached up and pulled the neck of her blouse down to show the bruises. "That was it. The bastard ever touches me again, I'll break his neck, crack his eggs, and set his nest on fire."

Peggy drank the last of her coffee. It was five o'clock. Time for her to start home.

"Want to go out tonight? See what's shakin' at the youth center? Like I said, I'm done with Arlin. He's outta my life, and a girl needs a little good time to forget."

Peggy considered. Her experience with going out in Greenwood at night had been sitting in the car or truck until someone brought her daddy out, too drunk to walk, so she could drive him home. She'd heard there were places where teenagers went. It might be fun to see what other kids did.

But there was Inez.

"No thanks. Maybe another time."

"You're sweet on someone, aren't you?" The waitress grinned. "Got you a big ole heart full of crush on somebody."

"I ain't got a boyfriend." Peggy pushed her coffee cup and pie plate back. "I don't need somebody to beat on me . . ."

"Who-ee," the waitress said, laughing, "I done pulled your chain, Blondie. I didn't mean to set you off."

Peggy felt her anger pass as swiftly as it had come. "It's okay. I just won't ever let a man treat me bad. Not ever."

"That's the way." The waitress stood up and untied her apron. "Well, I'm headin' to town for a little music, dancin', and sport. Let me know if you ever want to come along."

"Thanks." Peggy put her apron away before she hurried out the front door lest she be tempted by the offer and change her mind. Her walk took her through the downtown area, and she window-shopped as she went. It was June and not unpleasantly hot in the late afternoon. The summer stretched out before her with promise. She had a job and money of her own.

At the street corner she glanced at a news rack. Racial conflict was the headline, and she noticed that some Negro man's carport had been bombed in Jackson. Not long before, several Greenwood businesses owned by blacks had been burned. Violence in her household was inescapable. It seemed insane that anyone would deliberately engage in burning and bombing another, a stranger's home or business.

The display in a local department store caught her eye and she crossed the street, taking her time as she sauntered toward Basket Street and the horror of the day.

She arrived home to find her youngest brother, Michael, sitting on the steps. The door of the grocery was shut and locked, a sure sign that Gene was gone, and probably not working. She needed nothing else to tell her that Inez was not in the kitchen.

The long hours of standing on her feet and lifting heavy trays descended on Peggy with a weariness that made it nearly impossible to get up the steps. She forced herself across the porch and ducked into her parent's bedroom. Inez lay sideways on the bed, asleep. A bottle of whiskey, only an inch or so remaining, was on the bedside table. Without a word, Peggy went into the kitchen and began to put together something to eat. It was a shame she hadn't checked in the kitchen at the cafe to see if there had been anything left over from lunch.

By the time Sheila and her brothers finished with supper, the soft June dusk had given way to the glimmer of a waxing moon. She heard her father's boots crossing the porch, and she reached into the oven to pull out the plate she'd kept for him. Sometimes he ate; sometimes he didn't. But the food wouldn't go to waste. Someone would come in hungry and eat it.

Gene took his place at the table and ate the dinner she'd prepared. When she was certain he needed nothing else, she started out the back door.

"I want you to go over to Archie Hayes and get me something to drink."

Peggy stared, first at the darkness outside the door, then at her father. "I don't want to go over there now. I have to walk through nigger town."

"Won't nobody fool with you. You're gonna walk over there and buy me a pint."

Peggy tried to gauge her father's temper. Sometimes she could defy him. Seldom, though, when liquor was involved. "Daddy, it's dark. I don't like to go over there. Especially not with the trouble goin' on."

"I'll get my belt . . ." He left the threat unfinished.

"They're burning the Negro businesses." Peggy felt her fear grow larger at the thought. She'd had enough trouble in school being called a nigger-lover. She didn't need to be walking in the Negro section of town at night. She didn't need to be down there at all. The anger that simmered in town could as easily erupt against a white person, especially a woman, seen as sympathizing or flirting with Negro men as it could against Yankee agitators and uppity niggers.

Gene pulled money from his pocket and tossed it on the table. The change clattered. "Git goin' and hurry back."

"I'm not . . ." She looked into her father's bloodshot eyes. The words died in her throat. Picking up the money, she stuck it in the pocket of her shorts. The back door slammed hard behind her as she walked out into the night.

She knew the way to Archie's liquor store. She thought about stopping to see if Molly would walk with her, but her cousin had lately begun to date. Chances were she was out and having fun. Peggy didn't stop by her aunt's house but kept going. The moon sailed among the fringes of the trees overhead, and she stepped between shadow and light, concentrating on the patterns so that she wouldn't be afraid. To get to Archie's, she had to go straight through the middle of Greenwood's black section. In the distance she could hear the rich sound of laughter, the blues coming from a juke joint. The music was strangely comforting.

As she entered the boundary of the community, the smell of raw sewage draining into the open ditches drove her to the center of the road. Swaths of light shown between the unpainted boards of the shanty houses. Screens were unheard of.

She made her way to the tiny store where a group of men lounged. At the sight of her, all talking stopped.

"What she doin' here?" A large black man asked the question, and it was edged with fear.

"I came to get some Old Crow." Peggy felt like bugs had gotten inside her shirt. They were marching up her spine, tingling and dancing on her skin triggering waves of goose bumps. She could smell the fear on the men, the sudden anger. White folks were dangerous. White women could be lethal.

"Why'd you come here?" The question was an accusation.

"None of your business," Peggy answered sharply, her own fear making her aggressive. Something was very wrong. The Negroes were looking among themselves, eyes darting behind her.

"Get out of here." The large man spoke again, his voice soft and hard.

"I got money." Peggy reached into her pocket and brought out the crumpled bills and change that Gene had given her. "A pint of Old Crow."

"Git." The large man made a shooing motion at her. "Git back to your part of town before you fin' more trouble than you lookin' for."

"What's wrong with you? Where's Mr. Archie?" Peggy asked for the owner, a white man who often sold her whiskey for Gene. She'd come this far and she wasn't going home empty handed. Not with Gene waiting.

Suddenly she saw Archie. He came to the door, pushing it open so that light spilled out onto her face.

"Where's your daddy, girl?" he asked, worry plain in his face.

"He sent me for a pint."

He disappeared inside and returned with a package wrapped in a brown paper sack. "Your daddy's a fool sendin' you here. Folks see a white girl walking through niggertown, anything could happen."

"Damn!" One of the men swore softly into the night. He stood up, knocking over the fruit crate he'd been sitting on.

"It's Gene Albritton's girl," another black said. He placed a steadying hand on the man's shoulder. "You know Gene. Once he needs a drink, he don't care . . ." He left it unfinished.

"She got her liquor, now she can git!" The man took a step toward Peggy, who still held the money clutched in her fist. She thrust it out. "Here. Here's the money."

Archie Hayes took it from her, not bothering to count it. "Go home, Peggy." He looked at one of the men who'd remained seated. "Walk with her, Tom. Walk her to the edge." He shook his head. "Good Lord Almighty, anything could happen on a night like this." He seemed to speak to himself.

Tom rose slowly. He stepped out of the light of the door and waited. Clutching the bottle of whiskey, Peggy stepped back into the night, her heart pounding. She turned and started to run. Behind her were the soft footfalls of Tom, steady in the distance, marking time with her own.

Chapter Twenty

On June 12, 1963, Medgar Evers was returning to his Jackson home at 2332 Guynes Street just after midnight. As he got out of his car in the carport of his home, a rifle shot split the night.

Evers, mortally wounded, fell to the carport and attempted to crawl to the door. At his side were the T-shirts he'd been carrying in his arms. The slogan "Jim Crow Must Go" had been printed on the shirts, which he'd intended to use as a fund raiser.

The white shirts soaked up his blood as his wife came out of the house, saw him, and began screaming for help. A neighbor came with a mattress and loaded Evers on the mattress into his vehicle just as the law enforcement officials arrived to help. With a police escort, Evers was transported to a hospital, but he did not survive.

Near the scene of the crime a 1917 Enfield .30-06 army surplus rifle was found. The weapon was mounted with a six-power Golden Hawk telescopic sight.

Early on the morning of June 12 the Greenwood chapter of the NAACP received an anonymous call. "We have just killed Medgar, and you are next," was the message.

THE BRASS BELL over the door of Charmaines jingled merrily as Peggy pushed into work. Inez had started drinking extra early that morning, and Peggy had gotten into a fight with her when she'd snatched the liquor bottle and drained it into the Delta soil by the porch. Furious, Inez had fought like a wildcat, and Peggy's forearm was scraped raw.

Worse than her wounds, the chain of events had almost made her late for work. One thing she didn't want to do was arrive late. The money she was earning in tips—tight rolls of dimes, nickels, pennies, and quarters—had begun to add up. She had to keep her job, and no employer liked an employee who came to work late.

The cafe was empty as she swung through the door, sighing with relief. She'd made it right on the dot.

She stopped only three steps in the door, taking in the scene and what was wrong with it. Everyone was working as they should, but the silence in the cafe made her think someone had died.

"What's wrong?" she asked.

Mrs. Damguard shook her head and pushed back into the kitchen. Through the open door, Peggy caught a glimpse of Preacher, another of the black kitchen help. Her dark eyes were dulled with sadness as she washed the chicken parts that would soon sizzle in a pan of hot grease.

"What's wrong?" Peggy asked again.

"That NAACP nigger got himself killed last night in Jackson," one of the waitresses answered. Her voice was tired, worn away with what wasn't sadness but an acceptance of fact. "He just couldn't mind his own business."

"Jackson?" Peggy couldn't imagine anything happening in Jackson that would have such an impact on the people she worked with. Jackson was at least a hundred miles away. "Was he kin to someone here?"

"Naw, but it's going to make it hard for all of us," the waitress said. "Every single one of us." She got up as the door opened and the bell jangled a customer inside. "Here." She pushed the newspaper to Peggy.

Peggy took it, folded it, and dropped it down on the counter. There wasn't time to read stories in the paper. Reading and newspapers had never been high on her list of priorities anyway. The front door announced another customer, followed by three more.

"Mornin'," Peggy called out, surprised that even the men from the hardware store seemed troubled.

The small restaurant began to fill as the lunch crowd rushed in. Peggy took note of the specials, meatloaf and turkey and dressing. She pulled her pad out and headed for a newly arrived table of four. As she took their orders, she realized that whatever had happened in Jackson hadn't affected the appetites of the men who made Charmaines their regular lunch place. They might be quieter than usual, but they were eating with the same gusto they showed every day.

The newspaper, left on the counter, was scattered among the tables and finally gathered into the trash by one of the waitresses bussing a table.

By the end of her shift, Peggy had forgotten that tragedy had struck a Jackson family. The death of Medgar Evers seemed as distant as a flood in Missouri or a street mugging in New York City.

Chapter Twenty-One

The real heat of summer had begun to build, and Peggy blotted the perspiration from her upper lip as she took a moment from the bustle of Charmaines for a bathroom break. She'd come into work feeling headachy and nauseous, but her health wasn't of concern. Her symptoms had an easily traceable source—Inez and Gene, doing their best to kill each other, while dumping the minimal care of the younger children totally on Peggy.

She plucked the new gold tube from her pocket and ran the slick red color across her lips. It was a good shade, contrasting with her tanned skin and strawberry blond hair. Besides, she needed something to make her look more grown up. If the figure reflected back to her in the glass hadn't told her she looked no older than twelve, the customers would have done so.

Using a paper towel, she pressed off the excess lipstick and noticed that her hand was shaking. She'd almost tumped a pitcher of iced tea on one of the bank employees, and when Betty, another waitress, dropped a plate, Peggy had nearly exploded. Her nerves were shot.

As she stared into the mirror, she felt the hatred at her circumstances surging up inside her. Some folks teased her, saying that she was her Aunt Nellie Moye, Gene's sister, made over. Some said she had Gene's easy charm, when she chose to use it. Staring at her own reflection, Peggy saw only a sixteen-year-old girl who was desperate to get away from home.

Before she did something awful.

The smooth silver surface of the mirror gave way to a memory. She saw her mother struggling down the road, a stove on her back as her crooked legs inched toward home. Inez had wanted a stove to cook on so bad she'd carried it home herself when Gene wouldn't help her. From downtown Greenwood, Inez had hauled the stove on her back.

The image crystallized into anger that went from white hot to absolute cold. Dropping the lipstick into her pocket, Peggy pushed out into the restaurant.

"How about some more tea?" she asked a customer, smiling brightly.

"You are the most cheerful little girl," the man said, holding up his glass as Peggy picked up a pitcher from the counter and refilled it. "You must not have a care in the world, Little Blondie."

Peggy smiled. The nickname had stuck to her and begun to spread among the customers. She poured the tea, making sure a few ice cubes plopped over into his glass as well.

"I wish I was a child again and had my whole life ahead of me." The man chuckled and thanked Peggy for the tea. "You're one lucky girl," he said as he rose, dropping a quarter on the table.

Peggy made the rounds of her tables, taking care that all the glasses were filled and the table settings had everything from hot sauce for the greens to catsup for the burgers and fries. As soon as a table emptied, she cleared it off, whisked the tip into her pocket, and set up for the next hungry patron.

A loud argument rose at a corner table. The men weren't Peggy's customers, but she paused and looked over at them. Two men, sitting opposite from each other, were going at it. Another pair of men were at the table, but their faces were bent toward the steaming plates. They ate and ignored the other two.

"I can't believe he did it," one man said, his face red. He pushed back from the table. "He's not that dumb."

"Hell, he's gone around town bragging about it," a second man said. "You know he was wild about those guns. Collected 'em. I'm surprised he and that wife of his haven't killed each other in a shootout. They get to goin' at it and the fists and bullets fly."

The red-faced man stood up. "He's crazy as a run-over dog. That don't mean he's killed that nigger."

"It don't mean he's innocent," the man countered, his voice calm in contrast to the other man's anger.

"Well, if that nigger hadn't provoked it, he wouldn't be dead today. I say good enough for him."

"I ain't arguin' that issue," the calm man said. He pointed to his companion's plate. "Eat your food. We got to get back to work."

"They won't ever find him guilty."

The second man took a big bite of his rice and gravy, refusing to answer. "Pass the salt," he said to one of the other two men at the table. He accepted the shaker and passed it over his rice.

"There's not a white jury in this world will find him guilty." The red-faced man settled back in his chair and picked up his fork. "Not a jury," he said in a calmer voice.

Peggy nudged Betty. It was her section of the room where the men were arguing. "What's that all about?"

"Best I can tell they arrested somebody."

Peggy snorted as her gaze roved over her tables to be sure nothing was left undone. "Probably some of my kin. I only wish they'd lock up my daddy when he goes to beatin' . . ." She stopped herself. She'd made up her mind not to ever talk about her home life at the restaurant. "Who'd they arrest?"

"Some man used to work for the fertilizer company. Said he killed that NAACP nigger over in Jackson."

"You don't say." Peggy started across the room before the words were out of her mouth. Mr. Chaney had just walked in Charmaines and she wanted to be sure he got waited on proper. He was one of her favorite customers; she remembered the days when he loaned her and Sammy his horse.

"Sit right here, Mr. Chaney," she said, showing him a clean table in her section. "What'll it be for lunch today?"

"COME ON, PEG-A-LEG." Gene made a broad motion with his arm. "You want to drive? If you buy yourself a car, you got to learn to drive first." He waved her toward the truck. "Come on."

Peggy cut her eyes toward Inez. Her mother sat docilely in the rocker on the front porch. The motion of the chair was slight, and Inez looked as if she were far away. For the first time in days she didn't reek of whiskey.

"I'll stay here and make the boys some supper." Peggy didn't like the way Inez looked. It was almost like she'd turned into one of the late night horror zombies from television.

"Git your ass in this truck." Gene's charm had evaporated. "I want to go over to Lanie's and you're gonna take me."

Now that she knew the destination, Peggy also knew the reason. Gene had finished off the last of the liquor. It was no wonder her mother hadn't been drinking. The house was dry, and Gene hadn't been up to getting out to his stills to make his own.

"I got to wash out my dress for tomorrow," she said. She'd gotten bolder and bolder about defying her father. Gene was as mean as ever, but he wasn't as quick. Peggy had learned that sometimes it paid to be fleet of foot. She could fly in his face—as long as she could make a getaway. Once he had his hands on her . . . She looked down the road, mentally going over places to run. It was yet early evening, still too hot for anything except sitting. Folks would be home. There were plenty of places she could escape to if it came down to running.

Gene left the side of the truck, stumbled, regained his balance and came on at her. "I want you to drive . . ."

"I don't know how." Peggy had learned enough to get around town, but she spoke the lie with complete innocence. It did her good to know that she thwarted him at every turn, a small satisfaction in a long, hard day.

"You get up and come on or I'll make you wish you'd done what you were told."

Stalling for time, Peggy reached over and touched Inez's arm. Peggy's hand was tiny, but she could almost circle her mother's upper arm. It troubled Peggy that Inez's skin was cool. Almost as if the life was leaving her degree by degree. Now was not the time for a fight with her father. "Mama, I'm gone run Daddy to the store."

"Go on," Inez said, never breaking the pattern of her slight rocking. Her gaze went to Gene, but she didn't ask a question or mumble another word.

"Git in the truck." Gene stepped backward, eager to be off but half expecting Peggy to break and run.

Peggy stood. "Are you gone be all right, Mama?"

"Go on, girl." Inez rocked. "You need to learn to drive. One day you'll have a car of your own."

Peggy looked at her mother with growing concern. A car was completely out of the question. "We'll be right back." If she could only afford a car, she'd be able to go places, do things. She wouldn't have to rely on Gene to take her. Or dates. She'd been out some with friends of her brothers. As far as she was concerned, dating was another big trouble. The boys wanted to ride the back roads, drinking, until they came to some spot where they thought they'd pull up under a shade tree and try to hold her hand or kiss her.

Years of working hard beside Inez had given her muscles a tensile strength that served her well when she said no. She'd learned at an early age that fighting was the key to survival. If she had to, she fought.

She got behind the wheel of the truck. She'd driven a time or two before. Gene had always preferred Billy or Sheila as his drivers. Or Faye or Sammy. But they were all gone. Sammy had just married, and Sheila, too. All gone, and fighting just the way they'd learned at home. Peggy knew she wasn't going to live that way. She'd seen the television shows where families ate breakfast together and spoke with kindness. The men didn't drink and they worked, shaving their faces smooth and wearing clean suits. The women had time to fix their hair and makeup and cook delicious meals for the family.

And they smiled at each other.

That was the way her life was going to go, just as soon as she found the right man. A man, not some boy who shoved her back against the side of a car and tried to kiss her.

"Crank the damn truck," Gene growled. "Are you plannin' on sittin' here all night?"

She turned the key, pressed the gas and eased off the clutch. The truck rolled smoothly onto Basket Street, and she aimed toward town.

Gene rode in silence, content to let the wind blow through the open window and cool the heat in the cab. Peggy concentrated on shifting gears and watching for other cars. She liked the feel of control driving gave her, and she let her mind drift into fantasy, a time in the future when she'd be heading out of town and on her own.

At the corner of Carrollton Avenue and Bouie Lane, she pulled into the gravel drive of Lanie Howell's grocery store.

"I'll be right back," Gene said.

Peggy killed the motor and lounged back against the seat, knowing that her father might stay five minutes or several hours, depending on who else was there and how the conversation went.

Another vehicle pulled up, and she noticed three men were in it.

A tall, dark-haired man got out of the passenger seat and stared directly into her eyes. For a moment, Peggy held his gaze, unable to blink or look away. In the soft evening light, with the sun glinting on his neatly combed black hair, he looked strikingly like Elvis Presley. There was something in the loose, easy way he moved that made her swallow. He knew she was staring, and he invited her to look.

Ignoring the two other young men, he sauntered toward the truck.

"You're a pretty little thing," he said.

Peggy felt something go soft inside her at the sound of his voice. He wasn't a boy. He was a man.

He called back over his shoulder, "Hey, Inky, take a look at this peach."

The man called Inky laughed. "She's not ripe for the pickin', Lloyd. Better give her a few more years."

"I'm sixteen." Peggy spoke with defiance. She didn't mind that the customers in Charmaines thought she was a child. But this man, she didn't want him believing she was just a kid.

"Lloyd, you got somethin' waitin' on you at the house." Inky's voice was easy with suppressed laughter.

"You mind your own self," Lloyd said, walking up to the driver's window. "I found me some new business right here." His attention turned to Peggy. "What's your name?"

Peggy's hands tightened on the steering wheel. Her chest felt stretched hard and tight, and she couldn't breathe. She didn't like this man. It did something to her to look at him. His voice, the way he looked so much like Elvis, it made her feel all stirred up. "My name's none of your business," she said, staring directly over the steering wheel.

"I want to make it my business." He leaned down to the window.

The clean, sharp scent of aftershave came to her. It was a grown-up and sophisticated smell.

The door of the grocery opened, and Gene walked out, a brown paper bag held in one hand.

Lloyd straightened up at Gene's approach. "How you doin'?" he said.

Gene looked him over long and hard, taking in the black hair and the sure composure. "I'm fine. A lot better than you'll be doin' if you don't get away from my daughter."

"Lloyd Morgan's my name. You run that fish market over on Basket Street, right?"

"That's right." Gene opened the passenger door, but he didn't get in.

"I thought I might like to drop by and see this girl of yours."

"You drop by, you better plan on buyin' some fish." Gene lifted the sack to his mouth and drank out of the exposed bottle.

"Some fish might be nice." Lloyd was almost laughing.

Sitting in the truck, Peggy watched him out of the corner of her eye. He wasn't a bit afraid of Gene. Not a bit. In fact, he was playing with her father, just the way a kid might tease a snake with a stick. She chanced a direct look at Lloyd and saw the way his shirt laid hard against his chest. He wasn't skinny. There was plenty of muscle there. He looked down suddenly and caught her staring at him.

"You see somethin' interests you?" he asked.

Peggy turned the key, almost forgetting to depress the clutch. The truck bucked slightly, drawing a curse from Gene as he jumped in.

"I'll be seein' you," Lloyd promised.

Peggy lifted her hand out the window and shot Lloyd Morgan the bird. "You stay away, you hear," she said as she put the truck in gear and pulled out.

Behind her, easy and filled with confidence, was the sound of Lloyd Morgan's laughter.

Chapter Twenty-Two

The row of butter beans was not long, but the knee-high green plants were loaded with the plump green hulls that would yield the highly regarded speckled beans. Barefooted and wearing a pair of shorts and a halter, Peggy straddled the row of beans, picking as she moved slowly along, nudging a half-full tin pan along with her foot. It was hot, hard work, but the sun's relentless stare made her think of childhood and the times when she and Inez gardened together. Inez had talked then about her own childhood. Listening to the stories of laughter and kindness, Peggy had thought Inez was making it all up. Peggy realized that Ma Early had been right; Inez had never grown beyond a child in many ways. The viral infection had left permanent scars on Inez's mind as well as weakening her legs. Peggy didn't fully understand what spinal meningitis had done to her mother, but Ma had cautioned Peggy to look out for Inez.

At the sound of a truck coming down the road, Peggy looked up to check for Mike. He would be entering first grade in the fall, finally the last of the Albritton children. Peggy knew her mother had had a hysterectomy, and that because the doctors had cut on her, she wouldn't have any more babies. She didn't understand what had been done, but the relief was bone deep. No more babies at last. When Mike was finally in school, maybe she could think about leaving.

"Mike, get out of the road," she called to him, knowing he wouldn't pay an ounce of attention to her. She watched until the truck passed then stooped back to the hot row of beans. Gene would sell them in the store with some of the catfish he'd caught. Wiping her forehead with the back of her hand, she pushed aside the green leaves and hunted for the filled pods. She never minded gardening. In fact, she didn't mind the work of running a house and helping Inez—it was the fighting. That was why she had to get away.

She and Molly had talked about starting a new life together, maybe down at the Gulf where Biloxi and Gulfport were synonymous with freedom and a new way of life. She'd heard stories about the towns along the water. And there was Brookley Air Field in Mobile. There were jobs to be had there.

The truth was that Molly had mostly lost interest in their adventure plans. They still played cowboys and Indians on the weekends when Peggy didn't have to pull a shift at Charmaines or Molly didn't have chores. Things were changing, though. Molly had sprouted breasts and a way of walking and laughing that had boys falling all over themselves. After watching Mary Jean, Faye, and Sheila all court and marry, Peggy could read the writing on the wall. Molly wouldn't be leaving Greenwood unless she went with a man. So Peggy had decided to strike out on her own, just as soon as she had enough money saved for a car and a beginning.

There was always Memphis, or even Tupelo. Cities that beckoned. Any place where the land wasn't flat and parted into row after row of cotton. Any place where she could start a life, make a future that didn't include beatings and fighting and whiskey. If she could only convince herself to leave Inez. In all of her imaginings, when she got to the part of leaving her mama, that's when it all fell apart.

The sound of another vehicle came clearly on the still air. Since her back was aching from stooping over, she stood and scanned the yard for Mike. The little imp had disappeared. Grabbing the half-full pan, she stepped over the beans and started toward the front.

"Mike, I'm gonna tear the thunder out of your butt when I get my hands on you." She headed for the cedar tree, which had grown big enough to hide a small boy.

The dusty black truck pulled in front of the grocery, and Peggy glanced up. She stopped in her tracks as Lloyd Morgan got out of the cab. He threw her a smile as he entered the fish market.

Of all the people in the world, Peggy had not expected to ever see the tall, good-looking Morgan man again. An unfamiliar sensation made her body tingle and itch, a feeling that required some form of action, but Peggy didn't know what. She could run down the street, but something held her feet to the patch of dirt right in the front yard, bean pan balanced on one slender hip.

Unable to help herself, she inched toward the store to listen in on the men. Lloyd had surely come to buy fish. There was no other explanation.

"Give me seven of those tabby cats. I'll get my . . . mama to fry them up with some hushpuppies."

Gene pulled out the fish and wrapped them in white paper.

"I heard I might be able to get something to drink with those fish."

"Three dollars."

"Add it in with the fish."

Gene leaned below the counter and pulled out a jug. His brush with the revenuers had slowed his bootlegging down for a few months, but economic necessity and his own drinking problem had pushed him back into making mash.

"I saw that good-lookin' girl of yours out pickin' beans. Maybe I need some beans to go with my catfish."

"Peggy's only a girl." Gene cut his eyes up to Lloyd. "She's the last of my girls at home, and that's how I intend to keep it. She's got to finish school."

"I'd like to take her out some." Lloyd drew his wallet from his back pocket and pulled out a twenty. "I got a good weldin' job. I got a skill, and I could take her to some nice places."

"She's not old enough to get into a nice place." Gene took the money and made change. "Have a good day." He pushed the purchases across the counter.

Lloyd picked up the whiskey and uncorked the jug. "How about we have a little drink right now?" He offered the jug to Gene. "It's Sunday, and I got nowhere I have to be."

Gene took a drink and set the whiskey down. Without saying anything, he flipped on the television before he sat on the edge of his stool, waiting while Lloyd drank.

Outside, Peggy shifted the pan of beans. She could hear Mike around the back of the house, and she knew she should go back to the garden and finish the butter beans. Still, she lingered at the front of the store, slightly short of breath and dazzled by the sound of Lloyd's voice whenever he made a casual remark to her father. She could hear the television; the jumble of cheers and excited voices sounded like a baseball game. *Lassie* and *The Wonderful World of Walt Disney* were due on in a few hours. If Gene would let them watch. If she finished her garden work. She took a step toward the garden, stopped for an indecisive moment, and then went back for more eavesdropping. Finding out what Lloyd said, how he said it, was the most important thing that could happen to her.

"Peggy's only sixteen." Gene's voice sounded less firm, more mellow.

"Hell, sixteen's old enough. How old was your wife when you took up with her?"

"Times were different then."

"Inky said Slim Henderson told him all your other girls weren't older than Peggy when they started goin' out. She's plenty old enough."

"Have you taken a good look at Peggy?" Gene's question was peevish. "She looks like a child. What would a grown man want with a woman who looks like a little girl?" The question held a dark twist.

Lloyd's voice deepened with anger. "She looks ripe enough to me."

"Makes me wonder about you."

"Listen here, you . . ."

"Take your fish and your whiskey and go on. Go on away from here and leave my daughter alone."

"I asked you polite, but I don't figure I owe you any other questions."

Before Peggy could get away completely, the door of the store swung open and Lloyd stepped into the yard. He caught sight of her beside the store, but he walked on to his vehicle, putting the fish and jug on the seat before he turned around to acknowledge her.

The sun glistened in his dark hair, and the muscles across the back of his shoulders were manly. He walked like he was a king. Like Elvis moved, knowing that millions of girls were staring at him. And liking it. Except for Elvis, Peggy had never thought another such man existed.

"Come over here a minute, girl."

Peggy held tight to the bean pan and hesitated. Part of her wanted to go to him and another part told her to run as hard and fast as she could.

"Come over here. I'm not gonna bite you." He motioned her to the truck.

Peggy took a few steps and halted. It wasn't that Gene didn't want her to go out with Lloyd. Her daddy's displeasure wouldn't stop her. Lloyd Morgan was an unknown. The few dates she'd been on had been with boys her age, boys she could wrestle and subdue, or intimidate with her fierceness. Lloyd Morgan was like teasing fire with gasoline. There was always the chance that it would pouf into a giant ball of flame and burn everything around.

"You act like a whipped dog." Lloyd grinned. "Come over here. I got a candy bar for you."

The bribe of chocolate drew her closer. "What kind?"

"What kind you like?" he asked.

"Mr. Goodbar."

"Wait right there." Lloyd walked back into the store. He was gone hardly a minute before he came back holding the familiar yellow-and-brown wrapped candy. He held it out to her. "You're gonna have to come close enough to get it. I'm not throwing it to you."

The challenge finally got to her. "I'm not afraid of you." Peggy marched straight up to him, put the bean pan down, and waited.

He handed her the candy. "You sure you're sixteen?"

"March 7. That's my birthday, and I'm sixteen." She could feel him looking at her. It made her fingers fumble as she peeled back the outer wrapper, then the foil. When the first third of the candy bar was revealed, she held it out to him. "Want some?"

He shook his head. "No, that's all for you. I bought it just for you."

The shock of the words made Peggy's throat close on the sweet taste of the candy. She looked up at him to see if he was teasing her. Instead she saw something else, something that made her swallow the bite of candy without looking away. He'd bought the candy for her because he saw something worthwhile in her. Something he wanted. From her.

"Want to go for a ride with me, Peggy? Maybe we could go to a movie, or go fishin'?"

The chocolate coated Peggy's mouth. Thick and sweet, it promised a pleasure so intense that nothing else was like it. She held the candy bar lightly, so her fingers wouldn't melt the chocolate too fast. "You heard my daddy," she said.

"You're sixteen, girl. You're a grown woman. You can decide who you go out with and who not." Lloyd reached out and touched her jaw, his finger tracing down her skin. "You got about the prettiest eyes I ever did see." He eased into the truck and closed the door. Leaning out the window, he winked at her. "I'll be talkin' to you later on." He turned the truck on, put it in gear, and drove off.

Peggy stood in the front yard, candy bar melting in the heat of her hand as she watched him drive away.

Chapter Twenty-Three

"Mama, please." Peggy held the saucer with the buttered biscuit and syrup. "Just a little."

Inez turned her head away. "Thank you, Peggy, but I don't care for any."

Inez's manner worried Peggy. Lately Inez had drifted farther and farther away, to some place where people spoke with soft formality to each other, never raising their voices or arguing. A chill touched Peggy at the idea that her mother had gone to the past, or to some future where real life had given way to a cool, whispery half-death.

Force was the only way Peggy knew how to reach her mother. "Mama, you got to eat this. Now get ready to chew and swallow." She lowered the saucer, wary and careful. Inez could change in a flash. From a death-like trance, she could turn to rage. Especially if whiskey was involved. There had been more than one fight over a bottle that Peggy had hidden or destroyed.

She offered a bite of biscuit, but Inez stared straight past it.

"Mama, you don't weigh more than a wet cat. You've got to eat some of this. I've got a shift down at the cafe, and I can't go down to work and be thinking that you haven't eaten all day long."

"You shouldn't eat when you're not hungry. Gluttony is a sin, Peggy Ruth."

"You got to eat enough to stay alive." Peggy's exasperation was about to break out. Inez had to eat, and one way or another she was going to. Nobody else seemed to care if she starved to death. "Eat it, or I'll make you."

Inez caught the undercurrent of desperation, and she reached out to take a fourth of the biscuit. "If you insist." She ate it without enthusiasm.

Peggy handed her the plate, relief riding double with remorse. "I don't want to sound so mean, Mama, but you got to eat. If you get sick . . ." She didn't finish aloud. If Inez got sick enough to need a doctor, there was no telling what Gene would do. Gene's girlfriends were open knowledge to everyone around. Ma and Pa Early had given up trying to help. Inez wouldn't consider leaving Gene.

The loud honking of a car startled Peggy, the syrupy plate tilting dangerously in her hand. She thrust it at Inez. "Eat every bite, Mama," she ordered before she walked to the window.

Nellie Moye's big, black car idled in the yard, Nellie behind the wheel. Seeing Peggy in the window, Nellie laid on the horn again, long and without pause.

"Damn her," Peggy muttered as she hurried outside. Nellie was Gene's sister, and she was married to Bob Moye. Peggy had heard all her life that Bob had murdered a man down in Florida, changed his name, and moved to Greenwood. She didn't know if it was a family story or the truth, and she'd never dared to ask Aunt Nellie. A woman of bawdy good humor at times, Nellie could strike with the speed and surety of a cobra. She and Peggy had tangled before when Nellie had beaten and cursed Inez.

"Get your butt out here and let's go," Nellie said when Peggy walked up to the car window.

"Go where?"

"I got a job. One for each of us."

"I've already got a job."

"Well, you can have this one, too. I told those folks over at the Catholic Services that you were feisty and that you had a good imagination and could write. I said your spellin' and all needed some work, but that you knew how to make it sound right. We're gonna be part of the Job Corps."

Peggy blinked.

"Don't stand there lookin' like an owl just woke up in the sunlight. Get in the car."

"I got things to do here before I go to the cafe." Peggy thought about the long list of chores waiting in the house. "What's Job Corps got to do with me?"

"It's this new federal program where young folks can get trainin' to get jobs. You said you wanted to be a secretary. They'll show you how to type and do the things a secretary does."

"How much does it cost?"

"It's free, and better than that, I'm gonna work for them. They need volunteers, too. Now get in and let's go."

There were dishes to wash and the younger boys to think about. Inez had seemed more herself, and she'd eaten. Peggy ran her hands down her shorts. Working in the cafe was fine, but if she could get secretarial training, she could have a better life. The truth was, she was so far behind in school that she despaired of ever finishing. Secretarial training would be better than a high school degree. "Let me put on a dress. I got to go to the cafe at ten."

"You may not want a cafe job. Just hurry up."

Pushing the thoughts of what she ought to do aside, Peggy tore through the house and slipped into a dress. She was back at Nellie's car in less than five minutes. They headed down Basket Street toward the corner of Avenue I and Broad where Catholic Services were housed.

Nellie talked nonstop until they pulled into the parking lot. Glancing out the window, Peggy's hand froze on the door handle. "There's nothin' but Negroes here, Aunt Nell."

"It's white folks doin' the trainin'. It's so Negroes can find jobs." Nellie was getting out of the car. "Some white folks, the smart ones who aren't afraid, can learn here, too."

"I've heard folks talkin' about this place. There's gonna be trouble here."

"There's always trouble. Now you want to learn to be a secretary or not? Folks got a right to a job, no matter what color their skin."

Peggy got out. Nellie Moye was a contradiction. She'd beat and cuss and low-rate Inez and call a Negro laundress a lazy nigger to her face, and then turn around to work with something like the

Catholic church and Job Corps. Peggy didn't pay much attention to what was being said in the cafe, but she'd overheard enough to know that there was plenty of anger and resentment in town toward the new program. Threats had been bandied about.

"What's wrong, Peg-a-leg, you scared?"

Peggy started walking. The black faces that turned to her were young, and some of them were frightened. The idea made Peggy angry. "Why should folks in town care if Negroes want to learn to do a job? They fuss 'cause they say they don't work. There's nothin' wrong with this."

"You can learn a trade here, Peggy." Nellie opened the door and went in. "That's why I told them you'd help out."

Peggy stopped at the sight of a Catholic nun gliding toward her. "You must be Peggy," she said. "I'm Sister Joel. We welcome you into the program. We need young people of talent and good spirit. We need all the volunteers we can get."

Unable to resist, Peggy felt herself drawn into the room where skills classes were organized and young blacks were gathering in small groups.

Passing one of the large tables where forms and literature were neatly stacked, Peggy stopped. There was a flyer with the photos of six men on it. Two had been X-ed out. Peggy read the names, stopping at Emmett Till. She hardly recognized the features of the youth. He looked nothing like he did in the photograph she'd seen nearly ten years before. She stared at his face, ignoring the X that crisscrossed his features. Medgar Evers also had been slashed by an X. His name tickled her memory, but she knew only that he was a black man who'd been killed. The others—James Meredith, R. L. T. Smith, John Salter, Bob Moses—their names meant nothing to her. Meredith sounded vaguely familiar, but she didn't place him. Staring at the flyer, Peggy didn't hear the nun walk up beside her.

"Such a shame that hatred is printed and spread about, isn't it?" Sister Joel asked.

"They killed those two, and I guess it means the others are next."

Sister Joel moved her away from the table. "It's intimidation, though I wouldn't put it past the men who printed this to kill again."

Peggy thought about her mother, about the secret of Emmett Till that she'd never been able to tell. In one hot night, the Negro boy pictured on the flyer had been beaten, shot, drowned, and disfigured in such a grotesque way that the photograph of him still haunted her dreams.

"I want to be a secretary," Peggy said.

"Training will be done at the Job Corps Center outside of town. Your aunt, Mrs. Moye, has been hired as a driver. She'll bring clients in for training and help deliver meals to those who can't get into town. She said you would be good with writing and helping to train our young citizens to vote."

"I'm too young to vote," Peggy reminded her. The nun's touch calmed Peggy. As a girl, Peggy had listened to the gospel shows on the radio with Inez. They had sung the old hymns, and Inez had talked about God and Jesus and the way God's children were supposed to behave. Something about Sister Joel brought it all back, made it seem possible.

"You don't have to be a registered voter to help others register," she said. "The vote is the way to bring change, and every voter is important. Can you help?"

"Sure." If Sister Joel thought she could do it, she could. "I have a job over at Charmaines Cafe. I have to be there for the lunch crowd, but I can come back this afternoon."

"Thank you, Peggy. We need the help of young women like yourself. You're going to make a difference for a lot of people."

It had never occurred to Peggy that anything she did could make a difference for anyone. "I'd like that," she said, surprised at how deeply she meant it.

Chapter Twenty-Four

Darkness was just a faint promise as Peggy grabbed her sandals and eased out the front door. A whippoorwill cried sad and loud at the edge of the yard, and Peggy wished for something to throw at the bird.

Inez and Gene had fallen into a light sleep, and they had done so without inflicting major damage on each other. Both had eaten supper, and the younger boys were fed and busy watching television. Gene would undoubtedly throw a fit if he knew they were in the store, but that was her daddy's problem. At least they'd have something to keep them quiet and out of trouble. Lately, as they grew older and more adventurous, the lack of parental supervision had begun to show. It was never anything serious, but enough to keep Peggy worried that their childish pranks would blossom into serious troubles.

As she slipped past the store, she saw the gray flicker of the television and counted the heads before she hurried down Basket Street toward town. She'd agreed to meet Lloyd Morgan away from the house. She knew Gene disapproved of the older man. Inez was not happy with the idea of Peggy dating anyone. Lloyd had asked her to go out with him to have some fun, and for reasons she didn't fully understand, she'd accepted. When she got to the corner, she strapped on the sandals and started walking toward downtown. The yellow dress she wore was sleeveless and cool, and she'd bought it with tip money from her job.

She heard the car rolling up behind her, but she didn't turn around. She kept walking, trying not to let her heartbeat drown out her hearing. Things in Greenwood weren't the way they used to be. She had to pay attention. There were bad elements loose in the area. There were too many angry people. She forced her feet to keep going, straight ahead, a brisk walk, moving with a purpose.

"Hey, good lookin'. You want a ride?"

She recognized his voice, and relief swept over her. She waited for him to draw up beside her.

"I was afraid your daddy wouldn't let you come." He stopped the car and got out so she could slide into the seat with him.

"Daddy doesn't know I'm gone," she answered truthfully. "Where are we goin'?"

She'd been so taken with the idea of going somewhere with Lloyd that she hadn't asked any of the right questions. She hadn't known what to ask. It was Molly who wanted to know where they were going on their romantic first date. Molly had seen Lloyd and thought he was one of the handsomest men in the state of Mississippi. Maybe in the South.

"I thought we'd go over to Tchula. Meet some friends of mine. Do a little jukin' and dancin'. How does that sound?"

Terror struck Peggy to the core. First dusk had given way to a purpling twilight that promised a hot, velvet night, and being out with a man seemed suddenly wrong. "They won't let me in," she told him. Now he'd take her back home. "I'm not old enough to get in. I told you I was sixteen."

Lloyd revved the car and made the tires scream. "I got friends over there, Miss Peggy Ruth Albritton. Don't you worry about it. You'll get to see the inside of a juke joint first hand."

His words were a promise, and Peggy gripped the upholstery of the car as Lloyd pressed the gas harder and sped them through the flat blackness of the Delta.

"Where is this place?" Peggy finally asked when they'd traveled through the eye-blink town of Tchula and hadn't stopped.

"It's out by the train tracks, and a whole bunch of my buddies are gonna be there. There's somethin' you're really gonna like about this place." Lloyd reached across the seat and picked up her hand. "You are tiny," he said. "You don't look sixteen."

"I am sixteen. Born . . ."

"I wasn't doubting your word." Lloyd squeezed her hand then put it back down on the car seat. "We're almost there."

Lloyd angled the car in among the other vehicles parked in front of the shotgun style house. Loud music drifted into the open car window, and Peggy felt another thrill of fear and tingling apprehension. She'd been in a few joints before, but just long enough to buy her daddy a bottle and get back out. No place in Greenwood would ever let her stay longer than that.

The music seemed to float out of the joint and swell in the humid air. "This is Chuck's Place," Lloyd said. "They'll let you in."

Laughter mingled with the music. Peggy sat in the car and let the strange sounds touch her skin. She liked the music. It wasn't the rock 'n' roll she heard on the radio. There was a deep pulse to it, a throb that went deep and called for either dancing or tears.

Lloyd got out and came around to her side of the car, opening the door. He held out his hand and Peggy felt herself being drawn into the small club, taking the first step toward growing up. She smiled up at Lloyd as they walked through the door.

"Hey, Lloyd!"

He was immediately greeted by several shouts. In the darkness, Peggy made out Inky and Lloyd's cousin, Buddy Richardson. Lloyd introduced her to his sisters, Vicky and Shirley. They were beautiful girls in tight shorts and make-up, and their gazes roved over the men who weren't with their group. They all had bottles of beer or drinks, and several couples were dancing.

At the sight of the dance floor, Peggy felt a lessening of her anxiety. She'd never been in a juke joint before, and she wasn't much on drinking, but she could dance. From the first day she could stand and move, she'd danced. For the customers in the store, for Inez and Gene, her sisters and their friends, for Molly, and for herself. That dance floor was the one place where she'd never felt inadequate.

"You want a beer?" Lloyd asked.

"Seven Up," Peggy answered. She'd tasted corn liquor and beer, and both were nasty.

Lloyd laughed. "My date here wants a Seven Up," he said loudly to the man behind the bar. The laughter went through the group.

"You better be careful, Lloyd, or you'll have to change her diapers," one of the girls said.

Peggy felt her hands tighten into fists, but she accepted the cold, green bottle of soda and said a thank-you. As she tipped the drink to her lips, she felt everyone watching her. They were waiting, wondering what Lloyd Morgan saw in a scrap of a girl. She put the bottle down. "Can we dance?" she asked him.

Lloyd put his drink down so abruptly that a little sloshed out on the table. He took her arm as she started toward the dance floor.

Peggy let the music go deep inside, feeling it out for the rhythms, the tiny darts of movement and emotion. She thought of the day Verline Ellis had taken her to see Elvis so long ago. Verline had teased her about dancing on the stage with the singer. For a long time, Peggy had dreamed about that, a fantasy that gave such intense pleasure she refused to abandon it. Now, she looked up into the face of another handsome man. His hair was black, dyed like Elvis's, and he had some of the same lean, panther-like grace of the singer. There was something forbidden about him. Something of Elvis. And he was looking down at her like he had won her at the fair. She let the music go to her feet, and she started to move.

From the gathering of Lloyd's friends came whistles and cat-calls as she let go. She was only sixteen, thin and child-like she had never done well in school, and she was shy, but she had been born with a passion for dance. She closed her eyes and gave in to it.

They finished the number to applause. As Lloyd led her back to the table, his hand moved slowly up and down her back, a touch that Peggy recognized as pride and possession. He was telling everyone there that she was his girl. She belonged. She took a long swallow of her Seven Up and Lloyd ordered her another. Music poured around her, and now the small joint didn't seem so alien, so unfamiliar. It was just a group of boys and girls, some a good bit older than she, out laughing and dancing. It was okay.

"Who are those men?" she asked Lloyd, nodding at several tables of men who looked as if they were passing the time away without any real purpose.

"That's part of the surprise," Lloyd said. "There's a train track runs right by here. Some of those guys are engineers on the train. They stop in for a drink and get back on the next train."

Peggy nodded, though she didn't see what sort of surprise that might be.

"Let's dance." Lloyd pulled her out onto the dance floor for a slow song, and Peggy felt a moment of panic as he pulled her tight against him. "Relax," he whispered in her ear. "Close your eyes and let the music tell you. I'll do the rest."

Peggy shut her eyes and listened. Lloyd moved with a quick, clean grace that she found easy to follow. He felt the music the way she did. As they seemed to float around the floor, her body following his as naturally as if she'd been doing it all her life, she discovered she liked slow dancing.

"It won't ever be like this with anyone else," he whispered in her ear.

Peggy wasn't certain what he meant, but she believed him. There would never be another night like this.

"Hey, Lloyd, put that baby doll down and let's go find us a choo-choo," Buddy called out. "Time for a ride."

Peggy found herself being pulled out into the warm night. The excitement of the others seemed conducted to her by the humidity that touched her skin with wet heat. Lloyd held onto one hand while someone else grabbed her other and they ran in the dark. Unknown ground underfoot and the sense of being pulled forward into destiny, Peggy felt a freedom she'd never known.

The thin soles of her sandals felt the first rumble, and it opened her eyes. The ground trembled slightly, and there was a sound in the air, a storm riding in hard. But the wind was nonexistent and a mockingbird fussed at the rude interruption of the night.

"What's that?" she asked.

"Our ride," Lloyd said.

Though she couldn't see his face in the darkness, she could hear the smile in his voice. "It's a train," Peggy guessed.

"And we're gonna catch it." Lloyd tugged on her hand and the pack of young men and women hurried toward the approaching noise.

As they crossed the cotton field, the tracks gleamed like slivers of ice in the moonlight. Far down the tracks, Peggy could see the single glow of the light on the engine.

"It'll come by real slow," Lloyd whispered in her ear. "I'll get on first, and then you grab hold of my hand and I'll pull you up."

Peggy thought of the iron wheels churning over the rails. One slip and the outcome would be inevitable. She'd seen an old man limping around town, one who'd lost his foot under a train. If Lloyd didn't pull her up . . .

"It'll be fun," Vicky said. "Unless you're afraid."

"I'm not afraid." Peggy felt the rumble of the train in her knees. It was moving right up her body, taking control.

"When it comes, start running with it," Lloyd said. "I'll jump in and then grab you up."

The yellow light was headed straight toward them, riding a wave of metallic sound that sounded worse than the monsters on some of the television shows. "Don't let me fall," Peggy whispered.

"I wouldn't let anything bad happen to you. Not ever," Lloyd squeezed her hand and then he was running, pulling her beside him as he raced the black shadow of the train down the silvery tracks.

Peggy felt him jump. It was as if he leaped from her side, abandoning her to the metal monster that roared beside her. She held out her hand and ran. When she felt his fingers clutch hers, she was swallowed by relief, until she felt herself jerked up into the blackness of the open boxcar.

The open doorway banged her leg, but she landed soft, right on top of Lloyd. She could feel him laughing silently beneath her as she rolled off him and to the floor, scrambling to sit up. Beside her, he sat up, too. Liquid sloshed in a bottle.

"Have a drink," he offered, touching her cheek with the wet mouth of the bottle.

"Where are we going?" She'd forgotten to ask. For the first time since she'd slipped out past the grocery she thought of her mother.

"Just down the tracks."

"How will we get home?" She tried to sound nonchalant. "I mean, the car's back at Chuck's Place."

"There's a train comes back. We'll catch a ride on it." Lloyd's hand stroked her back. "Don't be worried, Peggy. There's no harm in havin' a little fun."

With a shriek, another person tumbled into the boxcar. A soft, female body bumped into Peggy as Lloyd's sister rolled into a sitting position. She drew a deep breath.

"Couldn't you pick another boxcar?" Lloyd asked, disgust thick in his tone.

"Lloyd, don't be startin' nothin' with a chicklet when you've got a cake in the oven," Shirley said. She crawled away from the open doorway where the black night swirled by.

"Shut up." Fury clipped Lloyd's words short.

"Come on, Baby Lloyd," Shirley said, stumbling as she tried to stand in the swaying car.

"What's she talkin' about?" Peggy couldn't see Lloyd in the darkness, but she could sense the tension in him. He'd said he was a welder. He'd never mentioned a thing about baking.

"My little sister's going to shut her mouth," Lloyd said. His voice had softened. "There's plenty of things I could tell about her."

Shirley's laughter seemed alive, predatory. "Calm down, tiger. You got a bottle in here?"

Lloyd shifted beside Peggy. There was the sound of liquid in a bottle once again. "Here, Shirley. Have a drink and shut up." Lloyd's voice was easy again, a long stretch of smooth road. "Just have a drink and let's all have us some fun."

211

Chapter Twenty-Five

"Peggy Ruth, you remember when we used to pick those scuppernongs out by the Yerger place? That was some fine jelly." Inez battered catfish filets and laid them out, side by side, in a platter on the kitchen table.

Peggy stood at the stove, her back and legs aching from the long day at Charmaines. As the hot grease began to bubble, she dribbled a bit of cornmeal in it to test the sizzle. The grease had to be so hot that the fish started frying the minute they touched it or they would become soggy.

The fresh filets were a surprise. Gene had gotten up at daybreak and gone fishing, returning with an exceptional catch, enough for Inez to have some to fry for supper. He'd cleaned them in the backyard, then disappeared, leaving Peggy and Inez to get supper on the table before he returned.

"What do you think, Peggy? Think the grapes are ripe, yet?"

The idea of scuppernongs caught Peggy by surprise. Inez hadn't talked about jelly in a long time. "I remember you working out at the Yergers'. You'd pick cotton till dark and then we'd hunt for scuppernongs." She eased the fillets into the grease, careful not to slosh it out of the pan and onto the eye of the burner. She slid a sideways glance at her mother and felt a moment of hope. Inez had slowed down on her drinking. Maybe she was coming back to herself. "That's some onion you got goin' there."

"It burns the eyes, but it'll give those hushpuppies some taste," Inez agreed. "Those were some sweet grapes we used to get out there." Inez finished chopping the big onion and mixed it in with the cornmeal left over from battering the fish. "Maybe we could find some this year. It's about scuppernong time."

Peggy flipped the fish in the pan. It was August, the month of relentless summer. Supposedly, the fish were jumping and the cotton was high. But the living had never been easy. Especially not with Gene. The night before, Gene had caught her stealing Inez's liquor and selling it back to him, a ploy that kept Inez from drinking. It also cut down on the number of midnight trips to Archie Hay's store that Peggy had to make for Gene.

Gene had tried to grab hold of her to beat her, but he couldn't catch her any more. She'd gotten too fast and agile for him, but he was looking for an opportunity to get even. She'd halfway expected to come home from work today and find the trouble she'd dodged the night before. Instead, Gene had brought in the fish.

She felt the sharp nip of an over-strained muscle near her shoulder blade and lowered the spatula. Soon school would start. Junior High. She was way behind everyone else her age, but at least she'd be in the building with the older students. No matter how far behind she was, she was determined to get through school. She had to perfect her reading and writing skills, even if she never got the hang of math.

Reading was vital to survival. Too often she had watched Inez move slowly along the aisles in the grocery store, unable to tell between plain and self-rising flour. Inez was at the mercy of the world. Peggy knew she had to have an education to look out for herself.

"Do you think those vines are still out at Yergers'?"

Peggy looked over at her mother to discover that while Inez had been rambling on about wild grapes, she had the hushpuppies ready to fry. There was anticipation in her eyes, a small flicker of wanting.

"We can go look. Maybe this evening, when it's cooler."

"Your daddy might ride us over. It would be good for the boys. They've never picked grapes to make jelly."

"Some homemade jelly would be good." Peggy lifted out the golden fillets of catfish and refilled the pan. The idea of riding with Gene made her uneasy, but chances were, he'd go off drinking and they'd have to walk anyway.

"Did I tell you?" Excitement jumped into Inez's voice. "We got a letter from Boyd. Gene read it to me and Becky. Boyd's doin' good."

"Boyd was always smart." Peggy felt the stab of pressure right in her twitchy back muscle. She had to finish school, to get a diploma. Her brothers and sisters had finished their educations, and they all seemed to be doing all right by themselves. She'd been taking the secretarial courses over at the Job Corps, but between working at the cafe and trying to keep Inez on an even keel, her progress had been slow. There was also the more exciting work of teaching Negroes how to register to vote. She didn't see where voting was such a big deal, but Sister Joel and the others made her feel that she was making the world a better place. They said they needed her, whenever she could make it. Her own education had taken a back seat to the voting work.

There was also Lloyd Morgan. He played the biggest role in her lack of advancement in her studies. Lloyd had swept her into a life of black nights, music that wound hot and cool through her bones, and carefree laughter. Lloyd encouraged her to take risks, to experience things like hopping the train. It seemed that every moment with Lloyd was filled with possibility. And the things he told her! Things that made her feel like she was special.

"Peggy Ruth! Mind that fish!"

Peggy glanced down to see that one side of the catfish was golden and crisp. It was time to turn it—and fast. She wielded the spatula with expertise.

"Call the boys," Inez said. "Gene'll be home any minute."

"Where is he?" Peggy knew he hadn't returned to the river, not after the haul he'd brought in earlier that day.

There was a hint of expectancy in Inez's voice. "Gone to the woods."

Anger burned hot and sudden in Peggy's heart. She lifted the fish from the pan, relinquishing the hot grease to Inez for hushpuppies.

"I'll get the boys." She walked out to the back yard to call her brothers, wondering if Gene had gotten his still up and running again. Lately he hadn't had time to cook mash, but that hadn't slowed his drinking, only Inez's. Liquor was a necessity of life for Gene. If he didn't make it, he bought it. But he didn't always share with his wife.

Lloyd drank, but never too much. He seemed to take enough just to ease the way from daytime to night. The men over at Chuck's drank, too, but it was part of the laughter and the soft feel of the summer evening on her bare arms. It was so different from the drinking that Gene and Inez did. Peggy couldn't help but wonder how the same thing could have such different natures.

She heard the rumble of her father's car pulling into the yard, and she yelled out at Ronald to get his brother inside for supper. They weren't hard to bring in. The smell of the frying catfish had been wafting out of the kitchen for the last thirty minutes, and the boys were ready to eat. They stampeded past her on the steps and headed for the table. Peggy followed them in.

"Somethin' smells good." Gene grabbed Michael by the waist and bounced him in his arms. "You're getting too big."

For a moment, Peggy felt as if a heavy curtain had parted, revealing a family supper-time scene that could have been. The tableau was perfect: her mother at the stove finishing the hushpuppies, Gene coming in from work, the children ready to eat, eager for the hot food. She knew that whatever it took, she would give it if only she could prolong this moment, stretch it out into a life.

"Peggy and I want to go pick some scuppernongs after supper." Inez looked at Peggy for confirmation before she looked at her husband. "We thought maybe you'd give us a ride down to the Yergers' where those vines grow wild at the edge of the cotton field."

Peggy felt Gene's speculative gaze on her.

"I might could do that." He was already reaching for the fish and hushpuppies.

Peggy stayed close to the back door as she watched her father. His sun-tanned face showed no hidden anger. It was almost as if he'd forgotten the liquor incident.

Inez interrupted her thoughts. "See, Peggy, I told you Gene would take us. We can get enough for some jelly."

"Some scuppernong jelly would be fine," Gene said, biting into the fish. "Mmmmm, this is good. That was a real sweet mess of cat, not fishy at all."

Peggy and Inez took a seat at the table. There was plenty of room now that so many of the children had struck out on their own. Only Ronald and Mike kept the table alive, talking about their adventures of the day.

"Where's the big man?" Gene asked, bringing silence down on the table. He concentrated on the hushpuppy he held in his hand as if it were a jewel.

Peggy ignored him, picking up her hushpuppy and biting into it, even though her stomach had knotted and threatened to revolt.

"Where's Lloyd?" Gene asked again.

"Workin'." Peggy knew she had to answer her father or it would only get worse. "He's workin' over at Barrantine's."

"More likely tryin' to decide what to steal."

The anger flared in Peggy. She was playing into Gene's hands, but she couldn't stop herself. "Lloyd's no thief. You can't stand it because he's got a job and you can't keep one."

"Peggy!" Inez reached across the table, clutching at and missing Peggy's hand.

"Those Morgans are no good." Gene bit into another piece of fish, taking his time. "Keep it up with him and you'll see. He'll run around on you, leave you with a passel of kids and no way to feed them. Folks know about that family, and they know none of those boys are worth a lick."

Peggy pushed back her chair. "I'm sick of you. You beat up on Mama and me, but . . ."

"Leave the dishes," Gene said, rising. "Let's go get those grapes if that's what we're gonna do."

"The grapes." Inez motioned the boys to their feet though the meal wasn't finished. "Let's go before it gets dark. We can come back and finish this up. Come on, Peggy. I need you to help me."

"Come on, Peggy," Gene mocked, "Lloyd won't die from waitin' for you. He'll just go see one of his other girlfriends."

Inez bent under the sink, tumbling things about until she came out with a large wash pan. "We're ready, Gene," she said, herding the boys out of the kitchen and toward the front door.

The muscadine and scuppernong vines that grew wild on the Yerger plantation were free for the harvesting to whomever wanted to pick them. The gold and purple grapes had to be crushed, and the hulls and seeds pressed out before good jelly could be made. With the convenience of store-bought jelly, many of the old-time jelly-makers had stopped the tradition. The grapes that grew in heavy clusters on vines that wound over trees and shrubs were often left to rot.

"If scuppernongs grew like kudzu, this state wouldn't be anything but one big jelly factory," Gene said as he parked beneath an oak. "You take your time pickin', I'm gone sit right here and watch." He pulled a half-pint from beneath the seat.

"Go on, children," Inez said, eyeing the bottle.

"Come on, Mama." Peggy nudged her with the pan. "You're the one who wanted to pick."

Inez never took her eyes off the bottle. It was half empty, and she watched as Gene put it to his lips, tipped it, and swallowed. He lowered it, his mouth quirking up in a thin curl. "Thirsty, Inez?"

She reached for the bottle, and he lowered it to rest on his thigh.

"Come on, Mama." Peggy grabbed Inez's arm and tugged her toward the vines where Mike and Ronald were already plucking the heavy fruit.

Inez twisted free of Peggy's hand. She went back to Gene and stood, waiting.

"Come on, Mama." Peggy urged. She glared at her father. Every time Inez was doing a little better, he got her started again. "I don't know why you have to do this."

Gene held out the bottle and let Inez take it. "Go easy," he directed, his sharp eyes taking in her consumption.

Inez handed the bottle back to him, picked up the pan, and went to the vines.

"You've got to quit drinking," Peggy said.

"If we fill the pan, we can make enough jelly to last the winter," Inez answered, already sighting a cluster she could reach from the ground. "Let's get to work. Then we'll have to get some sugar, if Gene don't have any in the store."

Peggy glanced back at her father and saw that he'd finished the bottle. He leaned back against the seat, one foot on the ground, watching them work. It struck Peggy that he might fall asleep. She wondered if it would be possible to drag him out of the car and run over him without having to go to prison.

When the pan was brimming over, the scuppernongs so ripe that the thick pulp split their skin to near bursting, Peggy carried it back to the car. Gene was snoring lightly, and she called his name to wake him up.

"What time is it?" Gene looked around at the mauve sky, darkening in the east to a bruised purple where it touched the long rows of cotton that stretched to the edge of the earth.

"Eight or so." Peggy didn't need a watch. "We've got enough scuppernongs." Inez slid into the front seat as Peggy motioned the boys out of the thicket and into the car. "It's time to go home."

"Get on in the car." Gene picked up the empty bottle and frowned. He dropped the bottle and grabbed Inez's arm in a grip that made her cry out. "You drank all the whiskey!"

"No! No!" Inez twisted until her thin arm was free of his punishing fingers.

"Mama didn't touch it except when you gave her the swallow," Peggy said from the back seat.

"You're so smart, I wonder if you could find your way home in the dark. Walking."

"I can find my way anywhere in Leflore County, and even around Tchu—" Peggy stopped before she said the little town of Tchula where she sometimes went with Lloyd to Chuck's. Gene didn't need to know Lloyd was getting her into drinking clubs, even though she still hadn't acquired a taste for liquor.

"You want to walk? Is that what you want?" Gene swung around so he could see Peggy. Ronald and Mike fell back into the seat, pushing their bodies as deep as they could go.

Unflinching, Peggy met her father's red glare. He'd had more to drink than the little bit in the bottle. She used her toes to feel up under the front seat until she located a second bottle. "I don't mind walking." Her shoulder blades burned with a steady fire, the kind that chars the rubble and weeds as it sweeps over a pasture. Her feet and legs had been hurting before she'd stood on them another hour picking grapes. She did not relish the idea of a seven- or eight-mile walk in the dark.

"Get out." Gene stared at her.

"Gene, don't leave her out here." Inez touched his arm. "There's strangers all over the county. Folks marching from one side of the state to another. Someone might get her."

"Well, they wouldn't keep her long." Gene eased back around to grasp the steering wheel. "Let's get on home. I can deal with Peggy Ruth when we get there."

Peggy leaned back beside her brothers, wondering which time it would be when she provoked her father that he struck her as hard as he hit Inez. That would be the time she surely killed him.

The car swerved into the other lane, and she heard the click of the radio and the burst of static as Gene tuned in to a station.

"Watch the road," Inez was gripping the dash. "Gene, please. . . . You shouldn't be drivin'. Let Peggy drive."

"Shut up! You want to make me wreck this thing."

"Gene!"

"One more word . . ."

The music came on suddenly clear. "Softer than satin was the night, um, um, bluer than velvet was the light, in her eyes. . . ." Peggy leaned back, focusing out the window as Bobby Vinton sang of a special moment captured forever. If she ever got married, she would wear a dress of blue velvet. A dress so plush and soft that just touching it would be an experience.

The disc jockey at the station broke in over the end of the song. "And now, Elvis Presley returns to the top forty."

"Return to sender, return to sender . . ."

Peggy forgot about Gene and the drinking and the trouble that probably waited at the end of the ride home. She closed her eyes and saw Elvis Presley, microphone in hand, singing. His hair dripping in one loose curl over his forehead, he sang with his chin tucked and his eyes closed, his lips almost kissing the microphone.

And he sang only to her.

"We're home." Mike pushed on Peggy's leg, waking her from the sleep of exhaustion. "Get out, we're home," he said again.

Peggy opened the door and got out. She pushed the pan of grapes to her brothers and was just turning to go in the house when she heard her father behind her.

"Hold up there, Miss Peg-a-leg."

She sighed. "What is it?"

"Ride me down the road."

Before she answered, Peggy reached under the front seat and pulled out the second empty bottle. "Haven't you had enough?"

Gene drew back his hand, but he hesitated. "Get behind the wheel. I need you to drive me over to Slim's."

"I'm goin' to bed." Peggy started across the yard. She was almost to the porch when she felt Gene's hand on her shoulder.

"Drive me over to Slim's." It wasn't a request.

Peggy thought of Inez. To fight with Gene in the yard would only insure that he would drag his anger into the house. Mike and Ronald would get upset, and Inez would likely get beaten. In the long run, it would be smarter to drive Gene to Slim's and get the whiskey. Then, they could come home, and she could slip into bed. Mrs. Damguard had asked her to work the breakfast shift in the morning, and she needed the money.

Peggy held her hand out for the keys. "You know I don't have a license yet."

"You're always wantin' to practice." Gene started toward the passenger side and stumbled.

Peggy got behind the wheel and put the car in reverse, feeling the tension of the clutch with her foot. When Gene's door was closed, she worked the clutch and the gas and eased into the road. She was getting smoother and smoother.

Slim's wasn't far away, but Peggy slowed as they approached. A group of Negroes were on the street, signs in their hands. Protestors had become more and more common, and Peggy eased by them as she pulled in front of the store. It looked like they were angry about Slim and the way he treated them.

"Look at them fools," Gene said. "What do they think they're doin'? Slim'll run their asses to jail."

Peggy had a pretty good idea what they were doing, but she held her tongue. Gene needed no provoking. He was partially drunk and out of whiskey. He was as mean as a cornered rattlesnake. He got out of the car, spit, and walked into Slim's. To pass the time, she listened to the radio, singing along with Chubby Checker and Little Eva as she slid down into the front seat. It wasn't full dark yet, and the sky was a rectangle framed through the car window.

Somewhere nearby, a blue jay was setting up a racket at some invasion, real or imagined, of its territory.

"Loco-motion," one of Peggy's favorite dance tunes, came on. Watching the protestors out of the corner of her eye, she felt a vague uneasiness. If she looked too closely, she might recognize some of the Negroes. And they might recognize her from the youth center. One thing she didn't need was for Gene to see her talking to a bunch of blacks.

Sister Joel said that everyone, white or black, had a right to cast a ballot and a right to receive an education. That sounded fair, but Peggy knew that Inez had never voted. Part of it was that she couldn't read, but another part was that she didn't look on voting as something a woman needed to do. Gene wouldn't like it if she took an interest in who served as sheriff. Elections were men's work. Men controlled it all.

The thought struck her suddenly. Control was the center of the fight. Folks who felt that casting a ballot was having control wanted to keep it all for themselves. It would have made a lot more sense if they were fighting over money.

Sitting in the car waiting on her father to come out, Peggy listened to the murmuring of the protestors that had the potential for trouble. That black men dared to protest was an invitation for violence that white men would gladly accept.

Eight songs had played on the radio, and there was still no sign of Gene. He was probably perched up at the counter, drinking away with Slim, but the longer she waited, the more uneasy she became. Unable to sit any longer, she started inside.

Just inside the door, she called out. "Daddy?" There seemed to be no one in the store at all.

"What are you doing in here?"

The angry voice startled her, and she whirled. A tall figure dressed all in white stood at the back of the room. She took in the pointed white mask that covered his face.

"Git back out to the car." Peggy recognized Gene's voice.

"Where'd you get that Klan robe?" She'd never seen a KKK outfit at home.

"This ain't none of your concern. Git back to the car."

Slim stepped out from the shadows by the counter. "You'd better do what your daddy says.

Peggy looked at Slim. "Where'd that robe come from?"

He shrugged. "It's just a joke," he said. "Gene'll be out in a minute."

Gene pulled off the white robe that looked like it had been made from a sheet. He dropped it into Slim's hands. "Look at them crazy niggers out there," he said, nodding toward the window where the protestors were barely visible in the failing light.

"Bunch of agitators and trouble makers," Slim agreed. "Times were when they knew their place." He looked at Peggy. "Like women used to."

Gene picked up the bottle of Old Crow from the counter. Almost half was gone. "I think we can take care of them for you, Slim." There was dark amusement in his voice. "Let's go, Peggy."

Glad enough to get out of the store, Peggy hurried to the driver's seat and got in, easing the car around carefully.

"Scatter them niggers," Gene said, pointing with his hand that held the bottle at the cluster of blacks.

Peggy looked at him.

"Hit the gas, girl."

Peggy's hands tightened on the wheel. "No."

"I said scatter those niggers." He grasped her arm, digging his fingers in hard. "Now!"

"No! What if I hit one?"

"They'll run. If they don't, it'll be one less nigger to worry about." Gene's fingers bit in deeper. "You put this car in gear and scatter them, or I'll do it and I won't miss."

"Daddy, please . . ." Peggy instantly regretted the pleading tone.

Gene's hands scrambled at the handle of the driver's door. When he finally got it open, he tried to push her out.

Clinging to the steering wheel, Peggy managed to close the door. "There's a ditch. We can't get over the ditch."

"You put it in first and give it the gas. It'll go through the ditch. Now do it."

Peggy lifted the gear shift into first and tested gas and clutch. In the near darkness, she couldn't be certain she could steer well enough to miss everyone. If Gene got behind the wheel, he wouldn't even try.

"Go!" Gene brought his hand against the back of her head, striking so hard that lightning shot behind her eyes.

Peggy felt the clutch pop under her left foot as she gassed the car over the ditch. Frightened cries streamed past the open window as bodies dove to left and right. In the gravel along the edge of the road the tires spun, swinging the back end of the car nearly around. Out of control, Peggy cried out with fear when she thought of someone ending up beneath the wheels of the car. At last she got the car straight and managed to drive down Carrollton Avenue. She checked into the rearview mirror, praying she would see no injured bodies lying in the road.

"You missed 'em all," Gene said, looking back out the passenger window. He finally chuckled. "That put the fear of the Lord in their black butts. That's what they need, a little fear and respect." He unscrewed the cap on the Old Crow. Tilting the bottle to his lips, he drank.

Chapter Twenty-Six

Peggy put her fingers around the cold fountain Coke in front of her and watched as Katie perched on a red stool at the long counter and measured three spoons of sugar into her coffee. All around them other teenagers were getting hamburgers and Cokes in the after-school rush at the Cotton Boll. Ever since Peggy had quit her job at Charmaines, she hoarded her small savings account for things other than food. For her, the soft drink was a rare luxury, but Katie had asked to talk. She had said it was very important.

"How's school?" Katie asked without looking at Peggy.

"Not so good." Peggy grinned. "Mama made me quit at Charmaines 'cause my grades were bad. She said school had to come before buying clothes. It just looks like I won't ever graduate."

"Maybe if you stopped going out . . ." Katie looked into the depths of the black coffee. "Peggy, Lloyd Morgan is married."

It took a few seconds for the meaning of the words to penetrate. "He is not." Peggy eased off the stool. "You're lyin'."

Katie examined the coffee as if it were the most fascinating thing she'd ever seen in a white ceramic cup. Finally she looked up. "I wish I was. His wife's name is Margaret. She's pregnant."

"That's a lie." Peggy took a step back. "Why are you comin' in here lyin' about Lloyd?"

"I'm not lying." Katie looked around the busy hangout and lowered her voice. Boys and girls were lined down the counter or sharing root beer floats at booths. Several had stopped eating and talking and were looking their way. "I'm trying to help."

"I thought you were my friend." Peggy felt the stab of betrayal. When she'd worked at Charmaines, several of the waitresses and regulars had discovered she was seeing Lloyd. No one had come right out and said Lloyd was married, but there had been hints so broad even she'd caught them.

"I am your friend. Peggy, he's got a wife."

"That's not true."

"Ask him." Katie twisted on her stool. "I wanted to tell you 'cause I know you wouldn't go out with no married man, if you knew."

"Lloyd's not married."

"How do you know that?" Katie started to reach out to Peggy but stopped. She dropped her hand in her lap. "Have you ever asked him flat out?"

"I asked him, and he said no."

"Then he's a liar as well as a two-timer."

Peggy felt the rapid pulse of her heart. Lloyd was the only good thing that had ever walked into her life. The only thing. He wouldn't lie to her. He couldn't. "How come he has time to take me out? We go out all the time. We go dancing and riding around. If he had a wife, he couldn't do that."

"A wife don't always have a say in what her husband does." Katie twisted her hands in her lap. "Peggy, please listen to me. Folks know about Lloyd. His family . . . Anyway, they think you know he's married. It makes you look as bad as him, like you don't care."

"I don't care!" Peggy flung the words. When she felt the stares of several of the other teens, she lowered her voice. "I don't care because it's not true. Lloyd Morgan is not a married man. I've met his sisters, and they never said he was married."

"Why would they tell you? Folks say they're cheap."

"Stop it!" Peggy glared at her friend. "You're just jealous. Lloyd's handsome and older. He's got a job and he takes me places. You're just eat up with jealousy."

Katie slid off the stool. "Don't do this, Peggy. Don't make this into something that's going to hurt our friendship."

"You're doing it. All I'm doing is finally telling the truth. I'm saying it just the way I see it. You're eat up with jealousy. You can't have Lloyd so you don't want me to have him. He wants me instead of you, so you're going to spoil it for me."

Katie picked up her books. "He's married, and nothing you say to me can change that. You don't believe it, you ask him. Ask him in front of his friends. Or ask his friends you like to run with so much. They're all probably liars and sneaks, but if there's a decent one among them, they'll tell you the truth." Katie side-stepped Peggy and pushed through the door and out into the late fall afternoon.

Standing at the counter, Peggy watched a gust of brown leaves twirl past her friend and fly across the street. School would be awful without her only friend, but Peggy was determined never to speak to Katie again. Not after what she'd said about Lloyd.

From a crowded corner of the room, Peggy heard her name. She turned to confront the high school boy who sat with three other boys in one of the booths.

"If it isn't little Peggy." He was talking to his friends but looking at her. "You know what they call Peggy Albritton. They call her Ankles, because no boy can put a hand higher than her ankles. But I'll bet it's different now that she's dating a man. Right, Peggy?"

His taunting tone made Peggy angry, but it also wounded. She turned back to her Coke and sipped a big gulp through the straw, trying to finish so she could leave.

The same boy spoke louder. "You can't get to first base with Peggy Albritton, but she can't get out of the seventh grade."

The boys' laughter was like a hail of pins raining down everywhere on her skin. She put the cola down and gathered her books. The best thing to do was leave—before she lost her temper and lit into the boy. She knew him. She'd gone out with one of his friends. Once.

"Hey, Peggy, does your fella know you're jail bait?" The boy made a bird-like noise. "Parchman quail." The laughter grew louder.

Peggy clutched her books to her chest and fled the hangout. It had been a mistake to go there with Katie. All of her life she'd been "one of the Albritches." One of the bad kids from "the Western front." One of the fish market kids. One of the bootlegger's kids. One of the crazy woman's children. One of the dumb ones. One of the ones who got held back in school. One of the nigger-lovers because her father was always drinking and fishing with blacks.

She tried to stop the angry thoughts as she ran toward home, dodging the falling leaves that swept toward her on the winds of an approaching storm. Never good enough. Never smart enough. Never . . . until Lloyd Morgan had stepped forward, pointed his finger at her, and said she had value.

She stopped at a pay phone and fished the coin out of her purse. She found her fingers were icy cold as she lifted the receiver and heard the dial tone. Katie had challenged her, and in doing so had given life to a worm of doubt that felt as if it were eating her from the inside out. She had to ask. She had to. No matter how mad Lloyd got at her. She had to ask.

Hands shaking, she inserted the dime and dialed the number she'd memorized but never thought she would call. A moment later she heard Artie Belle Morgan's voice.

"Baby Lloyd ain't here," Mrs. Morgan said. "Is this Peggy?"

"Yes, ma'am." Peggy could hear the pulse of her heart in those two words. She only hoped Mrs. Morgan could not.

"Is somethin' wrong?" Mrs. Morgan asked, a mingling of wariness and concern.

Peggy blurted the question. "Is Lloyd married?"

"What did he tell you?" Mrs. Morgan asked.

"He said no, he wasn't married."

"That's your answer then," she said.

Peggy started to ask if she was sure, but the words stuck in her throat. Lloyd's mama had confirmed that he was single. Katie was just talking mean, stirring up trouble.

"Peggy, where are you?"

"I'm goin' home from school." Peggy noted the heavy traffic on the road and realized it was near five o'clock. She was very late going home, and she'd not even given Inez a thought. "I have to go home."

"I'll tell Lloyd you called."

"Thank you." Peggy hung up the phone. She felt better, but not completely relieved. Lloyd's mama had said her son was not married, and surely she'd know the truth. Would Mrs. Morgan tell Lloyd she'd called, asking personal questions about him? A dagger of doubt slid through her ribs. Lloyd wouldn't like anybody asking questions about him. He kept his business private, and he liked it that way. But she'd had to ask someone.

She walked to the east, barely noticing the dark clouds building and the lightning that had begun to cut the darkness like Zorro's sword. She made it to the front porch before the downpour began.

"Peggy?" Inez came out of the kitchen. "I was gettin' worried."

"I had to stay after school." There was no point saying she'd stopped for a Coke with Katie. Inez would want to know how Katie was doing, and Peggy didn't want to talk about her.

"Lloyd called." Inez turned her back as she delivered the message. "He said he'd be by here at six to pick you up."

Peggy dropped her books. She'd planned to study for her math test, always her worst subject. It just wasn't possible to study when Lloyd was the alternative.

"When did he call?"

"A few minutes ago." Inez's voice held disapproval. "Peggy, he's too old for you. He's a grown man. Your daddy doesn't think much of him, wanting to go out with a girl who doesn't look sixteen. Gene said it's not right."

"Shut up! You just shut up!" Worn out with her own anxiety, Peggy had no intention of listening to Inez talk about Lloyd. "He takes me places. He cares about me! He makes me laugh."

Inez turned to her. "Any man can do that, in the beginning."

"You picked a fine one. Daddy beats you . . ." She clamped her lips together.

"Gene couldn't stop Mary Jean or Sheila. He can't stop you. But he don't like Lloyd, and he don't want him comin' around here. He said to tell you he'd better not catch Lloyd around the house any more."

"I'll meet him down the street." Peggy spun away and hurried into her room. She plundered through the wardrobe she'd purchased over the summer to find a dress that would make her look more grown up and keep Lloyd's attention focused on her. There were times in the dark bars that the women seemed to lean toward Lloyd a little too close. He never did anything to bring it on; it was just cheap and trashy women. They did it because she looked too young to stand up for her man. But folks around Greenwood were fixing to learn something different. Lloyd was the only good thing in her life, and she had no intention of letting gossips or trash take him away from her.

She put on the green dress that Lloyd liked. She was barely ready before quarter of six when she ran out of the front door and down to the corner to wait for him. Sometimes he was early, but mostly he was late. Often real late. But she didn't mind waiting. It gave her a chance to play out in her head how things would be, to think about where they'd been and what they'd done before. Lloyd always had some place to go and someone to see.

She almost jumped the curb when she saw his car coming, right on time. Before she'd closed the door good, she turned to him. "Daddy don't want you comin' to the house any more."

Lloyd shook his head. "The cow's out of the barn and Gene wants to close the door." He laughed.

Lloyd's laughter was one of the things Peggy liked best. There was a devil in it, an imp of don't-give-a-damn that soothed her like salve on a burn. There didn't seem to be much that bothered Lloyd Morgan. He did what he wanted and laughed at those who were shocked by his ways. Like an outlaw. Even the word carried a tiny thrill with it. Where she always had to tend to children and Inez, always had to carry the burden of responsibility, Lloyd just shrugged his shoulders and walked away from it. For the brief few hours she could be with him, she could pretend she had a little bit of the outlaw in her, too.

"Where are we goin'?" Peggy asked. Lloyd never made a date to go anywhere specific. He just picked her up and they went wherever he decided. Sometimes they just rode around the country, watching the moon and the stars burn up the night. Lloyd wasn't pushy like the boys her age. He kissed her, but when she told him to stop, he stopped. Inez had taught Peggy that the one thing of value she could bring to a man was her pureness. Peggy wasn't exactly certain about the process of how pureness got lost, but she'd heard bits and snatches of talk in the girls' bathroom at school and knew that it often happened on a back road. Once a girl wasn't pure, she wasn't fit for marriage.

"Why don't we go up to the lake and look for the ghost of that Indian woman?"

"Okay." Peggy felt a chill of anticipation. She'd heard all her life that there was an Indian woman buried up at Moon Lake at Clarksdale. She'd been hung for killing her husband after he beat her. The story went that she came out late at night, carrying an old oil lantern, to check the gravestones to find where her husband was buried, to be sure he'd stayed dead.

The flat cotton fields rolled past the window, softened by the night air into an even black that met the sky. The car tires sang a muted song, the sound drifting with the cool breeze through the open window. Teasing fingers of air lifted her hair, cooling the back of her neck. The nights were growing cold. Thanksgiving was only a few days away, and soon it would be winter in the Delta. She shivered and felt Lloyd's arm slip around her. She let him pull her across the seat to sit beside him.

"You feel good," he said, pressing her against his side.

"You feel good, too," she said, reaching up to touch his face. It had taken her a long time to be bold enough to touch him, but he'd encouraged it, teaching her what it meant to love her man.

"Here's the lake." Lloyd pulled up to a vantage point where they could see the moon reflected on the water. It had been a day with low humidity and the sky was clear and bright.

"This is a beautiful place." Peggy found it hard to talk with Lloyd. He was so much a man, he wouldn't be interested in the foolishness at school. She didn't talk about her home life with anyone. She found it easier to listen to him talk, or simply to lean back against him and feel his chest rise and fall in a rhythm that made her feel secure. Sometimes they would kiss the entire evening away.

His voice was low. "Mama said you called today."

Peggy listened hard, but she could hear no censure in his voice. "I did."

"She said you wanted to know if I was married."

Peggy's pulse started to race. She'd questioned Lloyd, and now he was going to tell her he wasn't going out with her any more. "Katie told me that you were, and that your wife was pregnant. She said everyone knew, and I had to know. I wanted to talk to you but you weren't there and . . ."

Lloyd eased his hand up and gently covered her mouth. "Hush up there a minute," he said. "You wanted to know if I was married, but you'd already asked me." His fingers caressed her cheek.

Peggy closed her eyes and swallowed, his hand still across her mouth, silencing her. Though the touch was gentle, she well knew how quickly a man could turn violent.

He swung his legs up on the seat and pulled her up his chest. One arm banded her waist and his left hand caressed her lips. He whispered the question in her ear. "You want to ask me again?"

For a few seconds, Peggy didn't answer, weighing the possible outcome of her need to know. Finally she nodded her head. Not knowing for certain was worse than being hit.

Lloyd's arms released her, and he allowed her to slide down into the seat so she could face him.

"Go ahead. Ask." He said.

"Lloyd, are you married?" The words seemed to pulse out of her mouth, not a sentence but a raw pleading of emotion.

"How could I be married, Peggy Albritton, when I'm goin' to marry you?"

Peggy could see the gleam of his teeth as he smiled at her. "What?"

"I'm askin' you to marry me." Lloyd reached across the seat and touched her face. "You're just the sweetest thing. I got to have you for my wife."

"When?" Peggy couldn't get enough air.

"I got some things to tend to first, but before too long."

"I got to finish school." Even as she said it, she knew it would never happen. There was no competition between finishing school and Lloyd Morgan. Lloyd wasn't the kind of man who would wait for her to get a high school degree.

"You can finish, when we're married."

The worst thought occurred to Peggy. Maybe he was teasing her, playing with her because she'd called his mother. Maybe he was punishing her by offering marriage, only to take it back later. "Lloyd, are you really askin' me?"

He reached over and pulled her into his arms. His lips found hers. When he broke the kiss, he stroked her hair. "You always smell so good. I always said I wanted to marry a woman who smelled good. Now I've asked, but you haven't answered."

"Yes." Peggy kissed him softly. "Yes, I want to marry you."

"Good, then we will." He turned the key in the ignition.

"Where are we goin'?" Peggy looked at the lake with longing. It was such a romantic place, and she wanted to be with Lloyd. Alone. Without all the noise and ruckus of a bar and the women eyeing Lloyd. He was hers now. Really hers.

"I got some things to tend to at home."

"It's not even eight o'clock."

"I got work early tomorrow. Got to start working hard to save up for us when we get married."

Peggy's arguments were deflated. They'd need a little nest egg to get going, to get their own place. She could imagine it, with curtains in the kitchen and a table where they could sit and eat together. "I'm gonna make you the best wife anybody's ever seen," Peggy vowed.

"I know you will." Lloyd circled the lake, headed back to Greenwood.

Chapter Twenty-Seven

Peggy tucked the lacy bra down in the bottom of the little suitcase. She'd spent the last of her savings on the new underwear and the overnight case to carry her things in. After tonight, Lloyd would be the one buying her nice things to wear. Dresses and panties picked out to please him.

After tonight. . . . She swallowed. Mary Jean and Faye and Sheila were married. So was Molly. They had all made it through the wedding night. They'd never talked about what had happened, so it couldn't be too bad. Peggy considered talking to Inez, but quickly decided against it. What a married man and woman did together wasn't something Inez would talk about.

Peggy listened to the pan rattling in the kitchen as Inez cooked. Her mother was doing better. It was okay to leave her. It was time. Not quite a month before on March 7, Peggy had turned seventeen. On March 1, Lloyd's divorce from his wife had come through, just after Margaret had given birth to a baby girl, Teresa Denise, whom Lloyd called Peanut.

Snapping the suitcase shut, Peggy glanced in the mirror. She looked no older than thirteen, even in the dress she'd borrowed from Faye for her wedding. It wasn't blue velvet, but it was a soft blue eyelet that showed off her eyes.

"Peggy?" Inez stood in the doorway. "I wish you wouldn't do this."

"Mama, you said you'd sign for me." Peggy felt a spur of panic. "You promised."

"Lloyd's not right for you. He lied to you. He's already got one baby, and actin' like he's not goin' to take care of that one."

"He had to lie. He knew I'd leave him." He'd explained it to her, how once he'd met her he'd stopped loving Margaret and how he had tried to talk his wife into a divorce so he could be free to marry

Peggy, but that Margaret had been stubborn, up until the very end, when she'd finally given in and accepted that he'd never love her because he loved Peggy.

"Peggy, lies are the traps of Satan. You have to tell the truth. Even when it hurts. The truth is the only way, you hear me. Always, always tell the truth. Lloyd's lyin' only shows he's not a fit man for you."

"Mama!" Peggy couldn't keep the desperation out of her voice. "I'm marryin' Lloyd tonight. There's nothin' you or Daddy can say or do to stop it."

"If your father catches you, he'll put a stop to it. Lloyd Morgan may wind up with an extra hole in his head."

The thought of Lloyd, injured or dying, made Peggy ache. "Don't say that, Mama." From her suitcase she pulled out the consent paper. "You got to sign this. Remember, Mary Jean and I taught you to sign your name. You can do it." She carried the paper and a pen to the kitchen table where Inez carefully marked out the letters of her name.

"I wouldn't do this except you need to get out of this house. You go at Gene all the time, and he's gonna hurt you."

Peggy kissed the top of her head. "Thank you, Mama. I'm gonna be happy."

"Marriage can be a bed of roses or a bed of thorns, Peggy. It's what you make it. Once you do this, once you give yourself to this man, it's for life. You remember that. Better or worse, richer or poorer, in sickness and in health, till death do you part."

"It's exactly what I want," Peggy said, folding the paper and putting it in her suitcase. Very carefully, she closed the latches, picked up the case from the bed and stood. "I love you, Mama." Unexpected tears filled her eyes. In agreeing to marry Lloyd, she'd refused to give much thought to the fact that she'd have to leave her mother behind. Now it was clear. She was beginning a new life. One without Inez.

"I love you, Peggy. You've always been my heart." Inez hugged her daughter. "Be happy. That's all I ask. Be happy."

Peggy broke free of the embrace and ran out the door, the suitcase banging her leg. Lloyd was going to pick her up in front of the Paramount movie theater. They didn't want to risk running into Gene and having a big blowout.

It was a beautiful evening. A storm had threatened earlier, but the April breeze had blown the clouds across the cotton fields, and there was the scent of wisteria on the wind as she passed a huge vine that had climbed a telephone pole, the purple flowers dangling like clumps of scuppernongs. With marriage to Lloyd, her life would be completely different. She would never go back to school—married girls weren't allowed. She would cook and clean and make a loving home for Lloyd, and for her children when they came. It would be perfect. So perfect. Not anything like her parents' marriage.

Most of the Greenwood businesses that she passed had closed at five o'clock. Chaney's Drugstore was still open, and she looked in the window as she passed, the suitcase tapping the back of her leg. The case wasn't heavy. She'd have to get the rest of her things after she and Lloyd got a house. He said they'd find a place to rent until they could do better. It would all work out after they were married.

She saw him coming down the block. The impulse to run away came on her so strong that she actually took a couple of steps backwards. A fear like she'd never experienced made her feel dizzy. Then she saw his face behind the windshield, his eyes on her and that dark sweep of hair that made him look so much like Elvis. He was hers. She had the man who would be hers for the rest of her life. She couldn't run away from that.

He pushed the door open as he idled at the curb. "Hop in," he said. "We got to get to the justice of the peace."

Peggy put her suitcase in the back seat and climbed in beside him. He pulled her up against him and held her tight as they drove out Highway 82 to Itta Bena.

The cafe they stopped before was modest but neat. Peggy opened her suitcase and got the permission paper signed by her mother. Lloyd's big hand engulfed hers as he led her up to the front door.

"Judge Rusty said he'd marry us," Lloyd said to the woman who met them.

She waved them inside and told them to wait a minute. A tall man finished serving platters of barbecue. Wiping his hands on an apron, he came toward them.

"I'm Judge Rusty," he said, holding out his hand. "So you're in the mood to tie the knot." He herded them through the cafe and into a small office. The Bible was open on the desk, and he picked it up.

Too nervous to look at anyone, Peggy concentrated on the floor. She heard the words, a flow of sentences that meant nothing and everything. She didn't have to hear them to know that by the power of God and the law, she was forevermore joined to the man who stood beside her.

Lloyd increased the pressure on her hand. "I do," she said.

In a few moments, Lloyd turned her so that he could kiss her. He passed some folded money to the judge, and Peggy felt him steering her out into the evening.

It was over. She was Mrs. Lloyd Morgan. Peggy Albritton was part of the past.

"Come on," Lloyd said, hurrying her along.

"What do we do now?" Peggy looked at her husband. They'd never talked about where they would go once the wedding was over.

"I've got some plans." Lloyd put her in the car and hurried around to the driver's side. Before she could ask any more questions, they were traveling down Highway 82 through the night. "I thought maybe we'd go to Greenville. Take a look at the Mississippi River."

Peggy had an image of a fancy hotel, one where she could stand on a little balcony outside the room she shared with her husband and see the river. She leaned against Lloyd's shoulder and smiled into his sleeve. It was going to be wonderful, perfect. Just like she'd dreamed.

Lloyd slowed the car, taking an old dirt road that wound behind the ruins of what seemed to be an abandoned plantation.

"Where are we going?" she asked.

"You ask too many questions." There was a ring of impatience in Lloyd's tone. "I can't wait any longer."

"Wait for . . ." Peggy bit back the question.

Lloyd left the dark and abandoned plantation house behind and pulled deep into the network of empty fields. In the moonlight, Peggy could see that the rows were straight and clean, the cotton barely a foot tall. Lloyd stopped, opened his door and pulled her out the driver's side with him.

Pressing her back against the car, he kissed her, long and hard, his hands beginning to work the skirt of her dress up.

"Lloyd!" She pushed against him, frightened. "Wait."

"I've waited and waited. You knew what getting married would be."

"Not here." Peggy braced her arms, but he ignored her efforts to hold him back.

His hand worked up her leg, and Peggy tried to twist away from him.

"Dammit, we're married." Lloyd's voice had taken on a note as dark as the night. "This is the way it's supposed to be."

"Lloyd, you're scaring me." For the first time, Peggy truly knew that the choice she'd made would change her forever. She was miles away from Gene and Inez. She was married. Lloyd had a right. She let her arms go limp.

"If you love me, you won't fight," Lloyd whispered in her ear.

Peggy didn't resist his hands as they tugged at her clothes and finally pulled her down into the still warm earth of the cotton field.

Above her the moon was a sickle in the sky. A blade, cutting the night. She tried to bite back the scream, but the pain was so intense she felt as if she'd been torn in half. Her cry echoed across the empty field, and she realized that it didn't matter to Lloyd that she cried out.

And there was no one else to hear her.

LLOYD PULLED THE car up to the side of the juke joint which had just begun to hop with the late evening partiers. Greenville was a river town, a port city on the Mississippi River. Straight from the cotton field, Lloyd had brought Peggy to the border of the state. Across the river was Arkansas, a foreign land to the young bride.

"What is this place?" She tried to sound normal, but something was very wrong. Lloyd had hurt her. She could feel the blood trickling out of her.

"This is Tilley's. It's a place I like to go."

"Can't we go to the hotel?" She needed a bathroom and some clean clothes.

"I got to celebrate. Yours is the first cherry I ever got, and it's time to celebrate."

"Lloyd, I don't want to go in there."

Lloyd opened the car door and got out. He slammed it and leaned in the window. "You can't anyway. You're too young. It ain't like Chuck's. They won't let you in here. Just wait in the car."

"Lloyd . . ."

He walked away before she could finish.

Loud music blasted out into the night before the door swung shut again, and Lloyd disappeared into the joint. Peggy found herself alone in the darkness. She eased her hand down between her legs. When she pulled it up, she saw the blackness and knew it was blood. There was so much blood, and it was going to ruin Faye's dress. She clamped her legs tight and waited, hoping the blood and the pain would go away before Lloyd came back out and wanted to get on with being married again.

THE GRAY LIGHT of dawn turned the dew to silver on the roof of Tilley's. Peggy watched the colors change to pink, then gold. The pain had stopped, but the bleeding had not. The door of Tilley's opened. Lloyd stumbled out into the new day. As he came toward the car, he was grinning.

"Let's go," he said, gripping the steering wheel to steady himself as he slid into the car.

"Where are we going?" Peggy asked.

"Home."

"Home?"

"To Mama's. We can stay there for a while. I've been out of work for the last few weeks and I don't have enough money to rent a place."

Chapter Twenty-Eight

After two weeks of pain and sporadic bleeding, Peggy finally went to see a doctor. The idea of submitting to an exam mortified her, but the fear that she was permanently ruined and the urging of her mother-in-law won out. The gynecologist told Peggy that she'd been torn inside. The doctor called Lloyd in and urged the new groom to give Peggy time to heal and to use tenderness and caution in the future.

Peggy returned, alone, to the small apartment that Verline Ellis had loaned the newlyweds until they could find money for rent. Still in pain and ashamed, Peggy had only to look out the front door to see her childhood home. The rooms where she and Lloyd were living were just across Basket Street from her parents' house. Peggy could see that her mother had been severely beaten for her role in helping Peggy marry, yet she could not go home for fear Gene wouldn't let her leave. Furious over the marriage, Gene had called every law officer he knew. His hope was to drag Peggy home and have the marriage annulled.

But Peggy was married, and neither her shock at life with Lloyd nor her father's ranting and raving could change that fact. She was Lloyd's wife, and she intended to remain so. No matter how many women decided Lloyd was fair game.

The ink was barely dry on the license before he was making the rounds of the Greenwood bars, taking up with women he'd had before, or finding new conquests. Though rumors were rampant, Peggy refused to believe that her husband's actions went beyond drinking and conversation. She knew he went to bars and hangouts where he drank, danced, and talked with other women. These were "flirtations," behavior forced on him by Peggy's health. Lloyd's idea of marriage was not a delicate wife who needed time to heal, and he let his wife know it.

Lloyd's work habits were as erratic as his fidelity. He often said he was going to work, when instead, he went to the Greenwood Grill or another local hangout where both women and liquor were cheap. Lloyd worked only when he chose—whenever his mother or Peggy had no cash. Artie Belle would give her "Baby Lloyd" money for alcohol, and Lloyd showed a strong need for liquor.

Still believing that if she worked hard enough and pleased her husband that she could save the marriage, Peggy cooked and cleaned and made sure she was made-up and well-dressed whenever Lloyd came home. When it became clear that Lloyd had no intention of supporting her financially, Peggy took a job as a waitress in The Alice Cafe, earning the steady wages that kept them struggling along.

Only a few weeks after the wedding, Lloyd was staying out until Peggy tracked him down and dragged him home. The dinner that she'd cooked would be ruined on the table. The family unit that she'd wanted and dreamed of had begun to crumble.

They had been married a month or so when one night Peggy turned off the gas beneath the pork chops and turnip greens, took off her apron, and colored her lips red with a tube of lipstick in preparation to go to the Greenwood Grill to find Lloyd. He was two hours late coming home, and if she didn't find him soon, every penny of his meager pay check would be spent on liquor.

Pushing open the screen of the apartment, she inhaled sharply. A man and an infant were standing outside the door. It took a few seconds for her to recognize Lloyd.

"Margaret said she wasn't gonna raise little Peanut," Lloyd said, stepping forward and thrusting the baby at Peggy. "The welfare gave her to us."

Peggy looked down at the infant. She wanted children. She wanted half a dozen. But not so soon. And not someone else's. Still . . . she blew softly on the downy fuzz of the baby's head and watched the dark eyes open and stare into her own.

"What'll I do with her while I work?" Peggy asked. "You spent your last pay check at the Grill, and one of us has to work regular and bring in some food."

"We'll think of somethin'." Lloyd had already lost interest and was looking behind Peggy, sniffing. "Is that pork chops?"

"Uh-huh." Teresa Denise's little fingers were curled around her thumb. "She's right pretty, Lloyd," she said, hefting the baby into the air. "A fine, healthy baby. How come Margaret didn't want her?"

Lloyd slammed in through the screen without answering. "Call her Peanut," he threw over his shoulder as he scraped a chair across the linoleum and sat down at the table. "Fix my plate, Peggy. I've got things to finish and I want to eat before I go out."

In less than ten minutes, he'd eaten the plate of food Peggy put in front of him. Pushing back, he stood and reached for the keys to the car. "I'm goin' over to take care of some things."

Peggy's back was tired from the long shift at The Alice Cafe and preparation of supper, but she'd learned the hard way that if she let Lloyd out of her sight, she might not see him again for several days. "I'll come with you," she said, leaving her barely touched food. She never understood how Lloyd could eat so fast.

"You'd better stay here and take care of Peanut," Lloyd said, already walking across the kitchen floor to the back door.

"We can get someone to keep her." Peggy felt the trap close tightly. "I'll call Annie or Sheila, or maybe Vicky could keep her," she said, thinking of Lloyd's sister.

"They're all out. It's Friday night." Lloyd was down the steps before the screen could slam. "See ya later," he said as he got in the car and drove away.

As if she knew her father was leaving, Teresa Denise began to wail. Peggy picked up the baby, absently clucking and rocking her in a motion that soon brought contentment and quiet. "I guess you need to eat," Peggy said, realizing she had no bottle, no diapers, no baby food. She went to her purse and looked at the five dollars left of her pay after she'd bought food for supper. After necessities for the baby, there wouldn't be anything left. She sighed as she hitched Teresa Denise on her hip and walked out the door into the early twilight and toward the grocery store where she would buy what she could for the baby.

Caught up in her domestic crisis, Peggy managed her job and the baby as best she could. The infant was not a unique experience; she'd grown up helping with her brothers and sisters and knew the ins and outs of childcare. It was Lloyd that troubled Peggy. No matter what she did, she couldn't seem to keep his interest. The focus of her world, always before directed at Inez, now shifted to her husband. The racial storm brewing over Greenwood and the state of Mississippi never entered her line of vision. Byron De La Beckwith was tried for the second time for the murder of Medgar Evers. The trial was the talk of the Delta, and for Peggy it meant nothing. Patrons of The Alice whispered the latest rumors and facts, gleaned from newspaper accounts or from friends of friends.

Among the evidence against Beckwith was ownership of the murder weapon, complete with a fingerprint. Beckwith's first trial, held in February of 1964, had ended in a hung jury. During the second trial, two Greenwood police officers again verified Beckwith's alibi that he was at a service station in Greenwood at one A.M. on June 12, 1963. The time factor and the distance between Greenwood and Jackson made it impossible for Beckwith to have been in both places at the time of Evers's murder.

The second trial ended in another hung jury. The all-white, all-male panel could not reach a verdict.

Beckwith returned to Greenwood a hero. A welcome home banner was hung from the overpass, celebrating Beckwith's lack of conviction. While the gossip swirled around Greenwood and all over the state, Peggy saw the banner and took no notice of what it meant. Lloyd's pay stopped altogether. Unable to make him tell her if he was working or not, Peggy started pulling a lunch and dinner shift at The Alice and taking Teresa Denise to Hilda Prescott to keep.

It was a balmy spring evening, and Peggy had finished a cup of coffee and a chat with George Anetopoulos, the proprietor of The Alice. The older man had taken a liking to Peggy, giving her an extra shift whenever he could. Lloyd's personal habits were well known among club owners, and Anetopoulos felt sorry for the scrappy young woman who was now saddled with her husband's child from a previous marriage. Anetopoulos's sympathies were with the lovesick girl who was determined, by sheer will, to make her husband love her.

"Check the salt shakers and napkins, Peggy," he said as she went to cash out a customer. The front door opened and the tiny brass bell jingled in a new customer.

Peggy eyed the woman who walked into The Alice. Her tight, tan riding britches were enough to attract attention—the wrong kind—but it was something else about her that made Peggy stop, metal napkin holder in hand, as the woman paused just inside the door. With her dark hair and slender frame, she was a pretty woman with the possibility of beauty, except for the wild look in her eyes.

The woman surveyed the room, taking account of everyone there. At last her gaze settled on the glass jar sitting beside the cash register. "Byron De La Beckwith Defense Fund" was printed in black ink and taped to the big jar. There were a few dollar bills and lots of quarters, dimes and nickels where patrons of The Alice had left their change to help defray Beckwith's legal costs.

Peggy reached behind the counter for napkins, trying not to stare at the handsome woman who was obviously looking for someone or for trouble. One of the other waitresses gasped, and Peggy turned back to look.

The woman's hand had been down by her slim side, but when she lifted it, she held a gun. The barrel swung in a one-eighty around the cafe, generating shrieks from the women and curses from the men.

"Put that thing down," a man yelled as he dove under a table.

"You givin' money to that bastard?" The gun came to a halt, pointed at the man under the table. Patrons backed into each other and the walls as the woman swept the room with the barrel once again.

Peggy ducked behind the counter, clutching the napkin holder.

The woman strode across the cafe, her long, sleek legs taking her straight to the cash register. Peggy peeked around the edge of the counter and saw the thoroughbred legs coming right at her. She felt her heart pounding against the metal container. In all of the fights and violence in her home, she'd never considered that a stranger might walk through a door and kill her. Now she knew it could happen.

"You can have my money." George Anetopoulos stood his ground behind the cash register, ready to open the drawer. "Take the money, just don't hurt anybody."

"I don't want your money." With her free hand the woman grabbed the Beckwith Defense Fund jar. "You listen and you listen good. Don't you give that son-of-a-bitch another penny for his defense fund. I'll kill every one of you that does. You raise another nickel for that SOB, I'll kill you all." Gun waving, she backed out of the restaurant, the jar clutched against her chest.

The door closed and the tiny brass bell jangled cheerily.

Peggy closed her eyes and tried to get the feeling back in her legs. Leaning forward, she peeked around the base of the counter. Several of the customers and some of the women who hung out in the cafe waiting to get picked up were under the tables, staring back at her.

"Who was that?" Peggy asked.

"As best as I can remember, that was De La's wife. I heard they ain't been gettin' along," one of the pick-up girls answered. She stood and pulled her blouse, which was too tight and too red, back down to her waist. "I can't believe that crazy woman come in here and stole De La's lawyer money." She brushed at her dimpled knees as she stood. "I think we oughta call the police."

Marvin Bradshaw brushed the dust off the front of his khakis. Drinking the last of his coffee, he set his hat on his head. "You call whoever you please, Ruby, but I'm gettin' out of here. De La and his wife shoot at each other all the time. There's no law says she won't come back here and shoot at me." He was out the door, not even bothering to wait for his change.

"Ain't that a shame," Ruby said, pulling her chair back to the table where she resumed eating the French fries she'd abandoned in such a hurry. "That woman ought to be horsewhipped. She should stand by her husband. It's a scandal, her stealin' his defense money and threatenin' to shoot anyone who contributes."

Peggy replaced the napkin holder on the counter. She had no earthly idea what all the fuss about De La Beckwith was, and she didn't care. She could only sympathize with the woman in the tight riding pants. Watching Gene and Inez and living with Lloyd had taught her a thing or two about standing by men—and wanting to kill them. She ran her hand along her ribs. Under her uniform was a long black bruise.

"Peggy." George waved her over to the cash register. "Why don't you go home? It's been a long day, and there won't be many customers. And maybe no more excitement."

"I don't want to go home." Peggy focused on the floor.

"You need some rest. You look done in, girl. But if you don't want to rest, maybe you could go by the jail and see Lloyd."

"Thanks, George." She tried to smile but felt tears instead. Lloyd had been arrested for parole violation. He'd never even bothered to tell her he'd been arrested for robbery before he married her. Now he was in the county jail, and no telling when he would get out.

"Things will get better," George assured her, patting her shoulder. "Maybe this will teach Lloyd a lesson."

"Maybe." Peggy swallowed back her tears. "Can I take Lloyd a piece of that lemon pie? Annie said it'll be too old to serve tomorrow."

George waved his permission, his head shaking.

Peggy put the pie in a cardboard box and hurried out of the restaurant and toward the county courthouse where Lloyd was being held pending a review of his parole status. As best she understood, he hadn't reported to his parole officer in months and he'd been picked up for writing bad checks. Now he was in a mess of trouble. She practically trotted along the streets as she worried about how she was going to get Lloyd free.

To her surprise, she heard her name called out. When she looked up, she saw Lloyd coming down the steps of the courthouse.

The rush of joy was almost crippling, but she managed a squeal and ran toward him, throwing herself into his arms, the pie still clutched in the white cardboard box. "How'd you get out? What happened? I was comin' to bring you some pie!" The words rushed out as she clutched her arms around his solid waist.

"Let's go get a drink." Lloyd licked his bottom lip. "I've been in that hell hole three days, and I need somethin' cold and wet."

Peggy looked around as if she'd been blinded by the sun. "We don't have a car, and we need to go on over to Hilda's and get the baby."

"Let's go to the Grill. Mama Ruth will be glad to see you. You haven't been in there in a long time."

"Not since Peanut came. But we need to go get her, Lloyd. Hilda's waitin' on me because I said I'd be there right after I got off work."

"No need to worry about all that, Peggy." Lloyd took her arm and moved her off the steps and toward the Greenwood Grill.

"Lloyd!" The anger flashed through her. "What's wrong with you? Peanut's your daughter."

"Not anymore, she ain't." Lloyd's fingers dug into her arm. "Now quit sassin' me on the sidewalk or you'll be sorry." His blue eyes had gone hot. "I want a drink, and I don't want no trouble from you."

"What do you mean, Peanut's not your daughter any more?" Peggy felt her heart beating in her ears, and she was afraid she wouldn't be able to hear Lloyd when he answered her.

"I gave her up for adoption. The police went and picked her up while you were at work."

"You gave Teresa away?" Peggy felt her face pull into a knot. She didn't understand. "You gave her away? Just like that?"

"I had to get out of jail, and I couldn't really take care of her. She's got a good home, and that family really wanted her. They wanted that baby, Peggy." He hustled her down the street. "Now it's all done, so forget about it.

"Who's got her?" Peggy dug in her heels until she left black marks on the sidewalk as Lloyd dragged her along. "Damn you, Lloyd Morgan, who has that baby?" Peggy tried to jerk free, but his grip tightened until she almost dropped to her knees from the pain.

"T. R. Lott. He's got a good job as a city policeman, and that's the best I could do for Peanut. Now shut up your whining, Peggy, or I'll take you behind that drugstore there and whip your ass."

Lloyd released her suddenly, and Peggy felt the hard cement of the walk bite into her knees. When he hauled her to her feet, she didn't resist.

"Anyway, Peanut was my baby, and I could do what I wanted with her. Now she's gone and there's nothing you can do about it so you might as well get over it." He kept a grip on her hand and pulled her along behind him as he walked toward Greenwood Grill.

Peggy followed without resistance, wiping the tears from her eyes with her free hand.

IN JANUARY 1966, Peggy learned that she was pregnant. More determined than ever to make her marriage work, Peggy cooked and cleaned like a wild woman. If she could only make herself indispensable to Lloyd, eventually he would have to understand that he loved her.

On August 3, 1966, their first child, Nelton Lloyd Morgan, Jr., nicknamed Butch, was born. While Peggy was giving birth, Lloyd disappeared without a trace. Six weeks later, penniless, Peggy moved in with her brother, Boyd, and started her daily searches for Lloyd. Her obsession with finding him drove her from bar to bar. There were rumors that he'd gone to Louisiana to work offshore or up to Chicago. At times it seemed she was only minutes behind him—he'd been seen in the Greenwood Grill or out at Chuck's. But whenever she arrived, he was gone. Unable to eat or think of anything except Lloyd, she barely managed day to day.

In the circle of her friends and family, there was no one who knew how to help Peggy. Her sisters and girlfriends had gone through marital difficulties. Some had divorced, some had endured. None could understand Peggy's inability to accept that Lloyd had abandoned her. They urged her to get mad at him, but Peggy only wanted him back. Not even the needs of her new baby could keep her away from the bars where she hunted for Lloyd. With each week, her health deteriorated and her friends worried that she had truly stepped over the line of sanity.

Finally, her weight down below seventy pounds, Peggy seemed to accept the fact that Lloyd was out of her life. Under the urging of her friends, she began to focus on trying to regain her life and take care of her baby boy.

Chapter Twenty-Nine

The lamp gave the bedroom in Mary Jean's house a soft, melon-colored glow. Evening had settled over the small house on Market Street, and though it was in the town limits, outside the open windows crickets chirred in a chorus that had lulled Butch to sleep. Peggy checked the light blue blanket that covered her son and stalled for a moment. She was better. Lloyd had been gone for over six weeks without a thank you or a kiss my ass. Her friend, Patricia Ann, better known as Trick, had finally convinced her that it was time to jump back into life. Mary Jean had consented to keep Butch for a few hours.

"Come on, Peggy. You got to live. You gotta start a life again. That baby needs a daddy, and we're gonna go out and find one." The slender young woman tossed her dark hair and pulled a compact and lipstick out of her purse. The red color seemed made for her full lips. When she finished, she planted her hands on her slim hips and gave Peggy an impatient look.

"I don't know, Trick." Peggy sat on the side of the bed. Her hand moved instinctively to touch Butch, to feel the wonderful texture of his perfect baby skin delicately flushed in the hot September evening.

There was the sound of footsteps on the wooden floor of the hallway, and Mary Jean appeared in the open doorway. "Go out for a while, Peggy. I'll watch Butch. Trick is right, you need to get out." She eyed her sister critically. "Lloyd Morgan is the worst kind of scum, abandoning his wife and him knowing you were 'bout to burst wide open with his baby. He's gone and good riddance. The best thing for you would be to go out and have a little fun. Maybe Trick can get you to eat something. You look like a stick."

Peggy looked across the room and caught her own reflection in the dresser mirror. She was only nineteen, but she looked so much older. The weeks without Lloyd had aged her. After the birth of Butch, she'd been unable to think of anything except finding Lloyd, of showing him his son, of making him want his wife and baby. The obsession had driven her to near madness.

That and worry about Inez. Peggy's mother was no longer strong enough to pull the cotton sack down the rows, so she "picked the ends of the rows," working in short hauls, resting in between. In an effort to get a job, she'd enrolled in a handicapped training program to learn to make pallets. The prospect of Inez getting job training particularly inflamed Gene. To prevent her from going to the training center, he often beat her to the point that she was physically unable to leave the house.

Anxiety overwhelmed Peggy. "I don't think I'm up to goin' out yet, Trick."

Trick walked across the room and knelt beside Peggy, taking her hands. "We'll go over to Tominello's and listen to some music," she wheedled. "What harm could it do, Peggy? If you don't go, you'll just sit here and worry. There's not a thing you can do this evening."

"I have to figure a way out of this." Peggy picked up a brush and ran it through her thick hair. Though Sheila had gotten the curls, she had enough hair for three people, thick and strawberry blond.

Mary Jean shook her head in disgust. "You can't fix a thing tonight, Peggy. When you do see Lloyd Morgan again, the best idea would be to shoot him." She sighed. "I'll keep the baby if you decide to go," she said, abandoning the doorway and her sister's hard-headedness.

"Come on, Peggy. I want you to go with me," Trick said, giving one last try.

"What for? Every man in town is crazy about you." Peggy didn't resent Trick her popularity. She was beautiful and she knew how to flirt. She'd tried to teach Peggy a few winsome ways, but Peggy had been too timid to even try. Her only talent, as far as she could see, was dancing.

"We won't stay long." Trick held up the keys to her car. "I'll bring you home whenever you say."

Peggy got up and went to check on Butch. He was a good baby and generally slept through the night. "Okay," she said. Trick and Mary Jean were right. She was going to have to pick up the pieces of her life and get on with it. Lloyd was gone. Even if he was in Greenwood, he didn't want to see his wife and the child he was now saying wasn't his. She might as well accept the fact. Her marriage was over.

Tominello's had a good juke box, and though she still hadn't acquired a taste for liquor, she could sip on a Seven Up and watch Trick turn the men inside out.

Trick pulled a cool summer dress from the closet. "Put this on," she said. "You've got to start takin' an interest in how you look, Peggy. Come on, I'll help with your make-up."

In fifteen minutes Peggy was dressed and made up. A touch of mascara and some lipstick had done a lot to brighten her face and her outlook. She got in the car with Trick with a tiny niggle of anticipation. This was the first public step in putting Lloyd behind her. They'd be sure to run into some of his friends at Tominello's, and it would be clear that she was done with chasing after him or sitting around and hoping he'd come home. She let the breeze coming through the car window blow away her hesitation as Trick drove through town.

The parking lot was crowded. Trick parked and got out, waiting for Peggy.

She lingered in the car, suddenly indecisive. "We'll leave when I say?"

"As soon as you say. The very minute you say so." Trick took her elbow and steered her through the door and into loud music and a haze of cigarette smoke.

"It's that good-looking Trick and, why, it's Peggy Morgan." The man who spoke did a little pretend bow at Trick. "Come sit by me, baby," he added.

Trick ignored him, shifting through the crowd to a table in the back. "We need a place we can sit down and be left alone," she called over her shoulder to Peggy. "We'll get our own table and when we're tired of a man, we can send him packin'." Trick winked at a guy at the bar and waved across the dance floor to another man who was holding a girl tight. At the sight of Trick, he loosened his grip.

"All you have to do is crook your little finger and they follow you like dogs after a hunk of beef," Peggy said. She admired Trick's easy flirtation.

"Men are easy to manage, Peggy. Your trouble is you don't want to manage 'em, you want to love 'em."

"Right." The word was bitter, but Peggy followed it with a laugh. "Not any more, though. I'm going to learn how to make them dance to my tune."

"That's the spirit." Trick turned to accept a kiss from a tall, handsome man who came over to the table. He aimed for her lips, but she gave him her cheek. "Good to see you, Tommy," she said, waving at another man who sat at the bar.

Drinks arrived at the table, and Trick blew a kiss to the man at the bar who acknowledged with a grin that he'd sent them.

"This is the life," Trick said.

"Sure." Peggy sipped at the small Country Club malt liquor that had been sent to her. It wasn't awful, but she'd rather have had a soft drink.

A voice boomed over the juke box and the laughter of the crowd. "Trick! Where you been, girl?"

Trick looked up at Rayford Steed winding through the crowded tables. "My, my," she said, smiling big. She leaned close to Peggy. "Rayford's been sweet on me for a while. Here he comes."

To Peggy, everything was moving too fast. Ever since they'd walked in the door, it was like a beehive had come to life. Everyone was running around, drinks in hand and music blaring, and Trick was the queen bee. The hive swarmed around her.

255

"Rayford!" Trick waved him over. "Get ready, Peggy, he's brought someone with him."

A wave of shyness forced Peggy's head down. She looked into her drink and finally managed to lift it and take the tiniest sip. She didn't want to meet another man, but she wasn't going to sit home with a broken heart. Lloyd had abandoned her. She swallowed the beer and put a smile on her face.

"Sh—!" The word exploded from Trick's mouth.

Peggy looked up. Behind Rayford Steed was Lloyd. His eyes were focused fully on her, and he had the dangerous, sad, Elvis look in his eyes. He brushed past Rayford and came to the table.

"Lloyd Morgan, you just stay away from here." Trick pushed back her chair and stood. She was bigger than Peggy but no match for Lloyd. "You've gone off and left Peggy and a new baby, and she has a right to go out and have some fun."

Lloyd shifted his weight from one foot to another. "Get me a drink," he said to Rayford.

"Sure." Rayford was more than glad to escape the sudden potential for violence between Peggy and Lloyd.

Peggy sought the easy words, the kiss-off gesture that had once come so easily to her. She wanted to lash him with her casual disregard. Instead, she spoke with hurt and anger. "Where've you been?" She pushed her drink to the center of the table. "I hunted all over the place for you."

"Takin' care of business." Lloyd's voice was as easy, as casual, as if he'd planned to meet Peggy at Tominello's after a regular eight-hour-shift at a job.

"Aren't you even gonna ask about your son? You've never even seen him."

"How is he?" Lloyd asked agreeably. "What's his name?"

"He's fine, no thanks to you. His name is Butch." Peggy held onto her chair. Hurt had been replaced by anger. The desire to fly up into Lloyd's face was almost irresistible. She wanted to bite him, to gouge out his eyes.

"Take me to see my son," Lloyd said.

"You don't have a right to see him," Trick broke in. "You run off and left Peggy without anything to eat and no way to pay the doctor bill. You've been sayin' he isn't yours."

"I've been over in Thibbadeaux working with Daddy. I had to make some money."

"You could have let me know." Peggy tried not to look into his eyes, but she couldn't stop herself. "All you had to do was let me know."

"Wasn't time." Lloyd took the drink that Rayford brought him.

"Let's all sit down and have a drink," Rayford suggested, pulling out the chair beside Trick. "How're you doin'? You're lookin' as pretty as ever."

"I'd be doin' better if you bought me a drink," Trick said easily. Rayford was gone like a shot, back to the bar.

"Take me to see the baby, Peggy," Lloyd said. "I want to see my son." He touched her shoulder. "No woman ever gave me a son before. Does he look like me?"

"A little," Peggy answered grudgingly. She looked at Trick, who shook her head. "Trick don't want to go."

Lloyd looked up at Rayford as he handed Trick a fresh drink. "Trick can stay with Rayford. You and me'll run over there and come right back."

"I'm not goin' anywhere without Trick." Peggy knew leaving with Lloyd would not be smart. He might seem fine, but at the drop of a hat he might decide to beat her senseless.

Lloyd lifted his chin at Rayford, who slipped a hand on Trick's arm. Lloyd spoke to Trick. "Let's go see the baby, and then we'll all go get somethin' to eat."

"Plenty of food right here," Trick said, picking up her cocktail. "No need to go anywhere Peggy doesn't want to go."

"Peggy, I got to see my son." Lloyd leaned so close to Peggy his lips almost moved against her cheek. "Please, don't deny me seein' my own son."

Glancing at Trick, Peggy knew she couldn't withhold the baby from his father. Lloyd might be a sneak for running off and leaving her and Butch, but he was her husband and the baby's father. "You can look at him, but that's it. I been talking to Mary Jean, and she's gonna help me get a divorce. No need in stayin' married to a man who can't take care of his wife and baby." She stood up. "If you want to see him, let's go, but we're comin' right back here, and I'm gonna see about being single."

"I just want to see my son." Lloyd put his hand on her waist and escorted her through the crowd toward the door.

"Looks like Peggy found her old man," a woman cat-called from the darkness of the bar. "I'm surprised she didn't get the blood-hounds from up at Parchman after you, Lloyd. She's been huntin' around town like a lovesick puppy."

Laughter erupted across the bar.

"Lloyd, you must have somethin' that little girl wants," the woman continued. "Maybe I should try some of it."

There was more laughter and Peggy stopped. She turned, trying to pinpoint who was talking, but the far reaches of the bar were too dark to see into. It sounded a lot like Big Linda, a woman Lloyd was known to fancy.

"Come on, Peggy, let's go see my son," Lloyd said, urging her along. "They're only teasin' you, just tryin' to start trouble because they know how much I love you."

Peggy couldn't distinguish the faces in the darkness of the bar. She put her hand on Lloyd's arm and called back. "Yeah, well you see who's walking out with him, don't you?"

"I don't know that I'd brag about that," Trick said softly as she brushed Lloyd's hand off Peggy and maneuvered her friend out the door and into the night. "Are you sure you want to do this?" she whispered. "This may not be a good idea."

"He needs to see his son."

"Quit whispering and let's go see my baby boy," Lloyd said, stepping between the women.

Peggy got into the back seat of the car with Trick. "Go over to Mary Jean's, and then we're comin' straight back here," she directed Lloyd. "If the house is dark, we can't go in. We're not gonna wake up the entire household. She's been good to help me, since me and Butch didn't have a place to call home." There were a lot of bones she had to pick with Lloyd. Lots of hurt.

Mary Jean's house was dark, but Peggy relented. Trick and Rayford remained in the car as Peggy led Lloyd into the house and back to the bedroom where Butch slept. Bolstered by pillows to keep him from rolling, he made small sucking noises in his sleep.

"Well, ain't he the little man?" Lloyd traced a finger through the baby's fine hair. "He looks like me, don't you think?"

"Maybe a little." Peggy wasn't ready to see too much of the Morgans in her son. "I think he looks more like Sammy."

"He's a big baby." Pride filled Lloyd's voice. "Yes, sir, he's a fine son."

"He is." The tenderness caught Peggy by surprise. For weeks she'd hunted Lloyd, and she thought it was only for herself. Now she realized that the search had been for Butch, too. Lloyd was his daddy.

"Well, he's gonna be one good-lookin' man." Lloyd stood up. "Let's go have a drink."

"I don't think so." Peggy looked at the sleeping baby. "I better stay here with Butch. You go on with Rayford and take Trick back to Tominello's."

"Come on, Peggy. We'll drive over to Indianola and find a place to dance."

Peggy shook her head.

"Come on." He reached over and grabbed her hand, drawing her to him. "I missed you. Let's go out and have some fun. We can talk about things, get some things straight so I can come home. We're married, and I miss my wife, my home."

"There's no home to come to," Peggy pointed out. "We had to move in with Boyd 'cause you abandoned us."

"I been workin', Peggy. I did go off, but I had to find a way to make some cash. I got some. I been over in Thibbadeaux working with my old man and I made some good money." He patted his pocket. "We can get our own place. Me, you, and my son."

Peggy looked at Butch. He was sound asleep, and Mary Jean was in the next room. She hadn't been out in months and months. Maybe Lloyd deserved a chance to tell where he'd been and what he'd been doing.

"There's a nice place we can eat over in Indianola. Trick and Rayford can go." Lloyd touched her chin with his finger, gently lifting her face up so that she had to look at him. "Just give me a chance, Peggy."

"You've had more than one chance, Lloyd. You ran off on me and Butch. You gave Peanut away. You . . ."

"But I always meant to come back to you, Peggy. I was always comin' back. You know that, don't you?" His fingers teased the line of her jaw. "I made us some money. Mama kept an ear out for you. I knew you were doin' okay or I would have come right back. Wasn't it better for me to work and save up some cash so we could have us a real place. A home with good furniture and stuff. We can have all that, Peggy. All you have to do is say yes."

"I don't know." Peggy couldn't look at him. More than anything in the world she wanted Lloyd to love her and his son, his baby boy. "You want to hold him?"

"Say you'll go with me. Just to Indianola."

"Only to Indianola, and then right back here."

"Let's get a move on it, then." He directed her out of the room with a firm grip on her arm. Once they were out the front door, he hustled her across the yard to the car.

"We're goin' over to Indianola to get somethin' to eat," Lloyd announced. "Rayford, let Peggy in the front."

"No!" Peggy got in the back seat with Trick. As soon as she walked out the door and left Butch behind, she had second thoughts about going off with Lloyd. He hadn't even bothered to look at the baby before he left.

Lloyd settled in behind the wheel. Leaning across the front seat, he opened the glove compartment and pulled out a bottle of whiskey. He took a swallow and handed it to Rayford, who also turned it up.

"You girls want some?" he offered it over the back seat to Trick.

She wrinkled her nose. "Not out of the bottle. I thought we were goin' to get a drink and supper."

"We are," Lloyd assured her. He took the bottle back and drank while he eased the car out of Mary Jean's yard and toward the western edge of town.

They broke the city limits with the radio going and the bottle passing back and forth in the front seat. Miles of Highway 82 stretched ahead of them and to either side were the flat cotton fields, almost ready for harvest.

"Look! Look up there on the side of the road." Rayford pointed out the windshield and Peggy and Trick leaned forward to see. A man was standing on the side of the road, thumb out for a ride.

"Let's get him," Lloyd said, whipping the car over to the shoulder. He came to a sliding halt in front of the hitchhiker. "Come on," Lloyd called out through the driver's window.

The man hurried to the car, hesitating when he saw the women in the back.

"Get in front," Trick said.

Rayford obligingly got out and let the man in the middle of the front seat.

"Where you headed?" Lloyd asked.

"West. To Louisiana."

"That's where we're goin', too," Lloyd said, pressing the gas pedal hard and handing the liquor to the hitchhiker. "Have a drink."

The man tipped the bottle up and took a healthy swallow. He passed it over to Rayford, who took another drink.

"Where you goin' in Louisiana?" the hitchhiker asked.

"Thibbadeaux. We got to go get my daddy. He's waitin' for me to come get him."

Peggy looked at Trick and saw the surprise and growing worry in her eyes. She leaned up to the front seat and spoke to Lloyd. "You said we were goin' to Indianola."

"I lied," Lloyd said, laughing. "We got to go get Daddy."

"I can't go to Louisiana, Lloyd. I got a baby."

"Mary Jean'll take care of him. It won't hurt."

"Lloyd, you turn this car around and take me and Trick back to Greenwood."

In reply, Lloyd let the car play across both lanes of the highway, forcing the on-coming traffic to dodge and weave. "We're goin' west, Peggy."

"I want to go home." Peggy felt the panic building. Trick's hand settled on her leg, restraining. She shook it off. "Take me home, Lloyd. I mean it."

"What you gonna do?" he taunted, lifting the bottle to his lips.

Reaching into her purse, Peggy found a rat-tail comb. It was aluminum and very sharp. Moving swiftly, she pushed the pointed tip into Rayford's neck. "Stop this car and let me and Trick out!"

"Lloyd!" Rayford had gone from amusement to fear. "Lloyd, she's got a knife at my throat."

His foot still on the gas, Lloyd swung around to investigate. "Peggy!" He swatted at her with one hand while still driving. The car swerved from lane to lane.

"Lloyd!" Trick screamed. "Stop the damn car!"

Slamming on the brakes, Lloyd brought the car to a gravel-slinging stop on the side of the road. "What the hell do you think you're doin'?" He turned to the back seat, pulling the comb from Peggy's hand. "A damn comb!" He tossed it at Rayford. "It's a comb."

"She was pokin' it in my neck, and it felt like a knife." Rayford was rubbing his neck. In the middle of the seat, the hitchhiker sat perfectly still.

Lloyd opened his door and got out. Reaching into the back seat, he pulled Peggy out by her wrist. "We got somethin' to straighten out," he said, dragging her around the car to the back. "Now you listen and you listen good, you're my wife and you'll do what I say. If I say we're going to Thibbadeaux, that's where we're goin', and if I get any more lip out of you, there's goin' to be trouble."

"You ran off and left me and Butch. I'm filing for divorce. Now you take me back to Greenwood." Peggy couldn't stop the anger.

"I gave you a warnin'." Lloyd stepped closer. "You want to get in that car and shut up like a wife?"

"I'm goin' home." Peggy walked away. She'd get back to Greenwood if she had to hoof it every step. She'd walked farther.

Lloyd's fingers clamped on the back of her neck. She felt herself jerked backward. Lloyd flung her against the trunk of the car, knocking the breath from her. Before she could react, he was on top of her, his hand up her dress and tugging at her panties.

"You're my wife. You're gonna do what I say."

"Get off me, you sorry bastard." Peggy got one hand free and raked it down his cheek. "Get off me, Lloyd. We're on a public road."

Lloyd retaliated by pressing his forearm on her throat, pinning her against the car. His other hand pulled her panties down. He began working at his belt buckle with his free hand.

"You're my wife," he said, his alcohol-laced breath hot and mean. "You'll learn one day that a man has a right, and he don't have to ask permission."

It felt like Lloyd was choking her, and Peggy fought the panic. He was going to rape her right on the side of the road if she didn't stop him. "You let me go, Lloyd Morgan, or I'll kill you." She could barely get a breath with his arm on her throat, but she bucked and fought.

"You're my wife and you'll do what I say, when I say it and how I say it." He pressed up between her legs.

Peggy bit back the cry of pain, fear, and outrage. Traffic whipped by, but no one stopped to help her. Inside the car was complete silence. Peggy slapped the back windshield, knowing even as she did that no one could help her. Lloyd was so much stronger, there was nothing she could do to stop him. She closed her eyes and tried not to scream. Even if Trick tried to help her, Lloyd would only hurt her, too.

When he was finished, Lloyd stepped back and pulled up his pants. "Now maybe you'll know to do what your husband tells you."

Peggy slid down the trunk, stooping to pick her panties out of the dirt. Stepping around the side of the car, she put them on. There was no way she could get back in the car and face Trick and Rayford.

Lloyd's grip caught her arm. "Get back in the car and shut up. We're goin' to Thibbadeaux to get Daddy, and I don't want to hear no more about it."

Peggy crawled into the back seat. Her body burned from the assault and she could taste the salt of her tears.

"You okay?" Trick whispered. Her voice was hoarse. "Peggy, you okay?"

"She's fine," Lloyd answered. "She just needs to remember that she has a husband. When she forgets, I'll just have to remind her again." Lloyd put the car in drive and tore out, pushing beyond the speed limit. "Hand me that bottle," he said to Rayford.

Peggy glared at the back of his head. In a quick hot change of emotions, shame had turned to anger. Lloyd Morgan had no right to humiliate her in such a fashion. He wasn't going to get away with it. She had to get back to her baby. She had to get away from Lloyd.

Trick lit a cigarette. "Maybe you should take a drink," she suggested.

Peggy shook her head, unable to answer. The only thing she wanted was to get back to Mary Jean's and to curl up in a tiny ball, Butch tucked snugly against her. She had to get away from Lloyd. She watched as Trick drew on the cigarette, the ash glowing orange in the dark of the car.

Peggy picked up Trick's cigarette lighter from the car seat. She held it in her hand, waiting as the men passed the near-empty bottle.

When Lloyd's attention was half on the bottle and half on the road, she flipped open the lighter and struck the flint. It took only a moment, holding the flame to the top of the car, to get the fire started in the head-liner.

"Holy shit, the car's on fire!" Rayford cried out. "Pull over! Pull over!"

Lloyd pulled to the side of the road, catching Peggy as she tried to make a break out of the back seat. Lloyd held her at his side while Rayford got Trick out of the back and then put out the small fire.

"Lookit him go!" Trick said, pointing to the edge of the cotton field where the hitchhiker was jumping rows and running as hard as he could in the opposite direction. "I guess he didn't like your company."

The blaze was out and Rayford moved to Trick's side. "I guess he didn't want a ride after all."

"Back in the car." Lloyd twisted Peggy's arm until her fingers released the cigarette lighter into the dirt. "You want to smoke, I'll light your cigarette for you," he said. "Now back in." He pushed her to the back seat. "We're goin' to Thibbadeaux, and that's the end of it."

They started down the road again. The lights of Indianola were visible in the distance, and at the edge of town Lloyd pulled into a gas station. A highway patrolman was sitting in his parked car. Lloyd gave him a look but drove slowly on to the pump. "Put in two dollars," he said to Rayford. "I got to take a leak. Don't let them out of the car. Watch 'em."

"Okay." Rayford rolled down his window and signaled the attendant over. "Two dollars," he said.

The attendant caught sight of Trick and hesitated. Even in the back seat, she was hard to miss.

Peggy drew his attention, motioning to the highway patrolman, making it clear that the women in the back seat needed help. The young man pumped the gas, took the money from Rayford, and disappeared into the service station.

Peggy gripped the vinyl seat, unable to do anything else to stop Lloyd from taking her and Trick.

"Rayford, I need to get back to Greenwood," Trick tried.

Rayford shook his head. "I ain't in charge of Lloyd, and here he comes."

Lloyd sauntered over to the car, refusing to allow Peggy or Trick to get out and go to the ladies room. "We'll stop some place where there isn't a cop," Lloyd said, starting the engine and heading out.

Peggy took a last look out the window. The patrolman was still sitting in his car, perched on the edge of the highway, waiting. As she watched, the lights of the service station grew smaller and smaller in the rear window. She'd given up hope that the attendant had decided to help her when she saw the red flashing light coming through the night atop a pair of headlights.

"Son of a bitch," Lloyd cursed. "This old heap won't outrun a cop." Still cursing, he pulled over and waited.

The officer walked up to the car, his hand on the big gun on his belt. "Get out of the car," he said, his voice hard.

"I got a license," Lloyd answered, reaching down to the seat.

The officer pulled his gun and leveled it at Lloyd's head. "I said get out of the car, and do it slowly."

Faced with the gun, Lloyd got out. The officer frisked him and left him standing, legs and arms spraddled against the car, while he got Rayford out and did the same search. Finally he looked into the back seat. "You two ladies get out." He motioned them away from the car. "Are you in trouble?"

"Yes, sir," Peggy answered. "We want to go home to Greenwood, and they were takin' us to Thibbadeaux, Louisiana."

"You know these men?" The patrolman kept his gun on Lloyd.

"Yes, sir, that one's my husband, but I don't want to go with him. He was kidnapping me, forcing me to leave my baby."

"You're married?" The officer lowered the gun slightly.

"We are, but he run off and left me and the baby. I'm filing for divorce, and he tried to kidnap me."

"Well, if you're married . . ." He looked at Lloyd.

"I'm tellin' you he was kidnapping us." Peggy's voice rose.

The cop shook his head. "I can arrest him for DWI, and I'll give you a ride back to Greenwood, but that's all I can do. No such thing as kidnapping for a married couple."

"A ride home is all we need," Peggy said, drawing Trick toward the patrol car. "You just get us back to Greenwood, and we can handle the rest."

Chapter Thirty

In the weeks following Lloyd's attempted abduction of Peggy and Trick, Lloyd did not return to Greenwood, at least not in any permanent way. He managed to get out of jail on the DWI charge and became an irregular presence in all of the old hang-outs where he and Peggy had once danced and laughed. Artie Belle made room for her Baby Lloyd when he couldn't find other lodging.

Though Peggy tried to avoid him, word of him floated back to her on the Mississippi breeze, teasing and tormenting her with rumors and images of him with another woman, teeth flashing and lean bodies swiveling as they danced and drank in some joint that had once been special to Peggy and Lloyd.

Living with her brother, Boyd, Peggy felt that she and Butch were a burden in a household that was struggling, even without the dead weight of her presence. Yet she had no money, no job skills to speak of, no means of support for an infant. There was no possibility of going home. Gene would not allow it, even if Peggy had been inclined to try. Prior to abandoning his family, Lloyd had broken Gene's arm in a drunken brawl. Gene had begged for it, slapping Inez around until Peggy flew at him, trying to stop him. Lloyd had stepped in and put an end to the scene. Gene didn't see it that way, and now his attitude was that Peggy had made her bed and she could lie in it.

As the late summer and early fall passed, day-to-day survival became harder to endure. Trapped, Peggy clung to the fragile illusion of a life where Lloyd, through some miraculous event, became the father and husband she had dreamed he would be. Somehow, she had to get him back so that miracle could occur. When she heard that he had taken up permanent residence with another woman, it was more than she could bear. She went after him, threatening the woman with physical harm. Lloyd came home, and the small family was reunited.

Lloyd promised to change, to slow his drinking and to find steady work. Peggy vowed to be the wife he wanted—perfect in the kitchen and with the baby, a tiger in the bedroom, and always ready to dance. The terms of the marriage were redrawn. They found another apartment and began again. This time they would make a home.

Casting aside the last shred of her rational will, Peggy stepped over the line into make-believe. If she pretended hard enough, it would be real. She had given herself to Lloyd, body and soul, and she had to make it work. Whatever happened, she had to make it work.

Lloyd's promises lasted barely longer than the time it took to utter them. The marriage limped along, with Peggy picking up waitress work whenever she could to have money to buy food and medicine for Butch. Always with the promise of going after the perfect job, Lloyd would take off for Chicago or West Virginia or Louisiana, leaving Peggy to fend for herself. During the lean times, Trick provided support and friendship, and Mama Ruth at the Greenwood Grill would often cook up a hamburger steak and mashed potatoes for Peggy and Butch, sliding the plate across the counter to the penniless girl.

Mama Ruth and Trick both encouraged Peggy to leave Lloyd. Peggy's sisters, who had married with varying degrees of success, also pushed for Peggy to sever her ties to all Morgans other than Butch. The harder they argued with her, the worse things got, the more Peggy clung to Lloyd. When he was home he cruised the bars and juke joints until dawn. If Peggy wanted to make certain that he came home, she had to go with him, sticking to his side like a burr.

He would sometimes leave her standing at the stove cooking supper to run and get cigarettes. Three days later, he would still be gone. To prevent his absences, Peggy had to follow wherever he went. Degree by degree, she tossed aside all autonomy. No longer a whole person, she became a shadow in Lloyd's world.

Lloyd took a job in Chicago. Although the Delta winters could get cold, Peggy had never experienced the brutality of weather like the bitter wind sweeping over Lake Michigan. Against her better judgment she had consented to go with Lloyd on another job hunt. With an infant less than a year old, Peggy found herself stranded one night on the side of a road with a broken-down car. The snow banks on either side were taller than her head. She was lucky and caught a ride before she and Butch froze. To her relief, Lloyd decided to head back to Greenwood.

In the spring of 1968, another brush with the law sent Lloyd packing for California, this time the Los Angeles area. Once again, Lloyd filled Peggy's head with the promise of a good job with good money, a fine life with a small bungalow house, the adventures of Hollywood just around the corner. As much as Peggy hated to leave Inez, she packed without complaint and headed west with Lloyd.

The assassination of Robert Kennedy brought law enforcement in the Golden Bear State out in such force that Lloyd decided he was less likely to be apprehended for some of his illegal maneuvering in Greenwood. As poor as they'd been when they left, they returned to the Delta.

Peggy discovered she was pregnant once again.

THE PORK CHOPS popped and sizzled in the cast iron skillet, and Peggy watched them carefully. She was holding up her end of the bargain, even if Lloyd was dragging a little on his end. He had moved them into a shotgun rental on the old McShane Plantation near Minter City some twenty miles from Greenwood. The house was as neat as she could make it with them living in one room with the baby and her pregnant. Hindered by her stomach, she used the broom to snare Butch's little clothes. She'd catch them on the end of the handle and lift them up. Even as big as she was, she cooked the pork chops for Lloyd's supper with a smile on her face. He'd given her some money for food, and he seemed to be working more. Or at least more regularly. Part of the agreement for living on the plantation was that he would work there, but Lloyd wanted more skilled labor. He knew about machinery and equipment, and he didn't much care for farming. Peggy liked the rhythm of the farm life. Even as big as she was, she still went out and worked in the cotton fields. What she didn't like was the fact that when Lloyd took the car, she was stranded seven miles from nowhere and without a phone. Still, it seemed that her husband had finally settled down. The prospect of another mouth to feed had made him grow up.

Lloyd left the house in the mornings and came home for supper. That's what Peggy knew about his work, and that was enough. With her stomach growing bigger by the day, she was determined to make Lloyd stay with her through the delivery of this baby. She'd been to the ob-gyn doctor in Greenwood and told him of her desire to deliver at home with a midwife. She'd selected Irene Lindsey from nearby Itta Bena to deliver the baby, and Irene was ready and waiting. The due date was less than six weeks away, March 15, and Peggy wanted it all to go perfectly.

By having the baby on the plantation with Irene assisting, she would show Lloyd what a woman suffered for her man. She would also follow in her mama's footsteps. Inez had delivered several children with the help of a midwife. Peggy's favorite story, though, was of her own birth, born in a cotton field and straight into her mother's and father's arms. Inez had always said what a special bond that had created between the two of them, and Peggy wanted this coming child to love her with the same intensity that she loved Inez. Based on the shape of Peggy's stomach, Irene had predicted that Peggy was carrying a girl.

In her mind, Peggy had replayed the scene a hundred times. She could see Lloyd's proud face as Irene handed him the crying baby.

Lloyd would bring the little girl up to Peggy and gently hand her over for her first milk. The baby would cement the bond between the four of them.

Butch's cry came from the living room/bedroom, and she took the perfectly browned pork chops out of the pan and went to check on the toddler. He was a tall boy with features that she hoped would grow to be as handsome as his father's. Lloyd had finally acknowledged that Butch was his son, and he had moments of pride in the child, but he didn't seem to love Butch the way she felt a father should. At the back of her mind was the dark memory of Lloyd's giving up his firstborn, Teresa Denise, for adoption. He'd never even blinked an eye. Of course Lloyd had never loved Teresa's mother the way he loved her. There had never been a family—he'd never really known the little girl he'd given away. Surely he could never do such a thing to Butch, or the child she carried now.

No, watching the birth process would make a difference in Lloyd, she was certain of it.

Chapter Thirty-One

Peggy sat in the chair beside the doctor's empty desk, waiting for him to return. The trip from Minter City into Greenwood in a car without springs had been more than uncomfortable. Anxiety had ridden shotgun beside her. The exam was over, and the expression on Dr. Meeks's face had affirmed her intuition. Something was wrong. Her gaze drifted over the certificates on the wall, absorbing none of the medical and legal jargon, sliding on to family photos and the smooth, empty expanse of the desk itself. The polished wood made her think of the china cabinet Inez had lost so long ago.

The door opened and Dr. Meek entered the room. He took his seat behind the desk and waited until she lifted her gaze to meet his.

"My strongest recommendation is that you check yourself into the hospital as soon as your labor begins," he said. "It isn't a good idea for you to have this baby at home."

"It's something I feel I have to do." Peggy's gaze fell. She was determined to deliver at home so Lloyd could be there. They wouldn't let him stay with her in the hospital, and he'd miss the entire thing. More than likely, he'd go off drinking and picking up women while she was giving birth to his child. The baby had to come at home. It had to.

"Mrs. Morgan, there's the possibility there was damage . . . when . . ."

"When Lloyd kicked me?" Peggy had not lied about what had happened to her.

"I think it would be foolish to risk having this child away from a hospital."

"Can you tell for certain something is wrong?" Cold fingers traced over her belly, making the skin draw and contract.

"Why take such a risk? At the hospital, we'll have every tool of modern medicine. At home, if you run into trouble, there might not be time to get you to the hospital." Dr. Meek looked beyond Peggy. "Your husband isn't reliable, Mrs. Morgan. If you count on him to get you to the hospital, it might be too late."

"Thank you, Doctor." Peggy stood up.

"Come back in a week," the doctor said. "That baby could come any time now, but we're still looking at the fifteenth."

Peggy clutched her purse tightly as she left his office and made her way to the front desk where she paid five dollars on her account. The doctor's words were tiny nails in her skin. They pricked and hurt as she walked outside into the promise of spring. It was the last day of February. March could still bring some cold spells, even snow, but for all practical purposes, the winter was over. And so was her pregnancy. The last few weeks had been hell. Lloyd was running wild, and she was too big and too pregnant to chase after him with the required energy. Soon, though, the baby would be born.

It was still early morning, and she had time to kill before Lloyd finished whatever he was doing and would be ready to go home. She would have to convince him to stop by Itta Bena to see Irene Lindsey. Peggy wanted to be sure the midwife was lined up, should the baby decide to come. Walking along the street, she window shopped and finally decided to check on Inez. She hated to go back home. If Inez was beaten black and blue, it would make her feel helpless. If her mother seemed better, unbeaten and more like her old self, it would make Peggy feel hope. She wasn't certain which was worse. Helpless or hopeful. Both were cruel sensations.

At 2012 Basket Street, Ronald was home from school. He said Inez had gone to pick cotton to earn extra money. Gene was working. A carpentry job. The store was locked tight, and Peggy checked through the house, finding only one bottle of whiskey. She poured it out in the backyard.

"Daddy's gonna kill you," Ronald said without emotion.

"He'd like to, but he won't." Peggy tossed the empty bottle into the trash.

"He'll just blame Mama and beat her for it."

Those words stopped Peggy cold. "Mama didn't have anything to do with this."

Ronald grinned. "That doesn't matter to Daddy."

Peggy noticed the blue mark high on Ronald's cheek. "What happened to your face?"

"I got into a fight at school." Ronald rolled his shoulders as if he were loosening up for another round with whomever had struck him.

"Don't be fightin'," Peggy said without any real conviction. She knew that in order to have any peace or respect from the other children, Ronald would have to fight. Just like she'd have to fight for Lloyd. It was the Albritton heritage.

"You look like you're about to pop," Ronald said.

"I feel like it." Peggy sat down in the rocker on the porch. "How is Mama, Ronald? Really."

He shook his head. "Some days she's okay, but some days she doesn't seem to know what's going on." He spit off the side of the porch. "Maybe she's getting a little worse. Daddy made her quit at the training center. He said she couldn't go back because it was for retarded people."

Peggy started to snap out a reply but stopped herself. Ronald was only repeating what Gene had said. "Mama is not . . . She's got epilepsy because Daddy beat her so much."

"She's been to Whitfield." Ronald had only heard the stories. He was too young to remember.

"Yeah, well Daddy had her sent there." Peggy stood up. She was getting too angry, and she was too big with child to accommodate a temper fit. "I got to be gettin' home. Get word to me if Mama starts gettin' worse, okay?"

Ronald looked at her with skepticism. "Sure, I'll just sprout a set of wings and fly to Minter City."

"Ronald . . ." Peggy tried to think of something to say that would mean something to her brother. "Mama loves you. Whatever else she does, she loves all of us children."

Ronald spit again. "Sure," he said, gazing down the road.

The weight of her sadness was more than the baby she carried, as Peggy started back toward Greenwood. Maybe she could stop in at the Greenwood Grill and see some of her friends. It had been a couple of months since she'd been out for a visit in Greenwood. She glanced at her watch. There was too much time to kill and her body was beginning to feel the weariness of the last days of pregnancy. Maybe Mama Ruth would let her lie down for a spell and rest her swollen feet.

Pushing into the cafe, Peggy was greeted by a blast of warm air and a cry of pleasant surprise. Mama Ruth came around the counter and hugged Peggy to her. "What a surprise! You're about to pop wide open, Peggy, girl."

"I am. The doctor said any time now, but probably not until March 15."

"It looks like twins," Mama Ruth teased. "Trick! Trick! Peggy's here."

Trick came out of the bathroom, adjusting the belt on her sleek dress. One look at Trick's perfect figure and flawless make-up, and Peggy groaned out loud. "I'm so sick of being pregnant," she said. Trick and Mama Ruth were the only sympathetic audience she was liable to get.

"Pretty soon the baby will be here and you'll be oohing and aahing and forgetting about how big you were and how much it hurt."

"I'm having this one at home," Peggy announced. The flicker of concern that passed between Mama Ruth and Trick pulled her up short. "What's wrong?"

"Not a thing," Trick answered. "You got a midwife?"

"Irene Lindsey."

"She's good," Mama Ruth said, nodding. "Lloyd gonna be there?"

"That's why I'm having the baby at home. Dr. Meek said I should go to the hospital, but they won't let Lloyd into the delivery room with me and I want him to see what a woman goes through. If he could only see it, maybe he'd understand better."

"I don't know . . ." Mama Ruth shook her head as she rose to her feet and got three cups of coffee and three slices of apple pie.

"Men don't care what women go through." Trick shrugged, not too bothered by that fact. "Have the baby at home if you want to, Peggy, but it won't make a difference to Lloyd. Lloyd's gonna do what he wants to do, and nothin' you do or say will change him."

"Once the baby is here I'll be able to stay with him better." Peggy picked up the fork. The pie looked delicious, but whenever she got anxious, she had trouble swallowing food. She'd tried to eat, for the baby. Now, though, her throat was closing.

"Eat that pie," Mama Ruth ordered.

Peggy took a bite, forcing it down in a swallow.

"What does Irene say about the baby?" Mama Ruth asked.

"She says she'll be there."

"I'd stop by and check on my way home today." Mama Ruth eyed Peggy's belly. "It won't be long now, and you don't want Irene goin' off to visit relatives or some fool thing like that."

"Okay." Peggy sipped her coffee. "I've missed talkin' to y'all. Living out on McShane's, it's hard to get into town like I used to."

"We miss you," Trick said, picking up Peggy's hand. "We're here for you if you need us, though. I'll come stay with you for the baby if you get me word."

"Thanks." Peggy grinned. "It's a little scary."

"You can do it," Trick assured her, squeezing Peggy's fingers hard. "You're the toughest little thing I ever saw. If you want to have this baby at home, you can do it."

"I'm gonna name her after you, Trick. Irene said it was goin' to be a girl, and if it is, I'll take part of your name."

Trick grinned. "I'd like that."

"You got all your baby things?" Mama Ruth asked.

For another two hours, the women discussed the baby and motherhood. The Greenwood Grill was more of a night spot than a lunch place, and the women had things to themselves until late in the afternoon, when Lloyd stopped by for Peggy.

"Take care of her," Mama Ruth warned, giving Lloyd the eye.

"I always do," Lloyd answered.

"She's gonna have that baby soon, Lloyd. You watch out for her. If it looks like there's any trouble, get her to the hospital," Trick said.

"I know how to take care of my own wife," Lloyd snapped back. He didn't much care for Trick or Mama Ruth interfering in his marriage.

"Bye." Peggy waved from the cab of the truck. "See you soon."

On the way home, Peggy convinced Lloyd to stop at Itta Bena to talk with the midwife one more time. Lloyd was not gracious, but he did find the neat shotgun house where Irene lived and waited in the truck while Peggy went inside.

Once out of the jouncing truck, Peggy realized that not all of the discomfort she felt was due to the ride.

Irene examined her patient and leaned back. "You gone have this baby tonight," she said slowly. "I'll have my things ready. When the water breaks, you send your man over here to get me."

Excitement tingled through Peggy. The baby would be coming, and very soon. "You really think it'll be tonight?"

"Tonight," Irene repeated firmly. "Have your man ready. When the water breaks, come for me right away. I'll be waitin'."

Peggy got dressed and hurried out to the truck. Lloyd sat with a fifth between his legs, the cap off and the bottle half empty. As Peggy got in the truck, he lifted it up and took a swallow.

"Irene says the baby's comin' tonight!" Peggy was flushed with happiness. "I can't wait."

"I can." Lloyd took another drink.

"You got to be there." Peggy had the first flash of true fear. "You can't go off and leave me tonight, Lloyd. What if I get in trouble and need help?"

Lloyd didn't say anything as he drove toward home.

Peggy gripped the door of the truck and forced herself not to press Lloyd. Even if he gave his word that he'd be there, it didn't mean anything, and if he saw how desperate she truly was, he'd make it a point not to be within ten miles of her. He hated desperation in any form.

They passed through the cotton fields and Peggy scouted the long rows for the tiny green tops of new cotton. It wouldn't be long. She was glad the baby was going to be a girl, and she was happy that the birth would be just on the budding lip of spring. Surely those were good omens for a little baby. She took deep breaths and kept her eyes out the window and away from Lloyd. She'd have to figure a way to keep him home. One that didn't cripple the truck, because he would have to go for Irene. She could do it; she just had to think of a plan.

Lloyd pulled into the front yard. He kept the engine running and turned to her. "Get out."

"Where are you goin'?" Peggy didn't budge.

"Down to the tool shed to work." His mouth hardened into a line, as if he found her responsible that he had a job he didn't much like.

"Ask Burshel Boatwright if he has any fish," Peggy requested. "If he does, tell him to bring them up here and I'll cook a mess of them for supper."

"Okay." Lloyd waved her out of the truck.

Peggy watched him drive toward the machine shed. Maybe he was going to work. Maybe he wasn't. She went in the house and began getting out the pails and brushes. She was going to give that house one good cleaning, from top to bottom, so the baby would arrive in a nice, sanitary place.

By late afternoon, the small house was spick-and-span. Peggy had felt the first rumblings of labor, and she had supper ready for Lloyd when he walked in. There was even a supply of liquor she'd gotten from Tommy Larry and hidden away. She'd give it to him to make sure he stayed on the plantation with her during the labor.

Lloyd ate the dinner, ignoring Peggy even when she gripped her stomach and suddenly sat down.

Peggy knew the baby was coming. With Butch, she'd been in labor thirty-six hours. She'd had no idea where her husband was. She had no intention of that happening again. No matter how much she wanted to go and lie down for a brief rest, she wouldn't. Lloyd would not get out of her sight.

They made it through the rest of the evening, and finally Lloyd was ready for bed. More than ready herself, Peggy laid down on her side and waited for sleep to release her from the low-grade pain and anxiety. She'd made it through another day. Pretty soon she'd have her baby at her side.

Peggy and Lloyd were both asleep when Peggy's water broke at just after one o'clock. Lloyd came out of a deep sleep swinging his arms and cursing.

"Quit pissin' on me!" he yelled at Peggy as he struggled out of the bed.

"Lloyd, it's my water." Peggy knew the process had begun in earnest. If she was going to the hospital, now was the time.

"Damn you!" Lloyd put his hand in the wet bed. "You've got the whole bed wet."

"My water's broken." Peggy tried to keep the excitement out of her voice. Lloyd wasn't good awake yet. "I think you need to go get Irene."

"I need some dry clothes." He stumbled around the room, knocking things over and pulling clothes down. "You got everything wet," he complained.

"Lloyd," Peggy was gripped by the first hard contraction. It took her breath away. "Lloyd, you've got to get Irene." She'd made her decision, but it didn't mean she wasn't afraid. If the midwife came, she'd feel much better.

"I can't go anywhere. There's no gas in the truck."

Peggy felt the panic hit along with another contraction. Lloyd had known he might have to go for the midwife. "Get Burshel or Harrison or some of the other men to take you. You've got to get Irene."

"You don't need no midwife. You've already had one baby. You know how it's supposed to go."

"I know how it's supposed to go. The midwife is to make sure it goes that way." Peggy thought of Inez. She'd delivered healthy babies with no professional help. She tried to calm herself with that thought. Inez was not even as big as Peggy, and she'd done all right. She took deep breaths and tried to relax.

"Let me see if I can find one of the boys." Lloyd's tone had taken on a grudging willingness. "I'll be back."

"You remember where Irene lives?" Peggy wanted to hold Lloyd in the house. If he got off with the men, there was no telling when he'd come back—or if he'd come back. He might forget about her and the baby.

"I remember where she lives," he snapped.

"Lloyd, you won't go off and leave me?" Peggy had not planned on being by herself. "You'll come right on back with Irene, won't you?"

"I'll be back." He slammed out the door without a backward glance.

Peggy took a seat in a chair and braced for the next contraction. The clock beside the bed ticked the minutes away as the contractions grew closer and closer together.

Peggy knew the ritual of birth, and the mucus plug was no surprise. The contractions came harder and faster, and she weathered them and paced the kitchen, constantly on the lookout for truck lights. An hour passed, then another.

There seemed no position she could find that would give her body comfort. Her back ached and throbbed, and when the contractions came, the force was enough to make her want to scream. Instead, she gritted her teeth and held on, waiting for Lloyd and the midwife. Surely they would be there soon.

When the contractions were only a minute apart, Peggy took to the bed and prepared to deliver the baby herself. There was no holding back. The infant was moving down the birth canal.

Just after five o'clock, there was the sound of a vehicle in front of the house. Lights swung, grazing through the windows of the bedroom, and Peggy heard Lloyd's heavy tread on the porch. She wanted to cry out with joy that he hadn't abandoned her, but another pain cut short all thoughts of anything except the baby.

Irene walked into the room, her bag full of medicines in her hand.

"Lordy, Miss Peggy, you havin' that baby all by yourself." She turned to Lloyd, who'd followed her in. "Look, Mr. Lloyd. That baby's head is crownin'. She'll be here directly."

"Let me get the boys." Lloyd was excited. "I promised them they could watch the baby bein' born."

"No!" Peggy had enough presence of mind to stop him. "I don't want them in here."

"I told them they could watch." Lloyd sounded belligerent and he smelled drunk. "They're right on the porch." He opened the door and waved the men inside. They hesitated on the threshold.

"Irene, make them get out," Peggy begged.

"Go on!" Irene shooed the men away from the door. "Miss Peggy don't want no fools peepin' at her privates while she's tryin' to have a child. Get on off that porch and go home!"

When she returned, Peggy was caught in another pain. Irene took her hand. "It's almost over," she said. "Just keep on pushin' and before you know it, you'll have a fine baby."

It took another twenty minutes, but by five-thirty, Peggy held the bloody infant in her arms. "Look, Lloyd, she's beautiful." She held the baby toward him.

"She's fine," he agreed. He did not offer to hold her.

"Push, Miss Peggy. Got to get that afterbirth out," Irene directed. She remained positioned to finish the job of birthing. "Here it comes, push hard."

Peggy held the little girl and pushed with all the strength she had left.

"Here it is." Irene took the tissue and looked at Lloyd. "Now, Mr. Lloyd, you gots to take this and eat it."

The command caught Lloyd completely off guard. "What?"

"You gots to eat the afterbirth so the baby won't be greedy and selfish." Irene held it out to him. "Get a pan."

"I ain't eatin' no such thing." Lloyd stood up.

"It's for the baby," Irene insisted. "If you don't eat it, she'll be so greedy she'll suck everythin' around her dry."

"She can be greedy." Lloyd backed away.

Irene pushed the pan into Lloyd's hands. "You won't eat it, then bury it."

"Where should I bury it?" Lloyd stepped back from the women.

"Bury it under that fire barrel out by the fence." Irene shook her head. "You want me to write you instructions?"

"Right." Lloyd backed against the wall.

"Now, Miss Peggy, you got to get on your feet," Irene directed. "Worst thing is laying around in bed. Get up and move to get the soreness out." Irene took the baby as Peggy managed to get to her feet. A sudden gush of blood stained her gown and ran down her legs to puddle in the floor.

"Mama!" Butch's stricken voice came from beside the bed.

In the process of the birth, Peggy had forgotten about her first child.

"Who hurted my mama?" Butch cried. He looked from Irene to Lloyd. "Who hurted my mama?" His tiny fists clenched.

"I need a drink." Before anyone could stop him, Lloyd cut through the kitchen and out the back door, the pan still in his hands.

Peggy swallowed back her tears and her disappointment. Watching the birth had not affected Lloyd as she'd expected. She turned to Butch. "I'm okay, honey. I just had a baby sister for you. I'm fine."

"What you gonna name this baby?" Irene asked.

Peggy looked toward the kitchen door where Lloyd had disappeared. "Her name is Marsha Ann. I told my friend Trick that I'd use part of her name, Patricia Ann." She looked down at the little girl and the hurt of Lloyd was eased. "This is little Marsha Ann Morgan."

Chapter Thirty-Two

Marsha Ann Morgan's official birth date was five-thirty A.M., March 1, 1969. Fifteen hours after the birth of her daughter, Peggy was dressed and with Lloyd in Tominello's. Although she didn't feel like dancing, she did—to keep other women from dancing with her husband.

The new baby had no effect on Lloyd's behavior. Peggy's hoped-for miracle of change did not occur. Marsha Ann's arrival simply created more work and more responsibility for Peggy. She was caught between meeting the needs of her children and trying to keep tabs on her husband.

As the weeks passed and the Delta softened into springtime, Lloyd's hours became more erratic. He was constantly dodging the law for bad checks, but no matter how thin his pocketbook, his charm could always get him a cold drink at the Greenwood Grill or Tominello's. Though almost everyone in the area knew Lloyd was married, it didn't matter to the women who leaned against him at the bar or let him run his hands along their legs in the back of a booth. Many of the women had regular jobs, and they had money to buy him a drink.

Left out on the plantation with no phone and no means of transportation, Peggy would find someone to watch the children while she hitchhiked into town to begin the bar-to-bar search for Lloyd.

When she did find him, usually back in a dark booth or belly-rubbing on the dance floor with some woman, Peggy flew into a rage. Her frequent attempts to beat up Lloyd or his girlfriends with soft drink bottles earned her the nickname of "the Seven-Up Kid." Blindly determined to make Lloyd stand up and assume his responsibilities, she refused to let him go and move on with her life. She had accepted Lloyd in a way that did not allow her to pull back. Life without him was inconceivable, and Peggy offered her love to him in much the same way she loved her mother—unconditionally. When it came to Lloyd and Inez, Peggy had no defenses, no means of protecting herself from their weaknesses.

Folks around town called her crazy. They ridiculed her, talked about the way she chased Lloyd down and fought for him. They whispered things about her mama, how Inez had never been right and how that was Peggy's heritage. At first Peggy ignored them. As the months passed and she found herself in the middle of degrading scenes she'd never imagined she would tolerate, she'd begun to wonder. She knew the difference between right and wrong. Inez had taught her. Lloyd, though, had blurred those lines. Her love, which she'd begun to suspect was not right, had taken her to some dark places. And yet she loved him.

Late at night or during an unguarded moment, she could feel herself breaking apart. Only the needs of her children—and her compulsion to find Lloyd—got her up and moving.

THE MORGANS' THIRD child, Tomeekca, was born November 9, 1970. Peggy had followed Lloyd over most of the Southeast as he either chased "a better job" or ran from the law. His offenses—beating his wife was not considered an illegal act—were never major enough to warrant an all-out effort by lawmen to bring him to ground. As long as he moved along, they didn't pursue him.

Lloyd's brother, Jimmy Dale Morgan, was not so lucky. He did time in Mississippi State Penitentiary in the mid-60s and was returned again for a three-year stretch in 1970. His crimes were similar to Lloyd's—burglary, robbery, larceny—but his luck wasn't as good or his charm as potent.

At 2012 Basket Street, the heavy drinking had finally taken a toll on Peggy's father. Gene had been institutionalized in Whitfield with delirium tremens, had dried out, come home, and returned to drinking again. Inez had tried several times, unsuccessfully, to stop drinking. The home situation was so bad that the welfare department finally intervened and took Ronald and Mike out of the home. The two boys were living with Faye and her husband, Mac, which was a point of much family friction. Gene refused to support them in any way.

Peggy's life had assumed its own pattern. Lloyd would work a little, spend the money in a joint on liquor and women, come home, and abuse her. She hunted down jobs for him and herself, saved what little money she could scrape together, followed Lloyd around to bars, pulled him from the arms of other women, and fought the women and her husband.

They moved frequently, leaving behind unpaid bills and a string of debts. They fought in public, earning bad reputations for Lloyd as an immoral womanizer and Peggy as a spitfire troublemaker with a crazy streak where Lloyd was concerned. The children followed along as best they could, never knowing when Lloyd would be home, always wondering if the next sentence would start a fight.

By the spring of 1972, Peggy had finally decided divorce was the only solution. The family had gone to New Orleans, where Lloyd's work lasted only a few weeks. They'd moved along the Mississippi Gulf Coast, trying out the shipyards and various machine shops. Lloyd was a skilled welder, but he could never stay at a job long enough to advance or acquire benefits. With the demands of the children and Lloyd's inability to assume responsibility, Peggy couldn't hold down a permanent job. Something had to be done. It was not that she loved him less. She was too tired and too poor to continually spin the fantasy.

She and the children were living at 1001 Dewey Street in Greenwood—Lloyd had disappeared yet again—when she contacted a lawyer and began to run an ad in the local newspaper notifying Lloyd of her intentions to divorce.

She opened the newspaper to make sure the ad was running. The lawyer had said it had to run for four consecutive weeks, a public notice of intent since Lloyd's whereabouts were unknown. Peggy knew if she really put her heart into it, she could find Lloyd, but the time had finally come when she didn't want to find him. Her obsessive grip on the marriage was loosening.

Looking over the top of the newspaper, Peggy took stock of her children. Butch was six, almost ready for the first grade. Marsha Ann was three, and Tomeekca two. They were handsome children. They were good children, too, and they deserved better than Lloyd for a daddy.

Peggy scanned the classified ads, finding the one she'd paid for. With a nod, she folded the paper and placed it on the table. She'd promised Lloyd's sister, Shirley, that she would drive her to the dentist in Itta Bena. Even though Lloyd was gone, Peggy saw no reason to mistreat his family when she had a car, a means to get her sister-in-law to the dentist. She folded the paper and rounded the children up in the car.

"Now y'all be good," Peggy cautioned the children as she prepared to leave them with a neighbor, Cathy, who had agreed to sit with them at Artie Belle's house. "I'll be back in an hour or two."

The trip to the dentist was uneventful. Shirley said the Morgans had not seen Lloyd in several weeks. Peggy didn't press the issue. She sat in the waiting room reading a magazine until Shirley came out, lip puffy and ready to get back to Greenwood. In little more than twenty minutes, they were pulling into the Morgans' yard.

"Thanks, Peggy," Shirley said, rubbing her jaw.

"Any time." Peggy kept the motor running and her hand on the gear lever. "Send the kids on out."

The screen door flew open, and Cathy pelted down the steps and into the yard. "Peggy, somethin' terrible's happened."

Peggy took in her wide eyes, the paleness of her face. "Has something happened to Mama?" Fear crowded out every other thought.

"No, it's Gene." The young woman composed herself. "You've got to go over to the hospital. Gene got into a fight with J. P. Henderson. I can't get the straight of it. Seems like he was hit in the head with a hammer or fell onto something sharp, I don't know." She took another deep breath. "They say he's gonna die."

"Daddy?" Peggy was stunned. "It's Daddy?" She couldn't believe it.

"You'd better get over there quick. Faye and Boyd have been lookin' everywhere for you."

Peggy looked past Cathy into the distance. "I told Mama he was gonna kill somebody or get killed. He just got too mean."

"Peggy, they want you over at the hospital." Cathy's forehead furrowed. "Your daddy's dyin'."

Shirley had gotten out of the car. "Just leave the kids here with us."

"Okay." Peggy's hands rested on the steering wheel, the motor idling. "I told Daddy I would take him over to Walls' Grocery to get the money when I got back from taking you to the dentist. They both get too drunk and too mean."

Cathy reached through the window and touched Peggy's shoulder. "You'd better go, Peggy. There isn't much time."

Peggy looked at her but instead saw her daddy standing at the counter of his store, his face angry and wounded as he told how he'd loaned J. P. a hundred and fifty dollars in good faith and how J. P. wouldn't pay him back. She and Gene had gone once to try and get the money, but J. P. didn't have it. Peggy had promised her father that she would take him again to recover the debt. Now it was too late.

She felt something shaking her, and she looked up at Cathy, who was rattling her shoulder with a strong grip.

"You okay to drive?" she asked. "I can drive you to the hospital, but you'd better get goin'. I'm sorry, Peggy, but they said it was just a matter of a few minutes."

"I'm okay." Peggy spoke through layers of cotton. Her own voice was muffled. She put the car in reverse and backed out of the yard. When she looked up, she was at the hospital.

Inside, Boyd, Mary Jean, and Faye were waiting. No one had gone to tell Inez. They had decided to wait until it was over.

"Daddy's gonna die," Boyd said as Peggy entered the small waiting room. "The doctor said there was nothin' he could do."

Peggy read the truth on her siblings' faces. "What happened?"

"The best we can make out, Daddy went to collect some money J. P. owed him and they got into some sort of push-pull. J. P. shoved Daddy and he fell into a bread rack and cut his head open," Boyd explained.

"That's gonna kill him?" Peggy had seen Gene inflict worse injuries on Inez. Much worse.

"It's caused bleedin' in his brain. The doctor said somethin' about drillin' a hole in his head to relieve the pressure, but he'd have to be flown to New Orleans." Faye paced the room as she spoke.

Boyd shook his head and sat heavily in one of the plastic chairs. "I checked with Jerry Bower. He said he'd fly Daddy in his plane, but the doctor said he wouldn't make it." He looked at Peggy. "You've got to do something. J. P. killed Daddy."

"Where's J. P.?" Peggy looked at her brother and sisters. "Is he in jail?"

"The deputies were here. They took statements." Faye shrugged. "It was bound to happen. Daddy spent every penny he got on whiskey. He never cared if his own children had clothes." The bitterness was clear in her voice. "If it hadn't been J. P., it would have been someone else."

"Where's Daddy?" Peggy had to see Gene before he died.

"They put him in a room," Mary Jean said. "I'll show you."

Gene, his head swathed in bandages, lay against the pale sheets. His breathing was shallow and harsh.

"He won't come to again," Boyd said. "It's just a matter of time."

Gene's gasping tore at Peggy. Though his eyes were closed, she saw the struggle to live in his face. She picked up his hand. "Daddy? Daddy?"

"He can't hear you, Peggy," Mary Jean said. "The doctor said he would never regain consciousness."

Peggy ignored her. "Daddy, it's me, Peggy. Can you hear me? Talk to me, Daddy." She clung to his hand, feeling the cool promise of death on his skin. For most of her life she'd feared and hated her father. Many times she'd wanted to kill him herself to protect her mother. Looking at him, cheeks sunken, air rasping in and out, she felt the hatred leave her. Gene would never harm Inez again. There was no longer any reason to hate him or fear him. He was her father, the first man she'd sought to please, the man who had set the pattern of her life. "Daddy, talk to me. It's Peggy."

His fingers curled around her hand and squeezed. The pressure held firm for several seconds then slowly released.

The harsh sound of his breathing ceased.

Chapter Thirty-Three

The summer was slipping past mid-June into the zenith of white-hot heat. Peggy drove the Ford along the quiet streets of Greenwood, the radio playing loud enough to drift out the open windows of the car and draw a smile from a housewife who stood on the sidewalk, putting out the trash. The dew had burned off the lawns, but the hour was still early. Several children were out on their bicycles, uncaring if the heat soaked their shorts and shirts. Though she had never had a bicycle, Peggy remembered when she and Molly had played and dreamed on summer days. It had not been that long ago, time-wise. She was still in her twenties. Yet so much had happened. She'd traipsed around the country after Lloyd, had three children, had come to a degree of maturity and a life she'd never bargained for, and finally knew the loss of a parent.

Gene was buried, and the arrangements for the funeral had gone smoother than Peggy had thought possible. The wake and the service were a blur. Only Inez had truly cried. None of Gene's children was overwrought with grief. He had inflicted too much trauma, too much tragedy and fear for copious mourning. At best, the children felt a collective sigh of relief. There would not be any more calls to the emergency room to gather around Inez, beaten yet again. No more fights and threats made by Gene—or against him—dragging his children into danger. It was over.

Lloyd had appeared for the funeral, acting as if he'd never been gone. With a few promises and a roll of cash to pay off the back rent and the bill Peggy had run up at the grocery store, he had sweet-talked his way back into the family.

A sudden movement to the left made her foot jam at the brake, and she took a deep breath. A boy careened around the corner of a white clapboard house, pursued by another laughing boy. She clicked the radio off so she could concentrate better. Peggy thought of her children. Butch and Marsha Ann were so happy that their daddy was home. Somehow, with just a kind word or a laugh, Lloyd made them ecstatic with happiness. He might ignore them for weeks, curse them, threaten them, slap them around, yet they crawled back to him when he crooked a finger and smiled.

They'd learned such behavior from her.

The knowledge daggered into her heart. That situation was about to change. She'd talked long and hard with Lloyd and put it on the line. He was either going to be a father and a husband, or he was going to leave. She'd dropped the divorce proceedings, but each time she made the decision to leave him, it was a little bit easier. Next time he forced her hand, it would be for good, and she'd told him so.

She turned left, headed in a round-about way to Basket Street to check on Inez. She was taking the long route, enjoying the summer day, the freedom from the children, and the sense that life might get better. For Inez, at least, things were bound to improve. Boyd had filed the claims for social security. Throughout his checkered employment career, Gene had worked enough to earn his pennies, and now Inez would have a small, steady income—and no one to abuse her.

Peggy's thoughts drifted to her father. Her image of him was clear, standing beside a nearly new green Ford, khaki pants creased. His thick hair was slightly long with a bit of a curl, and his lean face was alive with a smile. He was calling to his children to come and get something he had for them, some rare treat. Peggy had felt the warmth of his smile all the way across the yard, but she had hung back, afraid that if she approached the smile would turn into anger.

The film clip of the past stopped, and she held the smiling image of her father frozen while she examined it. Even now, she wanted that smile to be for her. Even if it was a made-up memory, she wanted Gene to look at her, to call her name special, to glance her way with a hint of pride and pleasure.

The picture faded and disappeared, replaced by the neighborhood homes slipping past the windshield of the car. The past was gone. Gene was dead and buried.

She turned at the corner of Slim Henderson's store, meandering around Greenwood, visiting the old haunts. It had been at Slim's that she had bought the beautiful red and white 1964 Ford she now drove. Slim had made her a good deal. She'd saved up the money herself, waitressing at The Alice once again. Slim had been a friend, but it didn't erase the memory of the night her father had made her scatter the black protestors. She might have killed someone. She almost did, and all because Gene and Slim had gotten liquored up and played the fool.

She felt herself falling down a black hole of bad memories, and she knew she had to stop. Hitting the brake on the car, she slid several yards in the loose gravel. She brought the car to a stop and did battle with her memory. Gene was gone, but the legacy of fear was not over. Not completely.

Hand shaking, she flipped the radio on again, listening to the disc jockey babble about high temperatures and the farmer's concern over a shortage of rain. The next record up was Freddy Hart's "Easy Lovin'."

At first Peggy didn't realize she was crying. It was a song she'd heard a million times in a hundred different bars and joints and small groceries where moonshine whiskey was sold in brown paper sacks. The song was a combination of Lloyd and Gene and the sadness that followed them into their homes like muddy footprints. Leaning against the steering wheel, she finally realized that whatever secret desires she'd had in childhood were forever passed. Her father was dead. The approval she hungered for would never come. Death was final and righted no wrongs.

In the privacy of the car, she cried until she felt as dry as a July cotton row. She tasted the dust of death, swallowing it as she started the car and drove on to her mother's. When she pulled into the yard, she knew she would never again approach the house in fear that her father was on a drunken tear, that he would lurch out the door and attack her, or that she would creep inside to find a new atrocity or horror committed against her mother. Perhaps there was some justice in death after all.

"Mama?" she called as she got out of the car and hurried up the steps. "Mama?"

"In the kitchen." Inez came to the doorway, wiping her hands on her apron. "I was making some breakfast. You want something? I got some fresh yard eggs."

Peggy shook her head. Since her marriage to Lloyd she'd had difficulties eating. When she was worried or upset, it seemed she couldn't force the food down her throat. During those times, her weight would drop to below seventy pounds, and she would suffer dizziness and blackouts. Gene's death and Lloyd's return had put her in a state of anxiety that made eating impossible. "You go ahead." She sat at the table and watched as her mother scrambled an egg and sat down to eat it.

"Are you okay?" Peggy studied her mother. Inez's hand trembled as she held the fork. Her epileptic seizures were more frequent, coming on her suddenly. It worried Peggy that Inez might be cooking or walking down the steps and suddenly fall into a seizure. Now there was no one in the house to watch her.

"I'm okay." Inez ate a bite. When she swallowed, she looked into her daughter's face. "I miss him, Peggy." A tear traced a slow line down her face. She lowered the fork to the table. "I don't know what to do now. For so long, everything was Gene. Now, there's nothing."

"It'll get better." Peggy spoke against the cold wind that suddenly blew over her spine. When Lloyd disappeared, she often felt as if her world had emptied of all meaning. Trick was always railing at her to get over it, saying how Lloyd's absence was simply a lack of cruelty and meanness and abuse. But for Peggy it was a life void of meaning. It frightened her to hear Inez say the same about Gene.

Inez shook her head. "It won't ever get any better. I look at the door and think maybe there's been a mistake, maybe he'll just walk through."

"And pick up something to hit you." Peggy knew the words were cruel, but she spoke as much for herself as Inez.

"Sometimes, Peggy, before you were born, Gene would come home laughin'. I remember so well. I'd be waitin' for him, supper cooked, and he would walk through the door and swing Boyd or Billy into the air and make them laugh. He was a good daddy then. A good husband."

Peggy had no answer for that. Lloyd had never been a good husband or any kind of daddy.

Inez picked up her fork and gathered a bite of egg. As she lifted it to her mouth, her hand shook so badly the egg fell back to the plate. She put the fork down and slowly got up and went to the cabinet. She got a glass and a half-empty pint of Old Crow. She measured out an inch in the glass and came back to the table.

"Mama, you got to stop that." Peggy sat perfectly still. It had never occurred to her that once Gene was dead Inez would continue to drink. Somehow, she thought the old Inez, the mother of twenty years past, would step out of the shell. The glass of whiskey in her mother's hand unleashed a million demons of anxiety. Peggy forced herself not to jump up and run.

"I'm gonna slack off some," Inez agreed, sipping the whiskey. "It's just my nerves are so bad. I miss your daddy." She took a bigger swallow.

"Mama . . ." Peggy didn't know what to say.

"When are you bringin' the children to see me?" Inez sipped.

"Maybe tomorrow." Peggy stood. "I got to get home. Lloyd's goin' over to Barrantine today to see about work. Maybe they'll hire him." Defeat colored her words and she couldn't help it.

"If Lloyd would just settle down and hold a job, he'd do all right."

"He would." Peggy didn't add what a big "if" that was.

"Come back to see me." Inez got up and poured more whiskey into the glass. She spoke to the wall instead of Peggy.

"I will," Peggy whispered as she hurried out into the June day that had grown oppressively hot. As she slid behind the wheel of the car, she entertained the thought of driving south, or north, or west. Just putting the car in gear and taking off, never to return. She could put it all behind her, the need and desperation and fear. If she could forget her mother and her children, maybe she could have a new life. Trouble was, she couldn't forget, not even for an hour. Shoulders slumped, she drove back to Dewey Street and her family. No telling what new mess Lloyd would have waiting for her.

She eased the car into the yard, skulking as she got out and moved toward the house. She'd been gone longer than she said she would. If Lloyd was awake, he'd be fretting and angry. He didn't like to be left without a means to get around.

The screen door closed silently as she entered the house that was too quiet to contain a man and three children.

"Lloyd?" She whispered his name.

"Is there any gas in that car?" Lloyd's question came out of nowhere, and Peggy spun to confront him. Before she could put up any defenses, his hand was on her throat, the fingers closing just enough to shut off most of her air. She had enough to breathe, but if she so much as shook a finger, Lloyd's grip would increase.

"Is there gas?" he repeated.

She barely managed a nod. She felt his grip loosen, and she sank against the wall. "Where are the children?" she croaked out.

"Hilda Prescott took 'em. I couldn't stand the racket. I got to go out."

"No." Peggy stood her ground, but only for a second. His hand flew out and slapped her so hard she fell against the wall and slid down.

"I've had enough of you telling me how things are goin' to be. A man doesn't let his woman push him around. I'm tellin' you good, Peggy, you stay up on that high horse and I'll beat you down off it. You got to take the wife's place. Women and niggers got to learn their place." He snatched at her purse, dumping the contents onto the floor. "Now where are those car keys?"

Peggy knew better than to rub her cheek though it stung like fire. "In the car." She could smell the whiskey on Lloyd's breath. It wasn't even lunch and he was already drunk. The best thing was to let him go. "Don't take my car," she said, adding, "please. I got to take Butch to get his school vaccinations. They won't let him in the first grade without those shots, and it takes a while to get them all."

"I got business." He finally focused on her. "You can walk to the health department."

Peggy swallowed a biting remark that was embedded in a lump of fear. Lloyd had a bad habit of taking the family vehicles and selling them for cash for liquor. She'd worked too hard to let him get hold of the beautiful red and white Ford.

"Okay, we'll walk. But I left some things in the car. I'll get them out." She could somehow disable the vehicle and save it.

She started out the door.

Lloyd's fingers caught her wrist and her body flew back to land against his chest. "What say we get together with Rupert and Nell tonight. Maybe do a little tradin' around in the bedroom."

Peggy tried to wiggle away from him. Lloyd was always trying to involve her in some sickness. "I'm not doin' that. I told you before, I won't ever do that." She felt the tears build behind her eyes. "That's not right, Lloyd. We're married. We're not for other people." She knew if she cried he'd laugh at her. "I don't want no other man but you." The last was a humiliating confession, but the truth.

"Well, I want something different. Something new. If you'd go along, Rupert might take a shine to you." He eyed her critically. "He likes 'em thin, and by God, you're as close to the bone as breathin' meat gets."

Peggy snatched her wrist free, losing all desire to save the car. "Go on. Get out of here." It seemed no matter what she wanted to happen, Lloyd always took a tactic that defeated her. "Just get out of here."

Lloyd ambled toward the door. His lean figure had broadened, filling out and swaying toward the stomach of a man who ate and drank too much and worked too little. "I'll be back later."

Peggy didn't answer.

He turned back to her. "Oh, yeah. Get you a baby sitter lined up for the weekend after the Fourth of July. We gonna go up to Parchman to see Jimmy Dale. I got word he's lonesome up there in the pen."

"You go. Take your mother." Peggy had no desire to visit Jimmy Dale Morgan in the pen. She had a sneaking suspicion Lloyd was carrying on with Jimmy Dale's wife. She had no proof, just the feeling. Lloyd had never given a care about his brother before.

"Well, you're goin'. You're gonna learn to do what you're told, or you'll be sorry. Folks already say you're crazy. Maybe I should have listened to 'em."

"Folks say you and your family are trash." She shot the remark back, for a moment feeling the resurgence of the old Peggy. When she saw him coming back toward the steps, she slammed the door and locked it. Lloyd was strong enough to tear it down, but it would make enough ruckus that someone would call the cops. Not that they'd do anything except tell him to stop. She slammed the thumb bolt home and backed away, just in case the thin wood gave quickly.

Lloyd didn't hit the door. "I could beat you to a pulp," he said softly. "But I don't want you all bruised and messed up. I'm goin' to

Parchman, and you're goin', too. We got another man who wants a ride over there to visit some of his kin."

"Who?" Peggy was instantly suspicious.

"Just a man. He's gonna pay for the gas and all." Lloyd continued to talk through the closed door.

Peggy felt a slight relenting. She and Lloyd didn't really have the money to go cruising the eighty miles to Parchman to pay Jimmy Dale a family visit. But if someone else was buying the gas, they could make the trip for nothing. "Who is he?"

"I forgot his name. Prescott set it up."

Lloyd had started walking away; she could hear the distance in his voice. Peggy peeked out the window and saw him get in the car. They'd go to Parchman to see Jimmy Dale—if they still had a car when Lloyd finished his "business."

Chapter Thirty-Four

The two men stood at the fender of the red and white '64 Ford. Their talk was desultory, and the stranger glanced at his wrist watch then lifted his hat just enough to allow a starched, white handkerchief to pass across his forehead. From inside the protective shading of the screened front door of her apartment, Peggy watched them. The stranger's suit was so sharply pressed the creases of his pants seemed to part the sunlight. His gangster-style hat gave him a look of sophistication. When he did speak loud enough for his voice to drift into the house, he had a cultured tone. High society. A planter. Peggy knew enough members of that elite class to recognize one when she saw him.

Although she'd been dreading the trip, Lloyd had insisted that she go, warning her that the man who would travel with them was very powerful. His name was Delay, and he had requested that she accompany them, Lloyd said, and since he was paying for the gas, Peggy could take the ride. Besides, Lloyd had told her, it wouldn't hurt to see Jimmy Dale.

Even though her brother-in-law was a repeat offender, Peggy bore Jimmy Dale Morgan no ill will. What troubled her was that Lloyd wasn't the kind of man who took to visiting his incarcerated relatives simply because it was the right thing to do. Something else was brewing with his sudden desire for an eighty-mile road trip to Parchman prison.

And the stranger. There was another fact that didn't add up to a complete story. It nagged at her that a man of his obvious background could surely have taken his own car on such a trip. Who might he be visiting in Parchman? Members of the upper class seldom did prison time. They were able to buy a better defense in the courtroom.

From out in the yard, Lloyd cast a glance of dark impatience at the screen door, and Peggy stumbled into the kitchen table in her effort to get away from his look. Lately, she'd begun to believe that Lloyd might kill her in one of his rages. He woke up and went to bed with a bottle in his hand.

"Peggy, get your ass out here!" Lloyd bellowed.

"Now, sir, women folks have to prepare themselves properly for a trip," the man said. "It's the duty of the gentleman to await with patience."

Peggy slipped through the screen door of the clapboard apartment and walked into the yard. Before Lloyd could gather his alcohol-dulled wits to say anything, the stranger made a stiff bow. "Mrs. Morgan," he said, "how do you do?"

Peggy was flustered. For a moment she thought about extending her hand for a shake, but it was such an unnatural act for her that she did nothing. Beckwith opened the passenger door for her. Without being told, Peggy slid to the middle. The men would want the windows where what little cool air there was would blow over them first.

"Let's go," Lloyd said to no one in particular as he started the car.

"Before we leave town, could we stop and get some chicken?" Beckwith looked around Peggy at Lloyd. "Those boys at the prison could stand some fried chicken."

Lloyd shrugged and pulled into a fast food joint where chicken was the specialty. Fifteen minutes later Beckwith came out, arms loaded with boxes and buckets of food. He put them in the back seat, the aroma thick around the containers that were showing the first sogginess of hot grease. "Thank you," he said as he resettled in the front seat.

The man's impeccable manners almost encouraged Peggy to respond with a "you're welcome." But a childhood with Gene and years of living with Lloyd had taught her not to speak when men were involved in their business, and this trip, whatever the motivation, could not be anything but man's business. There was a distinct line between the freedoms of being a man and the rules of being a woman. She'd learned the hard way that a moving vehicle was not the place to take Lloyd on, and the simplest courtesy was often misconstrued by Lloyd.

She remembered Carlos, a friend who happened to be male. Lloyd had almost killed him when he'd taken Peggy's side during a fight. The fact that Carlos had the wits of a child didn't stop Lloyd. If anything, Carlos's inability to really fight had made Lloyd that much more vicious. She blinked the memory away and practiced sitting as still and silent as she knew how.

While the men talked about crop yields and tobacco, farm equipment and national politics, Peggy watched the lush green rows of cotton slide past the car window. The rows were so long and perfect that they seemed to blur, whipping green-brown, green-brown, green-brown in a dizzying pattern. The highway paralleled the snaky curves of the Tallahatchie River, and periodically she caught a glimpse of the slow, yellow thoroughfare that had been a part of her childhood. When she glanced out the front windshield, sun devils danced on the asphalt, distorting the road into a gray, wavery line.

"That is a lovely red dress, Mrs. Morgan," Beckwith said in his high-tone way.

"Thank you, sir." Peggy kept her eyes rigidly on the road. Even though she had three children, she'd kept her petite figure. Men liked to look at her, which was a double-edged sword. While it made Lloyd proud, it also made him angry. She was acutely aware of Lloyd beside her. He seemed willing to let the compliment pass, for the moment.

To Peggy's relief, Beckwith halted his attempts to talk to her and returned to the topic of humidity. They were well into the eighty-mile trip to the state penitentiary when they passed a group of blacks ambling down the side of the highway, pushing and laughing at each other.

"The nigra was born into slavery and should have remained so," Beckwith said, almost as if he spoke to himself. "Northern agitators want to make out that it was us Southerners who invented slavery, but it was a fact of life in blackest Africa. They sold their own people as slaves. As a race they aren't capable of participatin' as full citizens. Now our fight to protect our society against the nigras is fallin' back."

Peggy half listened. Talk about Negroes was as common as an afternoon rain shower. The problem of what to do with the Negro logically followed when talk of crops and weather had been exhausted. Beckwith, despite his planter's manner of expression, was still a white man with the same sentiments of the men she knew.

"What is troublin' to see is that white men are shirkin' their duties. It is the white man's role to supervise the dusky races," Beckwith was saying. His tone was reasonable, but the emotion in his voice was thicker, stronger. "We are the natural rulers of the mud people and the mongrels, those that are less than human."

Not exactly certain what Beckwith was talking about, Peggy listened more closely. Whatever went wrong, it seemed the Negro was always to blame. Gene had done it—even as he fished and drank with them. Lloyd had begun to curse the blacks because he couldn't keep a job. Peggy knew it was Lloyd's drinking and lack of reliability that fouled his half-hearted attempts to work, but he never saw it that way. Like all the other men she knew, he found it convenient to blame Negroes. The men ranted and raved about blacks, and it made them feel better.

On Beckwith's side of the car, Peggy caught sight of the curl of the Tallahatchie River and knew that Minter City was close. Lloyd turned left on Highway 8, and they headed for Ruleville, where they would pick up Highway 49 West.

Beckwith, at first, seemed to be a higher class of man. As the drive continued, his speech grew angrier, more animated. He suddenly turned to Peggy, his eyes magnified behind his glasses. "Are you listenin', Mrs. Morgan? I'm tellin' you the way things are, and you're daydreamin' out the damn window." He leaned closer so that she could not escape his stare. "There's a problem out there and it centers around the Jew and the nigger."

Peggy found that she could not look away. Hatred burned hot in his eyes, and she felt as if he were violating her with calculated cruelty. A tiny droplet of spittle caught in the corner of his mouth as he ranted.

"Am I not right?" He waited for her reply.

Peggy could not answer. She could not talk to this man whose hungry look defiled and frightened her. Beckwith had not been drinking. It was not desire for her as a woman that she saw in his eyes. What he wanted was far more complicated. He took pleasure in his hatred, but a hatred fueled not by liquor or impotence at his social standing. She did not understand him at all.

"Don't you agree, Mr. Morgan?" Beckwith shifted his attention to Lloyd.

Peggy felt as if she'd been released from the clutches of a predatory bird, left to fall head over heels through the pale blue sky. When she regained her wits, she carefully kept her gaze ahead and watched the road for the landmarks that meant they were drawing ever closer to their destination. She pulled deeper into herself as Beckwith watched her with a pleased expression, addressing his remarks to her even though she sat rigid as a stick.

"Now, Mrs. Morgan, I'll bet you didn't know that the white race is the chosen race. The Jews claim that they are the chosen people of God, but they are not. They are mongrels, as are the blacks and others of impure heritage. I've read and studied this issue, and unless the white man takes a stand now, things are gonna git worse." He began to speak faster. "Look at it. We have niggers in our schools, niggers in our politics. And who's behind it? The Jews. We are the righteous, the chosen. We are the true Israelites. But God can't save us from the mongrels. We have to save ourselves. We must take action and take the power back from the mud people. My associates and I have taken a stand. We have taken action. . . ."

As the fields slipped by the speeding car, Peggy did her best to shut out his talk. Even if she ignored the words, she heard the bragging in the stranger's voice, the pure, ugly hatred that rose up inside him and poured out of his mouth. His words scalded her. His constant looks at her made her afraid to draw a deep breath.

At last she understood what he wanted, though he hadn't vocalized it. He wanted what Gene wanted, what Lloyd wanted, too. Only his tactics differed. He wanted to see her fear, to feel his power over her, to feed off the terror he generated in her.

In the privacy of the car, Beckwith confessed to knowledge of the murder of black children in a church, to knowledge of the bombing death of a Jewish man in Meridian. Rolling down the highway, surrounded by the flat acres of cotton fields, Peggy was a prisoner. The Delta was her prison, the men her jailers. Beckwith's twisted confession was a singing whip. Later, she would feel the bite of it in her flesh for having heard this talk. Beckwith and men like him were dangerous. They bragged to their women and later beat them for listening. It was a familiar pattern.

To block out his red-hot words, she thought of songs, of moments with her children, anything. The smell of fried chicken was overpowering in the car, and the stranger's voice cut at her, opening old wounds and making new ones.

Bryon De La Beckwith leaned back in the car seat, but his gaze behind his glasses was on Peggy. "I want y'all to know I killed that nigger, Medgar Evers, and I'm not afraid to kill again," he said. Then he added menacingly, "This better not never get out." He pulled his coat aside to reveal a pistol tucked in the waistband of his pants.

The threat was unnecessary.

Trapped between the two men in the front seat, Peggy breathed in the greasy chicken smell. Beckwith's link to the Evers murder terrified her. The smell of the chicken made her sick. Her mind registered the danger she faced and tripped the triggers of memory. The sun hung in the sky, and the car tires spun without traction on the highway. Nothing moved. Reality disintegrated into a moment of heat-glazed paralysis. "I killed that nigger, Medgar Evers. I killed that nigger, Medgar Evers. I killed that nigger, Medgar Evers."

Only the words seemed alive.

Beneath the words, an image filled Peggy's vision. She saw her mother, beaten to the point that only the slow trickle of blood down her forehead revealed she was still alive. The image of Inez disappeared, replaced by a photograph of what remained of a fourteen-year-old black boy. Emmett Till. Shot in the head. His skull beaten in. A cotton gin fan fastened to his neck with barbed wire. All before he was thrown into the Tallahatchie River. Peggy heard the name and the sound of male laughter as the photo was passed around the fish market. The laughter blended with the hatred as she heard her father and her Uncle Bob, joined by several of the neighborhood men, laugh about how "the nigger had struggled."

Peggy grasped at reality, looking out the car window to the ever present cotton fields. The rows whirred by, blending the strips of green and brown, converging at the horizon, just as the elements of past and present had suddenly come together in a moment so filled with terror that she thought she would surely die. The laughter of the men in the fish market rose out of the cotton fields and echoed hollowly in the car.

Beyond the laughter lay blessed blackness, and Peggy felt it coming toward her. Her body slipped to the left as she dove for the darkness and the comfort of escape.

Lloyd's elbow in her ribs made her suck in a gulp of air. "Listen to De La," he ordered.

"Don't say my name to the guards."

Beckwith's voice brought Peggy back to the present. Her stomach roiled at the greasy smell of the car as the Parchman check-in point appeared in the front windshield. She'd heard all her life that the guards carried rifles so powerful they could pick off an escaping inmate. Of course it was also said that a man didn't have to be attempting escape to earn a bullet in his back.

"Did you hear what I said?" Beckwith asked her in a sharp tone.

"What?" She was confused.

The braggadocio of Beckwith had given way to nervousness. "Don't say who I am, or we could all get in big trouble," he warned as they pulled up to where the guard could see into the car.

The smell of the chicken made the guard smile. He passed a clipboard into the car, and they all three signed in. Peggy used her real name but suspected that Beckwith lied. When they got out of the car to enter the building, Lloyd was thoroughly patted down, as was she. Byron De La Beckwith, arms loaded down with chicken and gun tucked in his pants, entered the prison without a physical check.

Lloyd's brother, Jimmy Dale, serving time for robbery and breaking probation, swaggered into the visitor's area. He was followed by two other men, one with a cold, black stare.

"Lloyd," Jimmy Dale said, slightly bemused that his brother had decided to visit. "What's shakin'?"

Peggy tried to keep her gaze on the floor, but one of the men who'd moved to a corner with Beckwith kept looking at her. Their talk was low, intense, but the dark stranger repeatedly shifted his gaze to Peggy. Watching. Calculating. Warning. She felt his eyes tuning into her, boring, carrying the cargo of violence she knew was no empty threat. The fear she'd felt in the car rose up inside her, threatening to snuff everything else out. Afraid she might faint, she found a seat and sat, making sure not to show any interest in Beckwith and the men he visited.

Lloyd and Jimmy Dale talked, and finally Lloyd drew her over beside him.

"Who is that man with Mr. Beckwith?" Peggy whispered. She still didn't want to look at the man. He spooked her badly.

"None of your business," Lloyd said.

"Who is he?" Peggy asked again. She wanted to know the name of the man who could frighten her with a look.

"He killed a man. The man inhaled flames down into his lungs. He inhaled fire, and that's all you need to know."

Peggy's gaze swung up to search her husband's features. "You knew this." It was an accusation. "You knew that man was a killer."

Lloyd looked down at her with cool calculation. "These folks know how to go about gettin' their way, Peggy. Just remember that and keep your mouth shut. Nothin' will happen to you as long as you keep your mouth shut." His grin was slow, relishing every moment of her fear. "Maybe it would even be best if you forgot you ever came here today."

Chapter Thirty-Five

But Peggy could not forget. The trip to Parchman with Byron De La Beckwith began a long downward spiral in her life. Each day she battled Lloyd's cruelty; her nights were filled with nightmare images of murdered black men, the cultured but deadly voice of Byron De La Beckwith and the dark eyes of the man Beckwith had visited in Parchman. Peggy didn't know who he was, but the look in his eyes terrified her.

Afraid that the Klan or some other vigilante group would kill her, Peggy decided that the only way to keep her and her children safe was to move. She fled the one place she'd ever known, the Delta. In her panic, Peggy was forced to leave her mother behind.

Peggy and her family relocated in Gautier, Mississippi, where she got a job at Ingalls Shipbuilding. She was one of the first female, AFL-CIO card-carrying boilermakers at Ingalls. She was a welder, and she had a skill. For the first time in her life she wasn't dependent on a man. But the long years of stress and the physical abuse took a toll. Peggy was hospitalized for a hysterectomy. While she was in the hospital, Lloyd took the car and all their new possessions and sold them.

After eight years of marriage, Peggy was granted a divorce on July 10, 1973. She returned to the Delta and got a job at Barrantine Manufacturing. With her welding skills and union card, she should have made a good living, but Peggy still hadn't learned a woman's place. No matter that her work was as good as, or superior to, the work of the white males. No matter that she showed up at work regularly. No matter that she pulled her shift with the same grit she'd learned at Ingalls. She was female.

Her worst mistake was in teaching another woman, a black woman, the skill of welding. Peggy had made friends with Linda

Quarrels, another single mother with children to support. When Linda asked to learn to weld, Peggy gladly obliged.

That decision earned Peggy the worst job assignments at the plant, and eventually both she and Linda were fired. Peggy returned to the Gulf Coast. Without her union wage, she could barely keep her family together.

For Peggy, the years 1975-86 were "the storm years." Alone, terrified, her faith in herself never strong, she was further weakened by one bad decision piled on top of another. Her options were severely limited, and her life was out of control, intolerable.

She had been taught that the right way for a woman to live was to align herself with a man, a mate, a husband. That was the irrefutable bond of life, the foundation of family. Peggy worked hard, but she needed an anchor to hold her steady during the more frequent storms of anxiety that left her shaking and terrified in the middle of the night.

Her mother, the only person she'd ever been able to count on, had set upon a new path of self-destruction. Unable to face life alone, Inez had married another abusive alcoholic, Charlie Phillips. Constant worry about Inez ate at her, but Peggy had nothing to offer her mother in the way of help or financial assistance. Peggy couldn't save herself, much less anyone else.

On February 5, 1978, Inez died.

The news came in a phone call from Peggy's brother-in-law, Mac. As soon as she answered the phone, Peggy knew it was bad news. Faye's husband wasn't in the habit of calling to make small talk. Peggy had last seen her mother on her birthday, when she'd taken Inez a cake.

"What's happened?" Peggy asked.

"It's Inez, Peggy. She's dead."

Peggy didn't react. Her dreams the night before had been tormented. The dark-eyed killer in Parchman prison watched her, waiting for her to slip up and tell the secret of Beckwith's confession.

Byron De La Beckwith's voice spoke in her ear, "I killed that nigger, Medgar Evers." There was the sound of a fist smashing into flesh and her mother's soft cry of pain, the smell of cigarettes and liquor, and the cheap perfume that came in the door with Lloyd.

Peggy had awakened with a sense of dread so overwhelming, she felt as if she moved through heavy water. Her present was a repetition of the past, and she was helpless to stop it.

"Did you hear me?" Mac asked.

"Mama?"

"She's dead, Peggy. You'd better come on up here. Faye and Mary Jean and Sheila are making the arrangements."

It wasn't until Peggy was called into the Greenwood Police Station to identify Inez's body that Peggy learned how her mother had died. Inez had fallen in a ditch walking home from a friend's house. The police believed she'd suffered a seizure of some type, possibly a heart attack or an episode of epilepsy.

Peggy looked at the photographs the police gave her and saw the worst. Inez's mouth was filled with dirt. She'd frozen to death in the ditch. The ice-covered body had been found early Sunday morning by an acquaintance when he'd heard Inez's little dog, Mugsy, barking and running frantically in the ditch.

The tenuous grip Peggy had held on her children and family was severed. Her life became a free-fall. The nightmare photograph of Inez, frozen in the ditch, was added to the other images that terrified her.

THE PEW IN the funeral home was hard, but Peggy found solace in the cool smoothness of the wood. Long ago, she and Inez had sat on such a church bench and sung together. Peggy remembered the smell of the song book, the thinness of the pages as her mother held it, pretending to read the words she knew so well by heart. Inez had seldom been able to sneak away from Gene and the duties of her children to attend church, but when she did, she took Peggy with her. It was their moment, a sharing that was special between them. Peggy focused on the memory of her mother's face as she sang. Inez had been so happy. So childlike and innocent in the pleasure of her singing.

From her seat in the funeral home chapel, Peggy stared at the simple coffin where Inez lay. Instead of the lavender she'd often told Peggy she wanted to wear when she was buried, she wore blue. Peggy had not been able to argue her sisters into changing, but she had held firm on one other point. Inez's favorite song. Her mother had repeatedly told Peggy to make sure that "Just a Closer Walk with Thee" was sung at her funeral. When Ma Early had passed, it was the song she wanted. Inez had told Peggy that when she died, she was going to join her mother and live in a better place. Peggy prayed that Inez had at last found a place where her childish vulnerability would no longer be used against her.

"Oh, Mama," she whispered softly so that no one else heard.

The minister continued to talk, and the words penetrated the cocoon of Peggy's memories. "Mrs. Phillips was a woman of God. She has merely returned to her home now. One of her favorite hymns was about walking with God, and I believe that's what she's doing now. Side by side, walking with her Savior. Let's sing now."

The words came back to Peggy though she hadn't thought of them in years. She clung to the memory of her mother, face soft with happiness as she held the hymnal in her hand and sang with innocent faith. If Peggy could only keep that memory in her mind, if she could hold onto that one, maybe she could survive.

At the close of the service, she and the other family members followed the coffin to Oddfellow Cemetery where Inez was buried. As the dirt struck the coffin, Peggy looked around her. Though she knew everyone at the graveside, she felt as if she were standing among total strangers.

PEGGY'S TIES WITH the Delta were truly severed. She'd never felt so alone and cast adrift. Struggling to feed her children, she moved to Mobile to work at Halter Marine Shipbuilding in Chickasaw. The daily struggle for survival consumed her. The years passed. Concern for her children overrode the old night terrors of Emmett Till and Byron De La Beckwith. Financial worry and exhaustion kept the past at bay until 1981, when Michael Donald, a black teenager, was beaten to death and lynched in Mobile.

Peggy picked up the *Mobile Register* one morning and read the horror story of another black youth tortured and killed. The past flooded back. She saw again the men laughing around her father's fish market, the ugly threats leveled against her mother, the bullying voice of Byron De La Beckwith—all of it was still out there.

In a panic, Peggy called the local FBI office and blurted out the story of her ride to Parchman with Byron De La Beckwith. Terrified of the consequences, Peggy knew she wasn't making a good impression on the agent. He treated her as if she was some kook. The agent told her the Evers case was inactive.

Peggy could tell the agent didn't believe a word she said. It was the same old story that her mother had lived and now she was living it, too. She could tell the truth and no one would believe her— except the men who committed such heinous crimes. She was trapped.

In 1983 Peggy found herself at the bottom. She'd had two surgeries and never asked her doctors what had been removed. Doctors were authority figures, not to be questioned. Doubled over with pain, Peggy couldn't provide for her three children. She began stealing food from a garbage dumpster behind a grocery store. When a store employee caught her and told her she had to stop, she knew she was at the end of her road. She could no longer provide for the children.

After repeated denials by Aid to Dependent Children, Peggy was assigned to Ellen Green, a case worker. Peggy repeated the details of her situation once again, but this time someone listened.

"Mrs. Morgan, you're sick. You need medical attention, and those children need a safe place to live." Mrs. Green pulled out her notepad and phone book and began the process.

Even with Mrs. Green's assistance, Peggy couldn't get into a Mobile hospital. But Mrs. Green did finally make Peggy accept that her children needed a safe place. Peggy didn't intend to put Butch, Marsha Ann and Tomeekca up for adoption when she took them to the Baptist Children's Home. She wanted a safe place for them until she could get back on her feet.

The look of the home was clean and comforting, and Peggy took what solace she could from that fact. When the paperwork to put her children into foster care was placed before her, she found that she couldn't read the typewritten words through her tears.

"Do you want your children adopted, Mrs. Morgan?" the administrator asked.

"No, ma'am." Peggy sat up. She only needed a temporary reprieve, a few months to get back on her feet. She had to find out what was medically wrong—the pain was crippling. And she needed a job, and some way to manage the fear that rode her night and day.

"But you do agree to a foster home if we can find a place that would be a good situation for your children?" the administrator asked.

"Temporary care?"

"Only temporary," the administrator assured her.

Peggy looked at her children who were standing outside the room in the corridor. Butch was seventeen, Marsha Ann, fourteen, and Tomeekca, thirteen. They stood silently. Tears dripped down Tomeekca's face, but Butch and Marsha Ann were stoic. Still, she couldn't make herself sign the paper.

"Mrs. Morgan, think of what would be best for the children," the administrator said.

For a split second, Peggy remembered the smell of the garbage dumpster where she'd tried to find food to feed her children. The sound of the pen scratching across the paper filled the room.

On the day she gave up her children to foster care, Peggy voluntarily committed herself to Searcy Mental Institution in Mt. Vernon, Alabama.

Peggy stayed one night in Searcy and was evaluated by the doctors the following morning. She was whisked away to an office upstairs and asked hundreds of questions, which she tried hard to answer honestly. After several hours, one of the doctors addressed Peggy.

"Mrs. Morgan, this isn't the hospital for you. Although you have serious problems that need to be addressed, you don't require institutionalization. We're having you transferred to the University of South Alabama Medical Center in Mobile. The doctors there will give you a thorough check up and the help you need."

Peggy stood up, not believing what she'd heard. "I can go?"

The doctor nodded. "We'll arrange transportation for you back to Mobile."

By that afternoon, Peggy found herself under the care of internist Dr. Ellen Sakornbut. The doctor did extensive tests on Peggy, but more than that, she listened. Once Peggy's medical condition was corrected, Dr. Sakornbut arranged for an appointment with a psychologist.

RAIL THIN AND unable to eat, Peggy smoothed the green dress over her bony hips. Glancing at herself in the mirror, she saw how far she'd let herself go. There was nothing left of the girl who'd once been one of the favorite waitresses at Charmaines. The image that stared back at her was of a woman, worn and fragile at the young age of thirty-nine. She'd lost the hearing in her right ear and she suffered headaches so intense they incapacitated her. Both were the result of Lloyd's beatings. She'd also been diagnosed with asbestosis. She could no longer hold up to the rigors of welding or the shipbuilding work, and she had no other training to fall back on. But she was determined to get well. Already her physical health had improved under the sincere concern of Dr. Sakornbut. And now she faced her first appointment with the psychologist.

Though she had accepted the appointment with Dr. Will Baker, she had no great faith that anyone could make her life better. She was going only because she had no other solution. She'd run out of places to run to.

Expecting only another encounter with someone from "the system," Peggy signed her name at the window in the main reception office and took a seat to wait for her appointment. Glancing around the waiting room, she couldn't help but wonder if the other patients were as terrified as she was. Although this fear didn't even compare to what she'd felt those first few hours in Searcy, she was still tied in a knot. Head tucked, she surreptitiously glanced around, watching the other patients as they read magazines or filled out paperwork. For the most part, they seemed glad to be there. That observation left a bitter taste in her mouth.

"Mrs. Morgan." The receptionist smiled as she motioned her into the inner offices.

Dr. Will Baker sat at his desk, but he stood when she entered the room. He motioned toward a chair. "Have a seat," he suggested. "I'm Dr. Baker."

Peggy took a seat facing the desk. Her gaze fell on an apple on his desk. In the light from the lamp, it was the most perfect piece of fruit she'd ever seen. The red skin glistened, as if it had been waxed and hand-polished. The curl of the stem had been crafted by an artist. Looking at the apple, Peggy felt a hunger so deep she'd never experienced it before. She had never wanted an apple so badly.

"Mrs. Morgan, why don't you take the apple," Dr. Baker suggested.

She looked up at him.

He motioned for her to take it. "Go ahead, why don't you eat it while we talk."

Peggy's hand reached out and lifted the fruit. It was as perfect in her hand as it had been in the light of the lamp.

"It's okay," Dr. Baker reassured her. "Just go ahead and eat. You'll feel better when you do."

Peggy devoured the apple. Wiping her hands on the tissue he gave her, she did feel better. She was ready to begin.

No one had ever listened to Peggy the way Dr. Baker did. He paid close attention as she tried to explain the terrors that ruled her life.

Peggy spoke of her mother, of the horror of her childhood and the helplessness of being unable to protect Inez from Gene. She cried as she told of her mother's death and how the picture of her, frozen in the ditch, tortured her at night. Through the sessions that began to stretch across the weeks, she told the psychologist about Lloyd and their relationship.

But the one thing she never mentioned was the secret of Byron De La Beckwith and his confession. She was too afraid to tell Dr. Baker about the racial incidents from her past, the horror of Emmett Till and the fear that Byron De La Beckwith would, somehow, come after her. Or send someone to get her. Sometimes, just on the verge of sleep, she'd hear Beckwith, that bragging tone in his voice. "I killed that nigger, Medgar Evers, and I'm not afraid to kill again."

But even as she walled off the secret of Beckwith's confession, with Dr. Baker's help she began to make inroads into some of her other emotional problems. Her erratic temper and her easy tears required patience. Dr. Baker hung with her, holding out the hope of recovery, and if not recovery, at least relief.

Chapter Thirty-Six

It was during this time that Peggy, always an avid newspaper reader, picked up a copy of the *Mobile Register* and read that a Jackson prosecutor named Bobby DeLaughter had reopened the case of Medgar Evers's murder.

She read the local newspapers obsessively, trying to find out what was happening in Jackson, Mississippi. She used what contacts she had in the Delta to try and glean what was going on with the case. She heard that Delmar Dennis, an FBI informant, had agreed to testify against Beckwith and that now Dennis was "in a world of trouble."

Peggy got word from family and friends in the Delta that they'd been visited by several former Parchman prison inmates. Those men were mighty interested in what Peggy might know about Byron De La Beckwith.

Peggy stood on the brink of a terrible decision. She'd made such strides to change her life. She'd worked so hard to put the demons to rest. Now her greatest fear was once again stirring. No matter how hard she tried, she couldn't escape the racial brutality of her past.

Certain she would be killed for her actions, Peggy knew what she had to do. What happened to Mr. Evers was a terrible thing, a wrong thing. And the man who did it had to pay. Peggy knew she had to tell the truth.

At first Peggy was distrustful of the Jackson, Mississippi, prosecution team. Her lifetime of dealings with law enforcement officials had shown her that in the eyes of the law, women weren't believed and they certainly weren't protected. She'd watched her mother hauled off to Whitfield too many times for trying to talk about Emmett Till.

Instead of calling assistant district attorney Bobby DeLaughter, Peggy called Dr. Aaron Henry, a civil rights figure and personal friend of Medgar Evers. Through Henry, she made contact with DeLaughter.

On February 22, 1990, Charlie Crisco, an investigator with DeLaughter's office, called Peggy. The prosecutors were very interested in what Peggy had to say, but several murder trials prevented them from visiting her for several months.

Those months of waiting were pure hell for Peggy. She expected to be killed. Her ex-husband, Lloyd, paid her a visit, warning her that if she told her secret to the prosecutors, she would sign her own death warrant.

The little girl who'd defied her abusive father stood once again. "Lloyd, I'm gonna tell the truth no matter what happens. Now you can just get out of here." She held her ground, refusing to show the terror that almost paralyzed her. Lloyd left, and so did her bravado.

Peggy's fear of Beckwith and his ilk was larger than Dr. Baker or Dr. Sakornbut. It ate at her day and night, and she made plans to run away. But when DeLaughter, Crisco and L. C. Bennett arrived at her home on September 6, 1990, she was there, waiting to talk to them.

She listened to DeLaughter and Crisco talk about the case, easing into the questions they'd come to ask her, and she began to believe in them. In contrast to so many men she'd known throughout her life, these were men who wanted justice. They talked about Medgar Evers's widow, Myrlie, and how she and her family had never known true justice. DeLaughter and his investigators wanted the murderer of Medgar Evers to pay for his crime. It was almost more than Peggy could dare to believe in.

The secret that Peggy hadn't been able to tell her therapist tumbled out of her mouth—but only half of it.

"Lloyd and I lived on Dewey Street in Greenwood. We were neighbors with Byron De La Beckwith. I don't remember exactly how it came about that we took him to Parchman, but we did. Lloyd and I did," Peggy told DeLaughter.

"I remember I had a 1964 Ford that I bought with the money I'd earned waitressing. It was red and white. It was a beautiful car and I'd bought it myself. Lloyd said we were going to Parchman to see his brother, Jimmy Dale, and that this man was going to ride with us. That was Mr. Beckwith. He was going to buy the gas."

And Peggy told it all, the fear that made her act irrationally; the dark, threatening eyes of the man that Beckwith visited; the belief that she'd be killed for telling the truth. The only thing she did not tell was Medgar Evers's name. She could not. She simply could not. She told the prosecution team that Beckwith had confessed to killing a black man, and that he had knowledge of other killings and bombings. And that he wasn't afraid to kill again.

"Mrs. Morgan, there's one question I have to ask," DeLaughter said as they were concluding the interview. "Why have you waited so long to come forward with this information?"

Peggy's voice filled with anguish that stemmed from a lifetime of being treated as a liar. "I did try to tell some people. I told a woman I worked with at Ingalls. She was with the NAACP. I told her all of it, and she just laughed at me and said I was crazy. And one time I called the FBI office here in Mobile and they said the case was closed. No one ever believed me, and I remembered what had happened to my mama when she tried to talk about Emmett Till."

Bobby DeLaughter and his investigators did believe Peggy. There was some confusion as to the year the Parchman trip had taken place, and the prosecutor and his investigators set out to pinpoint the exact time. They could roughly gauge it by juxtaposing the time Jimmy Dale Morgan was in prison and the time that Byron De La Beckwith was out of prison in Louisiana.

There were also prison records of the man Beckwith had gone to visit—the man with the terrifying eyes. Peggy thought his name might be Tommy, but she wasn't certain. It wasn't until later, when

Peggy was shown a selection of photographs, that she picked out the man Beckwith had visited in prison. He was Cecil Sessums, the Exalted Cyclops of the KKK in charge of the 1966 Klan firebombing murder of civil rights leader Vernon Dahmer in Hattiesburg.

DeLaughter and the investigators returned to Jackson to continue the task of assembling the elements of the case for trial. Peggy was left in Mobile, fully aware that she'd told the one thing that could never be told.

She had no doubt she was going to be killed.

Based on the things Peggy had told DeLaughter, Lloyd was called before the grand jury and forced to testify. Lloyd claimed to have a memory lapse about the Parchman trip, but he did volunteer that the prosecution should talk to Peggy if they had any more questions about the trip. Lloyd said Peggy had a terrific memory about such things.

Unaware that Peggy had already talked with the prosecution team, Lloyd tracked her down and threatened her if she talked to DeLaughter. He caught her alone at her trailer and told her that she would be killed if she attempted to testify. Lloyd invoked the power of the Delta men that Peggy had known all her life—the power of beatings and humiliations over women, the power of life and death. And then Lloyd held out hope. He promised Peggy that he would protect her.

"See, if you marry me, you don't have to testify. You don't have to testify against a husband. They can't call you as a witness, and I won't let anyone kill you," Lloyd said.

Feeling that the prosecution had dropped the case and possibly betrayed her, Peggy married Lloyd again. It was a hasty decision made in the fear Lloyd generated, but it soon became evident that Lloyd had lost his ability to control Peggy. She had changed. She fled from him, married in name only. She returned to Mobile and Lloyd disappeared.

The case against Beckwith was set to be tried on February 10, 1992. Peggy saw light at the end of the tunnel. If she could just avoid being killed until February, she'd testify and then it would all be over. Bobby DeLaughter would put Beckwith behind bars permanently.

Beckwith's defense team asked for a continuance, and the judge granted it, resetting the trial date for June 1, 1992.

Peggy's belief that Beckwith would be punished began to falter. It seemed like the same old legal system she knew too well—the only folks punished were the weak and the vulnerable.

The trial was postponed yet again, reset for September 8, 1992. The defense filed a motion to dismiss, claiming that Beckwith had been deprived of his right to a speedy trial, and that his rights against double jeopardy were also violated since he'd been tried twice in 1964, both trials resulting in hung juries.

In settling the due process issue before the court, Beckwith took the stand. In sworn testimony, Beckwith admitted to going to Parchman. When asked if he'd gone with Peggy Morgan, Beckwith responded "with a woman or a girl, a wife of a man, and that's all I remember." He also admitted to knowing Cecil Sessums.

When this information hit the newspapers, Peggy was terrified. It seemed the case would never be brought to trial, but her name had been made public.

The prosecution won the due process issue, but the defense succeeded in getting an emergency appeal granted by the Mississippi Supreme Court. The trial was postponed for the third time.

On Thursday, October 15, 1992, the Mississippi Supreme Court heard oral arguments on the speedy-trial and double-jeopardy issues. On December 16, 1992, the court rejected Beckwith's double-jeopardy claim outright, and decided not to decide the speedy-trial matter. Beckwith was ordered released on $100,000 bail.

The defense counsel, Jim Kitchens and Buddy Coxwell, petitioned the court for a rehearing, which was denied April 22, 1993.

Next they petitioned the U.S. Supreme Court to review the double-jeopardy claim. It wasn't until July that the court rejected the petition.

Since Peggy talked to DeLaughter in her Mobile home, almost three years had passed. She'd been informed of the trail dates set— and the cancellations. Not even the power of justice seemed to be able to detain Beckwith. He was out on bond and by legal manipulation was living as a free man. Peggy, in contrast, was on the run. She was afraid to stay anywhere long. Afraid to contact the people she loved. Afraid of everything.

The one bright spot in her life was the boarder she'd taken in because of her desperate fear. Joe Smith, a slender man, had a wiry strength and a calm way about him. He was becoming someone Peggy felt she could lean on.

During these years, Peggy vacillated wildly between running away and disappearing or riding out the trial—if Beckwith was ever brought to court. She lived with the possibility that someone would walk up to her in a grocery store or on the street and stab her or shoot her. In the world she'd known, women were as expendable as pets. DeLaughter had offered her a view of another world, a place where justice for a widow and her children was important. Peggy wanted desperately to believe in that world, and she clung to that dream. Often, when she was at a point where she felt she had to pack up and run, she would hear her mother's voice. "Just tell the truth, Peggy. Just tell the truth." She held on, hoping that DeLaughter wouldn't fail her.

At long last, the trial began. The first witness was called in January 1994. Peggy had been moving from motel room to motel room for the past six months, figuring a moving target would be harder to hit. Even though she knew DeLaughter was looking for her, she didn't contact his office. She trusted no one—she relied totally on her ability to keep moving.

When she finally called DeLaughter to tell him she would testify, he told her how to get to the courthouse in Jackson.

Instead of taking the route up Highway 49 that DeLaughter had suggested, Peggy, afraid the road would be ambushed, went over to Pearl River County and took the back roads. On the way she and Joe picked up her sister, Sheila, who'd agreed to accompany her.

The night before she was to testify, Peggy dropped a bomb on DeLaughter. "Mr. DeLaughter, I haven't told you the complete truth," Peggy said. She could see her confession affected him. "When I was in that car with Lloyd and Mr. Beckwith, Mr. Beckwith said more than I said. He said, 'I killed that nigger, Medgar Evers. He said the name, Medgar Evers."

DeLaughter took a breath. "You're sure of this?"

"I was just too scared to say the name," Peggy said. "I had to wait to be certain the trial would happen."

"Why didn't you tell me sooner, Peggy?" DeLaughter asked.

"I just didn't trust you enough. I have a problem with trust."

"Tomorrow, when you're called to testify, just tell the truth," DeLaughter told her, unintentionally echoing the words Peggy knew so well from Inez.

The next morning, Peggy was sequestered with Delmar Dennis and several others. It was a tense time. She understood Beckwith's defense team was going to tear her apart. DeLaughter had warned her that the fact that she'd been in therapy and was taking Xanax on doctor's orders would be used against her. Peggy understood.

What she didn't know was that a fierce battle regarding her testimony was taking place out of the hearing of the jury.

Defense attorneys Kitchens and Coxwell objected to Peggy's testimony regarding Medgar Evers's name. They also objected to any mention of bombings or testimony relating to the man, Cecil Sessums, whom Beckwith had gone to visit in Parchman.

Judge Breland Hilburn ruled that Peggy could testify to what Beckwith had said about Medgar Evers, but he cautioned the prosecution team of DeLaughter and District Attorney Ed Peters against delving into the subject of bombings. Court was reconvened and Peggy was called as a witness.

Peggy heard her name called, and she walked out alone.

When she entered the courtroom, she held a rock she'd found in Pearl River County. It was a symbol of the strength she knew she was going to need to get through the trial.

Peggy passed through the metal detectors. She'd dressed nicely for the trial, but she regretted her choice of high heels. She was trembling to the point that she was afraid she'd fell over. She focused on the spectators, forcing herself to walk what seemed like ten miles to the front of the court room. A white woman and a black woman were seated together, and they looked at Peggy.

She took a few more steps toward the witness chair and heard her mother's voice whispering in her mind. "Tell the truth, Peggy Ruth. Just tell the truth." She kept walking.

Beckwith sat to her left. The look he gave her warned her that she would be sorry for opening her mouth. Peggy shifted her gaze to the judge and followed the bailiff's directions to the witness chair.

Peggy risked a glance at the jury where she met the gazes of a black man and a blond lady. They were jurors, men and women who would sit in judgment on Byron De La Beckwith and what he had done. Peggy felt the first grain of hope. The two jurors seemed interested in what she had to say. They seemed willing to believe her testimony. Peggy felt like the good Lord was trying to show her that black and white, sitting side by side, were working together for justice.

She heard Inez's voice one more time, calming and reassuring. Peggy was ready to answer any questions asked of her.

IN THE CIRCUIT COURT OF THE FIRST JUDICIAL DIS-
TRICT OF HINDS COUNTY, MISSISSIPPI

STATE OF MISSISSIPPI NO. 90-3-495
VS.
BYRON DE LA BECKWITH DEFENDANT

TRANSCRIPT OF THE TESTIMONY OF PEGGY MORGAN
HAD AND DONE IN THE TRIAL OF THE ABOVE STYLED AND
NUMBERED CAUSE, BEFORE THE HONORABLE L. BRELAND
HILBURN, CIRCUIT JUDGE, ON THE 1ST DAY OF FEBRUARY,
1994.

PEGGY MORGAN

upon being called to testify as a witness for the State, after having been
first duly sworn by Hinds County Circuit Clerk Dunn, testified as follows,
to-wit:

DIRECT EXAMINATION BY MR. DELAUGHTER:

Q. Would you tell the ladies and gentlemen of the jury your name,
please?

A. Peggy Morgan.

Q. Okay. And how old are you, Ms. Morgan?

A. 46.

Q. Okay. And would you tell the jury where you lived in, say, the early
19—mid to—mid-1960s to mid-1970s?

A. 1000 Dewey Street, Greenwood, Mississippi.

Q. In Greenwood, Mississippi?

A. Yes, sir.

Q. Okay. At any time when you lived in Greenwood, Mississippi,
roughly during that period of time, would you tell the jury whether or not
you were ever introduced or became acquainted with the defendant in this
case, Byron De La Beckwith?

A. Yes, sir, I was.

Q. All right. Would you tell the jury whether or not you ever accompanied this defendant, or he accompanied you, on any particular trip?

A. Yes, sir, he did.

Q. Okay. And would you—would you tell the jury about that? How that came up and where you went.

A. Yes, sir. To the Mississippi State Penitentiary—

Q. Okay. Excuse me just a minute. You need to speak up a little louder. I'm having a hard time hearing you. If I can hear you, I know all the jurors can, okay?

A. Yes, sir.

Q. All right. Go ahead.

A. Mississippi State Penitentiary, Parchman, Mississippi.

Q. All right. And who was it that was—that you were—why were you going to Parchman Penitentiary.

A. To see my husband's brother and to take Mr. Beckwith over there.

Q. All right. And your husband's brother's name was what?

A. Jimmy Dale Morgan.

Q. Okay. And your husband's name was what?

A. Nelton Lloyd Morgan.

Q. Okay. And your then brother-in-law was being incarcerated at the penitentiary?

A. Yes, sir.

Q. Do you remember what day of the week it was that you made this trip?

A. Sunday.

Q. Okay. Now, the—was the defendant in this case also going to see your brother-in-law?

A. No, sir.

Q. Well, how was it that he came about going with you to the penitentiary?

A. Mr. Orlon Prescott said that he had a friend that needed to go to the penitentiary, and did we mind if he went with us.

Q. He being the defendant?

A. Mr. Beckwith, yes, sir.

Q. All right. Now, how did you get to the penitentiary from Greenwood?

A. My husband and I (sic) car.

Q. And what kind of car was that?

A. Umm—

Q. If you remember.

A. No, sir, I don't remember.

Q. Okay. Who drove?

A. My husband.

Q. And where did you sit?

A. In the middle.

Q. And where did this defendant sit?

A. The passenger's side, on the right side.

Q. All right. Now, at any time on this trip, Ms. Morgan, would you tell the ladies and gentlemen of the jury what, if any, statements that this defendant made concerning the murder or killing of Medgar Evers?

A. Yes, sir. He started talking about some bombings—

BY MR. KITCHENS: Your Honor, I object and move for a mistrial. The Court's ruling has been violated.

BY MR. DeLAUGHTER: That's not in violation. I specifically asked—

BY THE COURT: All right. Be overruled. Be overruled.

Q. All right. Go ahead.

BY THE COURT: Let's move along, though, if you would, Mr. DeLaughter.

BY MR. DeLAUGHTER: Yes, sir.

Q. Tell what he said in reference to the murder or killing of Medgar Evers.

A. Okay. He said that he had killed Medgar Evers, a nigger, and he said if this ever got out, that he wasn't scared to kill again.

Q. Okay. If what ever got out?

A. This trip to the penitentiary.

Q. And if it got out that what? I didn't hear what you said. That if this got out—

A. He wasn't scared to kill again.

Q. All right. And did y'all make it to the penitentiary?

A. Yes, sir, we did.

Q. All right. How long were you there?

A. We didn't stay for the full visiting hours.

Q. Okay. Did you return back to Greenwood that same day?

A. Yes, sir, we did.

BY MR. DeLAUGHTER: One moment, Your Honor.

(PAUSE IN THE PROCEEDINGS.)

BY MR. DeLAUGHTER: Nothing further, Your Honor.

BY THE COURT: Cross-examine.

CROSS-EXAMINATION BY MR. KITCHENS:

Q. Ms. Morgan, I'm Jim Kitchens, and I just had the opportunity to meet you for the first time this morning, correct?

A. Yes, sir.

BY MR. PETERS: Your Honor, we do want the record to show that they've had her name for two years, and have chosen to talk to her this morning; not that she was just introduced to him this morning.

BY MR. KITCHENS: I object to the side bar comment of Mr. Peters, Your Honor. He's—he's inaccurate in what he's saying. We've been looking for this lady, and have been unable to find her.

BY MR. PETERS: Thank you, Your Honor. They've had her name for two years.

BY THE COURT: All right. Gentlemen, let's not get into this kind of rhetoric.

BY MR. PETERS: He's the one that asked the question, Your Honor—

BY THE COURT: Go ahead and continue your cross-examination. The objection will be sustained.

BY MR. KITCHENS: May I proceed, Your Honor?

BY THE COURT: Your objection will be sustained.

BY MR. KITCHENS: Thank you, sir.

Q. Ms. Morgan, I believe you told me a little earlier when we had the opportunity to talk with you this morning that you live with different friends and relatives, and don't really have a place of your own, is that right?

A. Yes, sir.

Q. And I'm not trying to pinpoint where you stay, but you do live down in south Alabama in the Mobile area, don't you?

A. Yes, sir.

Q. And you just have a post office box, I think, down there some place, don't you?

A. Yes, sir.

Q. All right. Ms. Morgan, at the time that you are telling us about, you were married to a man named Lloyd Morgan, is that right?

A. Yes, sir.

Q. And he had a brother named Jimmy Dale Morgan?

A. Yes, sir.

Q. And Jimmy Dale Morgan was a convict serving time at the Mississippi State Penitentiary at Parchman.

A. Yes, sir.

Q. And that's not very far from Greenwood, is it?

A. No, sir.

Q. Can you recall about how far that is?

A. I would say approximately about 80 miles.

Q. How many times did you visit Jimmy Dale Morgan while he was at Parchman?

A. Maybe two or three times.

Q. And each time you would be with your husband, Lloyd, when you visited him?

A. Yes, sir.

Q. Were there other times when somebody besides just you and Lloyd went?

A. Not that I recall.

Q. There may have been but you can't recall, right?

A. Yes, sir.

Q. This has been a very long time ago, hasn't it, ma'am?

A. Yes, sir, it has.

Q. And I believe we discussed a little while ago that it's been in the neighborhood of 25 years or perhaps more.

A. Yes, sir.

Q. Ma'am?

A. Yes.

Q. And a lots has happened to you in that period of time, hasn't it?

A. Yes, sir, it has.

Q. Not all of it good.

A. True.

Q. Ms. Morgan, you did not know Mr. Beckwith on a close personal basis, did you?

A. No, sir.

Q. The morning that y'all went to Parchman, he was a virtual stranger to you, wasn't he?

A. Yes, sir.

Q. He wasn't somebody who had ever confided in you about anything in his life, was he?

A. No, sir.

Q. He was not somebody that had any reason to believe that he could trust you to maintain confidences.

A. Would you repeat that?

Q. I'll be glad to. Mr. Beckwith had no basis to think that you were somebody he could tell something confidential, and that you would keep it confidential.

BY MR. DeLAUGHTER: Your Honor, we object as to what the defendant thought. This witness would have no way of knowing what the defendant was thinking—

BY THE COURT: Rephrase the question.

Q. You had never talked with the man before in your life.

A. No, sir.

Q. You had not established any kind of a relationship or friendship or trust with him.

A. No, sir.

Q. He had never told you anything in confidence before.

A. No, sir.

Q. Do you know of anything that he knew about your background and your reputation or your trustworthiness?

A. No, sir.

Q. Now, Ms. Morgan, you were kind enough to share some very personal things with me as we talked to you, Mr. Coxwell and Ms. Ellis and I a few minutes ago.

A. Yes, sir.

Q. And I believe you understand I'm not here to embarrass you. I don't wanna do that.

A. Yes, I understand that.

Q. I—I need to ask you some of these things. Is that all right with you?

A. Yes, sir, it is.

Q. You have had some psychiatric problems.

A. Yes, sir.

Q. Psychological problems and psychiatric both; have been seen by both psychiatrists and psychologists over the last several years.

A. Yes, sir.

Q. And you are on some psychiatric medication right this minute, aren't you?

A. Some kind of medicine, yes, sir.

Q. Yes, ma'am. Is that Xanax that you're taking today?

A. Yes, sir.

Q. And you were prescribed this medicine by a doctor down in Mobile, is that right?

A. Yes, sir.

Q. And I believe you told me that this doctor herself is not a specialist in psychiatry, but work with doctors who are.

A. Yes, sir.

Q. And you are seeing this doctor for some of these long-term psychiatric problems that you have had.

A. (No audible response.)

Q. This is just a continuation of things you've been seeing doctors for over a long period of time?

A. Physical and—

Q. I can't hear you.

A. Physical and emotional.

Q. Yes, ma'am. You have—

A. Yes, sir—

Q. —some—some physical health problems, as well as some emotional problems that the doctor is helping you with.

A. Yes, sir.

Q. You have had some very serious traumatic things to happen to you in your life, haven't you?

A. Most definitely.

Q. You and Lloyd Morgan are not married any more, is that right?

A. Yes, sir, we are.

Q. You're still married to him?

A. Yes, sir, we are.

Q. You don't live together.

A. No, sir.

Q. And you've been separated for quite a long time.

A. Yes, sir.

Q. Mr. Morgan was abusive to you during your marriage.

A. Very much so.

Q. This contributed to your psychiatric problems.

A. Yes, sir.

Q. Your father was abusive to you when you were a child.

A. Yes, sir.

Q. That contributed to your psychiatric problems.

A. Yes, sir.

Q. Your father was murdered.

A. Yes, sir.

Q. That contributed to your psychiatric problems.

A. Yes, sir.

Q. And forgive me for mentioning this, because I know it's painful to you, but your mother froze to death, did she not?

A. Yes, sir, she did.

Q. And that contributed to your psychiatric problems.

A. Yes, sir.

Q. Your husband, you told us, carries on an incestuous relationship with one of his children. [Author's clarification: Not one of Peggy's children, but a child from another relationship.]

A. Yes, sir, he does.

Q. That contributes to your psychiatric problems.

A. No, sir, I don't think so.

Q. That doesn't bother you.

A. No, sir, it doesn't bother me.

Q. You have been diagnosed as having an anxiety disorder by psychiatrists.

A. Yes, sir.

Q. And that was some years ago.

A. Uhh—

Q. Ma'am?

A. My most recent diagnosis—

Q. That's your most recent diagnosis?

A. (No response.)

Q. Whatever—I'm not trying to put words in your mouth, and I only know what you told, so if that's not correct, please tell me.

A. Okay. Repeat the question to me again—

Q. Yes, ma'am. The diagnosis of anxiety disorder that you told me you have been given, is that recent or is that some years ago?

A. I don't know how to answer that question.

Q. All right. Then we'll move on to another question then. But you do—you have been diagnosed as having an anxiety disorder?

A. Yes, sir.

Q. And Ms. Morgan, you got in touch with the District Attorney's office here in Jackson, is that right?

A. I don't remember who it was.

Q. You don't remember whether they contacted you or you contacted them.

A. I remember I contacted them, and then they contacted me.

Q. All right. Now, Ms. Morgan, are you able even to tell us in what year Mr. Beckwith is supposed to have made this statement that you just quoted to the jury?

A. The mid-60s and mid-70s, somewhere in that—

Q. Anywhere from the mid-60s to the mid-70s?

A. Yes, sir.

Q. And you can't pinpoint it any better than that for the jury?

A. My first child—Lloyd and I got married in 1964, April the 3rd. My first child was born August the 3rd of 1966. My second child was born in 1969. So I know it was between those times.

Q. And Lloyd Morgan was with you at the time this was supposed to have happened.

A. Yes, sir.

Q. But you don't know where he is now?

A. No, sir, I don't.

Q. And he doesn't have any address as far as you know.

A. No, sir, he doesn't.

Q. Basically, your understanding is that he is a homeless person.

A. Yes, sir, he drifts a lot.

Q. Ma'am?

A. He wanders a lot, drifts a lot.

Q. Yes, ma'am. And you don't know that because you haven't heard from him in quite a while, have you?

A. The last time I heard from him was this past May. His—his daughter and him came to my house. They were in Mobile.

Q. All right. And that would have been May of 1993?

A. Yes, sir.

Q. And you and your husband, Lloyd, and Mr. Beckwith were all supposed to be in the same car when this occurred, is that right?

A. Yes, sir, we were.

Q. Just riding along through the Delta.

A. On our way to Parchman, Mississippi.

Q. And all of you, I believe you said in your statement, were sitting on the front seat.

A. Yes, sir.

Q. And how were you all seated?

A. Lloyd was driving; I was in the middle; and Mr. Beckwith was on the passenger's side.

Q. Yes, ma'am. And this man with whom you had never had a conversation in your life confessed to a murder to you at that time?

A. At that time, yes, sir.

Q. And the first time that you ever told anybody that Mr. Beckwith said that he killed Medgar Evers was when you talked to Mr. DeLaughter last night, less than 24 hours back from right now?

A. No, sir, I had mentioned it to other people, but last night was the first time I had mentioned it to Mr. DeLaughter and Mr. Crisco.

Q. You had been talking with the District Attorney's office here in Hinds County over a period of some four or five years about this, hadn't you, ma'am?

A. Yes, sir.

Q. Mr. DeLaughter, Mr. Bennett, and Mr. Crisco from the District Attorney's office came to see you in south Alabama quite a while back, didn't they?

A. Yes, sir. 9-6 of '89.

Q. I can't hear you, ma'am.

A. 9-6 of '89.

Q. 9-6-89?

A. Yes, sir.

Q. And they talked to you at length, didn't they?

A. Yes, sir, they did.

Q. And they tape recorded every word that you said.

A. Yes, sir.

Q. And in that statement, you never one time mentioned Medgar Evers.

A. No, sir.

Q. Ma'am?

A. No, sir.

Q. And though you say now that you have told other people this, you never told anybody in the District Attorney's office until last night.

A. You're talking about Mr. DeLaughter and Mr. Crisco.

Q. Anybody in the Hinds County, Mississippi District Attorney's office—

A. Correct, I've never told no one.

Q. Ma'am?

A. I've never told anyone, here in Hinds County.

Q. Until last night.

A. Correct.

Q. And you acknowledge, don't you, ma'am, that there are just a whole lot of things about this ride and what was said that you simply cannot remember?

A. Yes, sir.

Q. Ma'am?

A. Uhh, yes, sir.

Q. You don't have any accurate recollection of most of what was said on that trip, do you?

BY MR. DeLAUGHTER: Objection, Your Honor, if he wants to open this up, we'll be glad to do it.

BY MR. PETERS: Absolutely. He's asked—now he's asking questions, Your Honor, that we feel that she should be allowed to answer.

Q. Ms. Morgan—

BY THE COURT: Restate the question.

BY MR. PETERS: We want a ruling, Your Honor. We wanna know whether or not—

BY THE COURT: All right. Objection is overruled—

BY MR. PETERS: —she can answer that or not—

BY THE COURT: The objection will be overruled, to that one particular question. Certainly, if you venture any further than that, Mr. Kitchens, you will be opening the door.

Q. Ms. Morgan, again you're not even able to tell us what year this was.

A. It was between 1966, the mid-60s and the 70s.

Q. That's—that's as close as you can come?

A. Yes, sir.

Q. You made no memorandum or note about it at the time?

A. Note?

Q. Yes, ma'am.

A. No, sir.

Q. But you have been studying that statement that you gave to Mr. DeLaughter, Mr. Bennett, and Mr. Crisco.

A. They handed me the statement this morning.

Q. Yes, ma'am. And you had a copy of it in your hand when we were talking back there, didn't you?

A. Just overlooking it, yes, sir.

Q. Yes, ma'am. And you never told them during that statement anything about Mr. Beckwith saying that he killed Medgar Evers.

A. No, sir, I didn't.

BY MR. KITCHENS: Thank you.

BY THE COURT: Redirect.

REDIRECT EXAMINATION BY MR. DELAUGHTER:

Q. Ms. Morgan, could you tell the jury whether or not any of the traumatic things that the defense attorney asked you about, did any of those occur prior to the trip to Parchman that you explained to the jury?

A. Explain that to me just a little bit better, Mr. DeLaughter, please.

Q. All right. The traumatic events that the defense attorney asked you for which you sought some psychologic aid and assistance, did any of those traumatic events occur prior to—before you went to the trip to Parchman?

A. No, sir.

Q. Okay. That all came afterwards?

A. Yes, sir.

Q. Okay. And after you—either during this trip or right after this trip, Ms. Morgan, would you tell the jury what, if anything, this defendant told you to—to try to maintain your silence?

A. Yes, sir. He told me that it better not ever get out, and he carried my husband and I over to his apartment—

Q. Speak up.

A. He told—told me that this better not never get out, the trip to Parchman, and he invited my husband and I over to his apartment, and his apartment was full of guns.

Q. And what did he say?

A. He just told me that the trip to Parchman had better not never get out.

Q. Okay. And how did this make you feel?

BY MR. KITCHENS: Objection, Your Honor, as to how it made her feel. We think it's really irrelevant—

BY THE COURT: I sustain the objection.

Q. What effect did this have on you telling or not telling anyone else about this?

A. It put a fear in me, and I knew not to say anything.

Q. Now, you mentioned that the first time we talked was, I believe, in September of 1989, when it was me and Investigator Crisco and another investigator by the name of Bennett, is that right?

A. Yes, sir.

Q. Okay. Now, after that 1989 conversation in your home in Mobile, Ms. Morgan, when was the next time that—that you and I talked about this trip to Parchman?

A. Last night.

Q. Okay. So although several years have passed, it's not like we have had continuous conversations—

BY MR. KITCHENS: Object to leading, Your Honor.

BY THE COURT: I'll let her answer the question.

Q. We've not had continuous conversations over a period of four years, have we?

A. No, sir.

Q. And when we talked last night, did I ask you why you had not told me in 1989 the specific name of Medgar Evers?

A. Yes, sir.

BY MR. KITCHENS: Your Honor, we object to continually leading the witness.

BY THE COURT: I'll let her answer that question.

Q. And your answer to that was what?

A. Repeat the question, Mr. DeLaughter.

Q. Did I ask you why you haven't told me the name of Medgar Evers?

A. Yes, sir.

Q. Would you tell the jury why you waited until last night to tell me the name of Medgar Evers?

A. Because of the lack of trust. I didn't know who to trust sometimes. I have a problem with trust and who I'm talking to.

Q. Now, I believe you said that you had contacted the District Attorney's office back in 1989, which led to us coming down there to talk to you, is that right?

A. Yes, sir, I think—

Q. Okay. All right. Why did you call the District Attorney's office?

A. There was something that came up saying that—

Q. No, just—what were you—what was your purpose—what were you trying to accomplish by placing a call to the District Attorney's office?

A. Thinking that there was something there that would merit—that it should be brought forward.

Q. Okay. Speak up a little bit. What did you say?

A. If there was evidence there that should be brought forward.

Q. Okay. At that time in 1989, were you interested in being a witness, and coming into court and testifying?

A. No, sir.

BY MR. DeLAUGHTER: Nothing further, Your Honor.

BY MR. KITCHENS: Your Honor, may we have some brief recross?

BY THE COURT: All right.

RECROSS-EXAMINATION BY MR. KITCHENS:

Q. Ms. Morgan, I want to be sure you understood some of the questions. Mr. DeLaughter asked you whether any of these traumatic things that I had to ask you about on cross-examination had occurred before this trip you told us about.

A. No—

Q. One of them was the child abuse that you suffered. That occurred before the trip, didn't it?

A. Yes, sir.

Q. And you said that contributed to your psychiatric problems.

A. Yes, sir.

Q. Your husband was abusive to you.

A. Yes, sir.

Q. Before the trip and after, wasn't he?

A. Yes, sir.

Q. So you didn't understand the question, did you, that he was asking you?

A. No, sir.

Q. Now, ma'am, though you have not talked to Mr. DeLaughter, according to what you just said, other than last night and in September of 1989, you've certainly known how to get in touch with him, haven't you?

A. Yes, sir.

Q. He left you a card, I'm sure.

A. Yes, sir.

Q. When he was down there.

A. Yes, sir.

Q. With the telephone number and address of his office and his name on it.

A. Yes, sir.

Q. Mr. Crisco has been in touch with you since then, has he not?

A. Yes, sir.

Q. Mr. Crisco is the investigator, or one of them, that came with Mr. DeLaughter.

A. Yes, sir.

Q. And the District Attorney's office called you about coming up here, and told you when you needed to be here, and all those things.

A. Yes, sir.

Q. And so you've had a good bit of communication with that office, haven't you?

A. Just recently.

Q. And today is, what? Tuesday? I'm losing track of the days, but is this Tuesday?

A. Yes, sir.

Q. And you've been in Jackson since Sunday, haven't you?

A. Yes, sir.

Q. Staying in a hotel.

A. Yes, sir.

Q. And you've known exactly how to pick up the telephone and call the District Attorney's office anytime you wanted to.

A. Yes, sir.

Q. Yes, ma'am. Now, Mr. DeLaughter asked you on redirect examination what motivated you to make the call that you first made about this case to somebody in Jackson, is that right?

A. Yes, sir.

Q. And the truth is, it was as a result of a threat from your husband, wasn't it?

A. No, sir. The threat came afterwards.

Q. The threat came afterwards?

A. Yes, sir.

Q. Your husband threatened you about this at some point in time.

A. Twice.

Q. To get you to testify?

A. To get me to testify?

Q. To talk about Medgar Evers.

A. Not to get me to talk about him.

Q. You don't know where he is now, where Lloyd Morgan is at this time—

A. No, sir, I don't.

Q. You're not afraid of him?

A. Yes, I'm afraid of him.

Q. If you were to see him, you would be?

A. Sir?

Q. If you would see him?

A. Yes, sir.

BY MR. KITCHENS: All right, Ms. Morgan. Thank you.

BY THE COURT: (To the Witness) You may step down.

BY MR. DeLAUGHTER: One thing, Your Honor.

BY MR. PETERS: Based on his question.

BY MR. DeLAUGHTER: Based on a question he just asked.

BY MR. PETERS: It was a brand new matter brought out by—

BY THE COURT: Mr. Peters, I don't need any help from you, please, sir. Yes. Go ahead.

FURTHER REDIRECT EXAMINATION BY MR. DELAUGH-TER:

Q. What did—what did Lloyd Morgan threaten you with?

A. He told me I better not come here and testify. He said I was gonna wind up dead.

BY MR. DeLAUGHTER: Nothing further, Your Honor.

(WITNESS EXCUSED)

Chapter Thirty-Seven

Peggy sat at the kitchen table of her trailer. She'd testified and come home. The trial had ended, but the jury hadn't reached a decision yet. She kept one eye on the small television across the room, which was turned to the five o'clock news. She'd been back in Mobile for four days. It was Saturday, February 5, the anniversary of her mother's death. It was always a hard date for her, but since she'd testified four days earlier, the past had eased its grip on her a little. By telling the truth, she had finally vindicated her mother.

Joe Smith, the boarder who'd turned into Peggy's supporter and her soon-to-be husband, walked past the sliding glass door and busied himself in the yard with the white, half-Spitz dog he was so fond of. Bear had really taken to him, and it pleased Peggy to see the two of them together.

She didn't expect to hear any news about the Beckwith trial. She'd waited all week, and she seemed helpless to do otherwise. She'd called the local CBS affiliate the day before and asked if they had any indication of how the trial was going. The reporter had told her that the jury was out, but that deliberations could take as long as eight weeks.

She looked at the business card she'd gotten from a Jackson reporter in the crush that surrounded her after she'd testified. She hadn't wanted to talk with the reporters, but Sheila, her sister, had insisted. The reporters had swarmed over her until she was totally confused and frightened. In the melee, she'd never found Myrlie Evers. Peggy had hoped to give her the small stone she'd held during the trial, wanting the other woman to have a share of "the rock of strength."

Outside the trailer, Bear barked and whipped around the yard in a circle, playing with Joe. At the sight, Peggy couldn't help but smile. She thought about putting on a pot of coffee. Night was falling, and Joe would want something hot to drink when he came in.

"This is the CBS evening News with Dan Rather."

She glanced over at the small television set and wondered what Dan Rather was doing working on Saturday.

"A verdict has been reached in the murder trial of avowed racist Byron De La Beckwith. . . ."

Peggy sat up and blinked.

Dan Rather stared straight into her eyes, delivering the message only to her. " . . . Beckwith has been found guilty. . . ."

Peggy gripped the table.

She erupted from her chair, a wild cry bursting out of her.

The front door was flung back on its hinges and Joe ran into the room. "Peggy, what's wrong?" He looked around to see who was hurting her.

"They found him guilty!" Peggy pointed to the television where people were commenting on the verdict.

"The jury brought in the verdict?" Joe was amazed at the speed of the decision. He looked at Peggy, who had begun to cry. "What are you going to do?" he asked.

Peggy only shook her head. "I don't know," she finally managed. "This has been hanging over me for so long, I don't know." She found a tissue and brushed the tears from her face. Through all of the turmoil, the running and the hiding, Joe had tried to help her. She'd nearly drowned him in a river of her tears. Now he was worried about her again. "Maybe we should do something to celebrate," she said.

Joe grinned at last. "Yeah, let's put on a pot of coffee.

345

Chapter Thirty-Eight

Peggy and Joe stood in the Greenwood cemetery, staring at the marble headstone that marked Inez's grave. Leaning down, Peggy placed the fresh flowers at the head.

"Those eyes of Cecil Sessums's don't stare at me any more," she told Joe. "Ever since the trial, they've been taken away." She stood up and looked at him. "I'm not goin' to live any more in fear and bein' scared all the time. I'm not goin' to live in lies and fightin'. On February 5, when that verdict came in, I was reborn. This is a new life."

Joe waited, knowing that Peggy spoke as much for herself and her mother as for him.

"I've done some terrible things in my life, but I'm not lying about them. Anybody who asks me is goin' to get the truth."

Peggy's hand touched the cold gravestone. "The credit goes to Mama. She tried to teach me right. She did the best she could."

When Peggy started out of the cemetery, Joe fell in beside her. "Are you hungry?" he asked.

Peggy shook her head. "No. It's goin' to be a long drive home to Mobile. Maybe we should get started." She turned back once to look at the splash of bright red roses on the grave. "Mama loved red roses."

Joe opened the car door and helped Peggy in. It was a cold, raw day and he hurried around to get in the car. He cranked the motor, then waited as Peggy looked back at her mother's grave.

"A new life, Mama," Peggy said softly. "Thank you."

Epilogue

Today Peggy lives at the end of a newly paved road. She and Joe are raising her grandchildren, Marsha Ann's two girls. The rickety trailer has been removed, and a new house sits in the middle of the immaculately maintained lot.

A chain link fence protects the children and Bear and Dobey, the two small dogs Peggy cares for. There's plenty to eat and time to spend with the grandchildren she loves.

"I could never make up to my own kids what happened," Peggy said. "But I can take care of these grandchildren and give them a good home."

She's married and changed her last name, but time has not erased the woman she was, Peggy Morgan, a woman determined to tell the truth.

The therapy with Dr. Baker and testifying at the trial against Beckwith have given her a voice. She's a fighter for her community and a woman who won't be silenced—no matter what political correctness dictates. She draws a line in the sand where fair is involved, and she stands up for it. In doing so, she's come in contact with people like the Mobile and Prichard police chiefs, the mayors of both cities, and former Alabama state senator and attorney John Tyson Sr., a man she adores. She no longer fears authority figures and is quick to praise or criticize, depending on what she thinks is needed.

She's actively organized the young people on her road to form a litter patrol. She and the kids clean the community, picking up aluminum cans to sell and buy gasoline for weed-eaters and shrubbery and flowers in their continuing efforts to keep their small community clean. "I'm trying to teach the younger generation that doing for others is the best reward life can offer," she said.

Beautification of her neighborhood is symbolic to Peggy. She plants trees and shrubs, giving the plants special names that symbolize the progress she's made in her life.

Symbols are very important to her. "I want to change the bad things into good things," she said. "Take KKK for instance. For most of my life, that's stood for hatred and cruelty and meanness. Now, I've decided I won't let it mean that any more. To me, it's going to mean Kind, Kinder and Kindness. That's what I want it to come to mean for everyone."

If Peggy had her way, everyone in the world would be treated with kindness. The dark terrors of her childhood and the brutality that her mother endured would be vanquished. The terrible hate and prejudice that led to the deaths of Emmett Till and Medgar Evers would never exist.

It would be a world of truth and justice.

The End

Acknowledgments

This book has been a long and sometimes strange journey. It is appropriate that it ends at a publishing house called River City. Carolyn Newman, publisher, saw the worth in one woman's story of survival. Ashley Gordon, editor, gave great direction and expert navigation in guiding the book to publication. Their professionalism and help have made the process a real pleasure.

As always, my agent, Marian Young, was the best representative a writer could have.

Throughout the writing of the book, I've had help from many others. Carolyn Males was instrumental in shaping the book, as was Steve Greene.

The members of my critique group, the Deep South Writers Salon, gave sound advice and helpful criticism. We've been together a long time, and though there were raised eyebrows at my step into nonfiction, the group was always supportive. Whenever Jan Zimlich, Alice Jackson Baughn, Rebecca Barrett, Susan Tanner, Renee Paul, and Stephanie Chisholm speak, I listen.

I also thank Bobby DeLaughter for his careful reading of the manuscript and his generous involvement in this project.

Jerry Mitchell was a big help in gathering facts and transcripts. And Elizabeth Langston never gave up on this book. I thank her for her belief in me.

But the real credit for the book goes to Peggy, a woman with enough courage to survive and to speak the truth.

Sources

For those interested in this aspect of Mississippi history, there are a number of good books to read. Listed below are books I relied on heavily.

Mrs. Mamie Till-Mobley died this year, but she had been working with a Chicago lawyer, Chris Benson, on a book about her son's murder entitled *Death of Innocence: The Story of the Hate Crime that Changed America*. The book is set for release in October of 2003 from Random House.

DeLaughter, Bobby. *Never Too Late: A Prosecutor's Story of Justice in the Medgar Evers Case.* New York: Scribner, 2001.

Massengill, Reed. *Portrait of a Racist: The Man Who Killed Medgar Evers?* New York: St. Martin's Press, 1993.

Vollers, Maryanne. *Ghosts of Mississippi: The Murder of Medgar Evers, The Trials of Byron De La Beckwith and the Haunting of the New South.* Vol. 1. New York: Little, Brown, & Co., 1995.